D1795072

£99

001056

Credit Insurance

Credit Insurance

HOW TO REDUCE THE RISKS OF
TRADE CREDIT

vwvwvwvwvwvwvwvw

DICK BRIGGS AND BURT EDWARDS

DUDLEY COLLEGE OF TECHNOLOGY

LIBRARY

WOODHEAD-FAULKNER

NEW YORK · LONDON · TORONTO · SYDNEY · TOKYO

368·87 BRI

001056 ✓

Published by Woodhead-Faulkner Limited,
Simon & Schuster International Group,
Fitzwilliam House, 32 Trumpington Street,
Cambridge CB2 1QY, England

First published 1988

© Dick Briggs and Burt Edwards 1988

Conditions of sale
All rights reserved. No part of this publication may be reproduced, stored in a retrieval
system or transmitted, in any form or by any means, electronic, mechanical,
photocopying, recording or otherwise, without the prior permission of the publisher.

*Please note that in order to avoid the clumsy repetition of 'he or she' the male pronoun has been
used throughout.*

British Library Cataloguing in Publication Data
Briggs, Dick
Credit insurance; how to reduce the risks of trade credit.
1. Credit insurance
I. Title II. Edwards, Burt
368.8'7
ISBN 0-85941-176-1

Designed by Geoff Green
Typeset by Pentacor Limited, High Wycombe, Bucks
Printed in Great Britain by A. Wheaton and Co. Ltd, Exeter

Contents

vwvwvwvwvwvwvwvwvw

Foreword

vwvwvwvwvwvwvwvwvw

For many years now it has been a matter of some regret to me personally that there has been so little written about credit insurance, let alone the compilation of a reference manual to advise on the different types of cover, whether domestic or export, that are now available in the London market. Therefore, when first approached by the publisher with a view to assisting in the production of such a book, I was greatly enthusiastic and agreed to help find someone to fulfil the task.

I believe the partnership of Burt Edwards and Dick Briggs has produced a fully comprehensive and exciting reference book for all those existing and potential users of credit insurance, as well as those working within this specialised line of business.

The credit insurance industry prides itself on adapting to the changing needs of the marketplace and, as a result, it is difficult to keep pace with the adjustments in cover and additional facilities that inevitably occur. I am therefore all the more indebted to Burt Edwards for having agreed in the first instance to write the book, and to Dick Briggs whose later cooperation ensured that the book was as up to date as could be reasonably expected.

Good sound credit management is a prerequisite to the provision of credit insurance cover and in no way should it be viewed as a substitute. For this reason, credit insurers keenly support the desire to develop more competent credit managers and this book makes a very useful contribution to this process.

The credit insurance industry owes a considerable debt of gratitude to Burt Edwards and Dick Briggs for this major production. They are both to be congratulated and thanked for all the hard work that has been put into the creation of this long overdue, but much needed, and most valuable record.

John E. Phillips
Director and Chief General Manager
Trade Indemnity plc
1988

Foreword

vwvwvwvwvwvwvwvw

I am pleased to be able to join with John Phillips in contributing to the Foreword to this important new study on credit insurance which I very much welcome.

I am naturally inclined to think in terms of *export* credit insurance, but I recognise that many of ECGD's customers are confronted with the problems of trade credit in the domestic market as well as overseas. While there are clear differences in the risks presented by each sector – and ECGD's recent experience of having to meet heavy claims as a result of the world debt crisis serves to underline this – there remain equally important similarities. The need properly to manage and control credit exposure, to understand the risks involved and to be aware of what the credit insurer can do to help, apply equally to both domestic and export trade credit.

I see two roles for this book. First, through its thoroughness and clarity, it will demystify a subject which has for too long been considered the preserve of experienced experts. It should, therefore, serve as a helpful guide to newcomers. Second, for the already experienced practitioner, it will provide a very useful work of reference.

In its description of the nature of trade credit, the problems it presents and the solutions offered by credit insurers, this volume will be of enduring value to those who refer to it. Over time, though, improvements and changes will be made to the services which credit insurers provide in order to meet the changing needs of their customers. Given the emphasis which the authors place on providers and users understanding each other's needs, they will, I am sure, endorse my plea that companies, whether actual or potential users of credit insurance, should keep up to date on what the credit insurers offer and never hesitate to test us out as to whether we can meet their particular need.

I have no doubt that a wide range of people will be grateful that Dick Briggs and Burt Edwards embarked on this formidable task – and completed it so successfully.

Malcolm Stephens
Chief Executive
ECGD
1988

Acknowledgements

vwvwvwvwvwvwvwvwvw

Our thanks are due to John Phillips and Malcolm Stephens for their consistent support and encouragement in this venture. In compiling the technical material in chapters 8, 9 and 10, we have enjoyed valuable help from:

Trade Indemnity plc
Export Credits Guarantee Department (ECGD), London and Cardiff
The Credit Insurance Association Limited
American International Underwriters (UK) Ltd
Barclays Bank plc
Credit and Guarantee Insurance Company Limited
Insurances of Credit
Mr Geoffrey Lynch of Roberts and Hiscox Ltd at Lloyd's
Mr Alastair Malcolm
PanFinancial Insurance Company Limited

For their guidance on the international scene we are indebted to:

Mr Derek C. W. Hill, Secretary General, International Union of Credit and Investment Insurers
Mr Klaus Oppenheimer, Secretary General, International Credit Insurance Association
Mr Hugh Dowell of Trade Indemnity plc

Table 2.3 on page 21 is reproduced from *Key Business Ratios*, Dun & Bradstreet Ltd, with their kind permission.

Part One
Trade credit

vwvwvwvwvwvwvwvwvw

1

A glance at the present scene

vwvwvwvwvwvwvwvw

In the UK, the majority of trade revenue is unprotected against the risk that it will never be received by sellers. 1984 saw 14,000 UK corporate insolvencies with a further 6,000 personal bankruptcies. Although these figures were then an all-time record, they occurred again in 1985, '86 and '87. Every year, thousands of companies go out of business owing vast sums of money to thousands of other companies. Subsequent payments by liquidators are usually negligible, so why does business allow itself to suffer these awful profit haemorrhages? Are they avoidable? Could the losses be recovered in any way? Do company directors, responsible to their shareholders, make objective decisions about their customers' ability to pay their bills? Or do they sell first, and worry later? Consider the following facts:

1. A proportion of sales revenue is lost by most companies every year because of the insolvency of some customers.
2. Protection against insolvency losses can be purchased from credit insurance companies.
3. A minority of trade sales is protected by credit insurance.

This book is based on the apparent illogicality of the third point. It looks at trade credit, how it is used and its effect on profits. It also looks at business failures, how they happen and what can be done to reduce their damage to individual suppliers. Because selling on credit implies trusting customers to pay at a later date, the book concentrates on the protection against nonpayment which is available from insurance companies. Throughout, we explain corporate and underwriting attitudes to covering the risks, to try to see why there is so little take-up of the facilities available.

THE BUSINESS OPPORTUNITIES OF CREDIT INSURANCE

An obvious implication of the general state of under-insurance is that there are significant opportunities for credit insurance companies and specialist brokers to increase their business, and for trading companies to plug their profit leaks. In order to satisfy their respective needs and exploit the opportunities, suppliers and users both need to understand better the strengths and weaknesses of the existing scene. On balance, the initiative needs to come from the sellers of the product, i.e., the credit insurance companies themselves. They face the classic marketing challenge of a widespread lack of product knowledge by potential buyers, that is, industrial firms. Despite the marketing efforts in recent years by some providers, especially Trade Indemnity plc, there is still a lot to be done by insurers in general. As well as market research to identify buyers' needs, and product analysis to get pricing right, the main need is to revise advertising and selling methods so that no businessman is left unaware of the product, and a majority becomes aware of reasonable detail. For corporate directors and financial managers to be unaware of the range and benefits of available credit insurance protection is a serious professional shortcoming. Just by looking into the case for cover benefits are achieved because, invariably, weaknesses of in-house credit controls are identified. The most widespread weakness is probably that staff are not clear about their duties or levels of authority, so that credit is allowed without anyone making an objective assessment.

SELLING TO A MIXTURE OF RISKS

Sales revenue could obviously be protected by selling for cash only. If credit were allowed only to no-risk customers such as government or 'blue chip' companies, there would be virtually no bad debt loss but there would still be the expense of slow payments. However, sales volume and profitability would be severely restricted and commercial realities dictate that credit sales have to be made to all kinds of customers, whether good, average or risky. If volumes are to be maximised without painful levels of bad debts and slow payments, sellers have to identify the risks within their mix of customers and manage them.

THE DIFFERENT NEEDS TO BE MET BY THIS BOOK

'There is very little literature on credit insurance.' This comment was made by Mr P. J. B. Carson in an article for the Chartered Insurance Institute in 1977. Although he was referring to the scarcity of reference material for his article, his observation is still valid. Of course, every credit insurance company and all the major broking firms have their brochures and sales aids, mostly excellent in themselves, but individually biased in their purposes. Trade Indemnity has to be commended for putting out the message on behalf of credit insurance in general, within their publicity material for their own purposes. The panoply of business books covering financial management treat the subject of credit insurance very scantily indeed. And this despite trade receivables being usually the largest responsibility of any financial director! As the task of managing receivables is usually delegated to credit managers, it is no wonder that the insolvency-prone economic scene of the last few years has seen a rapid growth in the credit management job in industry, both in numbers and seniority. And the previous dearth of credit management books has changed, in line with this trend, with an increasing trickle of offerings which do indeed contain information on credit insurance.

We have looked at the ability of the credit insurance industry to meet four needs:

1. Potential buyers of credit insurance need to know of the wide variety of facilities – with some interpretative comments.
2. Credit insurance companies need to understand traders' problems – their risks, commercial pressures and ability to control losses.
3. Existing users need to understand much more how they can help the underwriting decision process and the settlement of claims.
4. Users, underwriters and brokers – in fact, everybody involved – need to overcome buying and selling objections by being better informed on the details of risk, cost and profit justifications.

We have taken this approach in the belief that the book is needed just as much by the providers of credit insurance as by its purchasers.

Our twin objectives are as follows:

1. To stimulate every kind of business into looking consciously at whether profit can be increased from the use of credit insurance.
2. To help maximise the business for those in the supply side by clarifying the problems of firms selling on credit.

WHY ARE SALES UNDER-INSURED?

The reason for the authors' collaboration was to use our accumulation of experience of corporate credit management and marketing of credit insurance. We share a concern that a fundamental anomaly exists in UK business today – that credit insurers are more numerous and flexible than ever before, yet despite insolvencies at record levels, most companies still do not protect their major cash asset. Is this by choice or accident? Sometimes it is a conscious decision following an objective study. In other cases, poor selling of the insurance cover is responsible. But usually, it is due simply to companies not looking into the possibilities. There is also the 'drop out' factor, where some of the few companies who do insure, discontinue cover for a variety of reasons. The most common reason is probably a rough calculation that premiums have exceeded claims!

We take a good look at the substance of trade credit, in both home and export sales, to see where problems arise. Correspondingly, we look at the capacity of the underwriting market and its willingness to cover traders' risks and, by deduction, the short-comings. A typical gap between the two sides is the frequent difference of opinion about what a credit limit should be – surely a good example of the need for a better dialogue?

CREDIT INSURANCE: NO SUBSTITUTE FOR CREDIT MANAGEMENT

Good managers know from experience that credit insurance should never replace a company's own management of its credit risks. Poor credit management will restrict the insurance cover available, or increase its cost, whereas demonstrably good standards of risk control not only encourage underwriters to provide cover, but also enable traders to negotiate better rates. In this vital area of negotiation, we say that the use of specialist brokers can achieve better cover and costs.

CREDIT INSURANCE AS ANOTHER TYPE OF INSURANCE

There is a good case for comparing the need for credit insurance with protecting any other asset. The benefits of life, fire and other traditional insurances are well understood. Companies know they must protect themselves against losses of premises or vital stocks. It is accepted that such insurances can restore operating positions fairly quickly; and decisions tend to be concerned with premium cost compared to the costs of other forms of security. There is no shortage of information, nor do companies overlook protection or 'not bother' to protect themselves. Even when some large companies decide on 'self-insurance', it is a conscious decision after a major study. Yet no decision at all may be taken to protect the riskiest asset! It is not often that companies seek out credit insurance cover; it usually has to be sold hard as if it were a luxury.

CREDIT MANAGEMENT TODAY

Although credit management is one of the fastest growing corporate professions, it is barely recognised in many companies and totally absent in others. Most companies just sell and hope to get paid. Some take on all available business in the belief that today's profits will be covered by tomorrow's bad debts. But bad debts are only the tip of an iceberg which threatens the corporate ship. The dangerous mass of the berg is the interest cost of slow-paying customers, usually ten times or more greater than bad debts for any one company. It is surprising, since slow debts harm profit and competitiveness so much, and lead on to actual bad debts, that more companies do not commit a fraction of sales income to managing these risks at a senior level.

THE EXTRA RISKS IN EXPORTING

In international sales, only some 30% of UK exports are insured, yet in addition to the normal payment delays and bad debts in foreign markets, export profits have been hit, in recent years, by the inability of nearly two-thirds of the world's governments to remit hard currency after customers have paid locally. The protracted negotiations for rescheduling foreign debts have produced severe problems for those exporters not carrying ECGD or other export credit insurance protection. This 'transfer' risk has been the prime factor in the rapid growth of the private, or non ECGD, insurance market in the 1980s. And while the transfer risk is the main worry, there are many other actions by governments which frustrate the intended performance of export deals. The imposition or cancellation of import licences by hard-pressed foreign governments is a popular (for them!) way of reducing FX spending.

CREDIT INSURANCE: NOT THE SAME AS FACTORING

It is important that credit insurance is not confused with factoring. Insurance is purchased to replace insolvency losses whilst allowing companies to manage their own day-to-day credit risks, collection of sales proceeds and interface with customers. The factoring service is sold by subsidiaries of banks to provide a combination of credit management and funding of sales. The factor makes credit checks, decides credit limits, processes the supplier's invoices through a sales ledger and collects from customers, all for a fee based on a percentage of turnover. A large proportion of invoice value is advanced without recourse, for sales made within the limits set. The factoring company may itself purchase credit insurance cover for the risks it takes on and its charges include the cost. A simple comparison would be that credit insurance is a facility to reinforce a company's own credit management, whereas factoring does the entire credit task for a company.

SPREAD OF RISKS AND SELF-INSURANCE

Good credit management across industry, with risks identified and well spread, would make it highly unlikely that there would ever be a 'domino effect' in business failures, where a large insolvency hits a series of suppliers who have become too dependent on the next one in the chain. But since good risks management is not yet widely in place, there are many examples of domino collapses or, at least, severe damage. Before credit insurance or credit management ever came on to the scene, a sound business maxim was, 'Don't have too many eggs in one basket', i.e., it is important to obtain orders from a variety of customers. This is often forgotten in the rush for sales growth, when more and more orders may be welcomed from a single customer and nobody notices or cares that its insolvency would be disastrous.

Every company should ask itself, 'What size of bad debt would damage our financial health or lose us a valuable outlet?', then look in the sales ledger to see if such exposures exist. If so, credit insurance may be the answer, together with a fresh approach when prospecting for orders.

Well-managed companies try to maintain a balanced portfolio of types and sizes of customers, in different sectors, for good marketing reasons. This automatically spreads the credit risks, often without the company even realising it. Although balanced marketing is an excellent form of risk control in itself, it allows potential dangers through if normal controls are neglected or over-ridden.

In the same way, companies who decide to self-insure, by allocating substantial revenue to a reserve fund, can experience high losses if that method encourages over-risky orders to be taken just because of a convenient 'bucket' for hiding losses.

As management policies, self-insurance and risk-spreading both need day-to-day control and periodic review to compare actual experience with that intended, in the knowledge that credit insurance is also available.

THE MARKET OF IGNORANCE

Except for the relatively few insured companies, and those with policies of self-insurance or well-spread risks, there is a widespread ignorance of credit insurance. It is not usually the responsibility of corporate-insurance managers. The receivables asset is normally managed by staff of the financial director, treasurer or company secretary. But specialist brokers know that there is little knowledge of credit insurance facilities at that executive level. Decisions and pressures tend to occur at a lower level, where the benefits of protection are more readily understood. One inference of this is that a fertile market exists for marketing which is aimed at beneficiaries rather than always at top people.

FREE CREDIT INFORMATION ON CUSTOMERS

There is a considerable treasure house of financial information on thousands of companies in the UK and abroad held on file by the major credit insurers', such as Trade Indemnity plc and ECGD. They store not only the usual commercial agency reports and official data from company registries, but also the valuable knowledge of credit levels allowed by their policy holders. Added to declarations of overdue accounts and actual claims, the total represents a good picture of receivables risks in each industry at any one time. Enlightened managers of credit make the most of this indirect benefit of free data as well as the more obvious direct benefits of cover.

THE OVERALL PICTURE OF RISK IN TRADE CREDIT

Back in 1959, the Radcliffe Committee Report reminded the UK business community that trade credit was between two and three times greater than bank lending in overdrafts. The risk for companies is much higher than that for banks, who have much more visibility of a debtor's current situation through the ability to demand balance sheets and cash-flow projections. A trade creditor can rarely make such demands. A bank charges interest and takes security on assets to cover its loan. A trade creditor normally does not. In the 1950s, Mr P. Bareau wrote that the growth of capital in industry had not kept pace with business growth on short-term credit. In other words, the ratio of most companies' external debt had deteriorated – how much more so since then, as the developed world has seen volume growth and price inflation as never before. Trade debtors average about 72 days of sales value in the UK, on payment terms usually at 30 days. In any one industry, companies competing with similar products to similar customers may vary in their credit perform-ance between 50 and 150 DSO! The national picture of credit tolerance is one of high vulnerability to bad debt losses.

THE IMPACT OF CREDIT ON THE CREDITOR

Theoretically, working capital is dynamic. Students learn that companies borrow to build stocks, turn stocks into sales and thus receivables, then receive cash to pay off creditors (including the bank), then put fresh borrowings into new stocks and sales to repeat the sequence. In practice, companies in a regular way of business have balance sheets showing a fairly constant value of receivables matched by static short-term borrowings. A company's receivables asset is therefore a fairly permanent investment of borrowed funds. But the return on this investment, if measured at all, is not measured in the same way as the return on capital assets. The cost in interest of borrowed funds for financing debtors is a major business expense. A company borrowing at 15% p.a., with a net margin of 5%, loses that profit if the customer has not paid after four months. The cost of replacing a totally lost investment, i.e., a bad debt, is also very high. A company making 5% net has to sell twenty times the value in new business to recover a lost debt.

THE NEED TO MANAGE CREDIT WITH THE HELP OF CREDIT INSURANCE

Progressive companies have come to recognise that they must manage debtors as a major company task, not as a spare-time one or one at a junior level. Job-holders who may have had the responsibility in the past, such as the sales manager or chief accountant, do not have the time needed or the specific expertise for the daily work. As well as the more easily understood role of 'debt-collector', the credit manager is concerned with assessing the credit period and the value of each order; i.e., can the customer pay it within the terms allowed?

Professional credit managers are still a relatively rare breed in the UK, more numerous than in mainland Europe but not nearly as well established as in the USA. We look at the duties of credit managers and their place in the decision-making hierarchy of UK companies. Just as credit insurance is not a substitute for credit management, the lack of credit management is not an automatic case for insurance. What is the use of buying, say, 80% protection when internal credit controls are so bad that many claims would be made with the uninsured 20% being higher than the net margin? Other actions are also required to control the credit risk. A detailed review of procedures will almost certainly reveal the need for a senior person to be in charge of credit from day to day.

The other side of the coin is the attitude of companies who believe that because they have strong credit management in place there is no case for spending money on credit insurance. We show that the most effective systems are those which squeeze profits even out of risky customers by a mixture of good, 'hands-on' risk management and supportive insurance cover.

TYPES OF CREDIT INSURANCE

We look at all the major forms of cover available. In both home and export business, there are schemes for whole turnover, at fairly low and standard premium rates (because the risk for underwriters is spread), and specific account cover, at relatively higher rates. Premium sometimes depends on the degree of credit control and, in some cases, insurers will investigate the trader's procedures. Some insurers offer cover on a 'catastrophe' basis, where the seller can specify his normal, acceptable level of annual bad debt loss and then be covered only for losses above that level. Cover can be negotiated with most insurers as an equation of the percentage of cover, the claim delay period and the premium payable.

Each credit insurance company believes it is different from its competitors and has its own special place in the market. The word 'complementary' is used by insurers, who all state that they do not believe in meeting competitors head on. It seems that most trading companies are not aware of the alternatives available to them. Again this points to a business opportunity for brokers and insurers in the ways they get their product information to potential buyers.

PAYMENT OF CREDIT INSURANCE CLAIMS

Insurers pay insolvency claims at defined dates after losses are proved, usually on the appointment of a receiver or liquidator. This is a considerable benefit to insured sellers in cash-flow terms, since it could be a long time later that actual dividends, if any, are distributed to creditors. Cover is available for 'protracted default', normally payable six months after due date. However, when all possible collection steps have been taken during this waiting period without success, the buyer is probably in an insolvent condition anyway, even if not formally declared. Export claims can be for a wider variety of risks in addition to insolvency and default, and different percentages of losses are payable at defined time-scales. All these kinds of cover are examined and compared in some detail in the chapters that follow.

COLLECTION AGENCY ACTION

During cases of protracted default it may be advantageous to use the services of a commercial collection agency, possibly that of the credit insurance agency itself. Where the buyer is in default but still apparently solvent, a third-party agency will either succeed in collecting or else prove the uncollectability of a debt. It is usually the 'third-party' effect of the agency which succeeds where the buyer has ignored the payment requests of his friendly seller.

CREDIT INSURANCE AS AN AID TO FINANCE

The fact that a company's receivables asset is protected by credit insurance makes it a better bet for a bank or other lender, as well as to financial analysts and potential new owners. The asset base is more secure and attractive than an uninsured company's. Projected profit levels, which are otherwise subject to wide variances according to the collectability of sales, are more reliable. Policies can usually be assigned to banks as security for loans, and interest rates may be lower for borrowings to support insured assets.

WHERE CREDIT INSURANCE IS NOT A GOOD IDEA

We look at situations where credit insurance is not cost-effective, such as where individual debts are small or the risks are well spread over a large turnover. When brokers examine a sales ledger, the resulting 'who owes what' analysis can be very useful to a company even if the final decision is not to insure. Quite often, consultants find that no objective study has ever been performed.

THE STRUCTURE OF THE BOOK

Although the credit insurance subject itself is vast, we have added credit management material to it because the two topics are so well linked in everyday management practice.

We look first at trade credit in home and export sales to understand its use, commercial pressures and costs. We then divide the problems between commercial, or customer, and political, or country, risks because they are quite different. A company's concern about the less obvious political risks depends on its kind of business and its exposure in the riskier countries. Consider the relative prospects of an exporter of luxury bathrooms to a Third World market which has declined from importing millions of dollars' worth of extravagances to now being unable to afford basic needs, and an exporter of metal cans to the same market for that market's own exports of tinned fruit to earn desperately needed hard currency.

We look at how companies assess their risks, investigate customers and markets, operate controls to limit the possible damage, collect their debts and measure results for possible improvements. This leads us to the general principles of credit insurance which have stood the test of time and coped with recent pressure for innovations, such as greater selectivity of poorer risks at a marketable price.

Some space is given to the history and evolution of the market, with its reinsurance facilities. The development from the early part of this century was prompted by Mr Cuthbert Heath, the 'father' of credit insurance, and is fascinating in itself but also useful in seeing what is and is not possible.

We compare policy wordings and conditions, to help understand the alternatives. In export credit, we explain how UK sources match or better the facilities available to foreign sellers.

Despite the 'pros and cons' approach throughout the book, we still have a separate chapter at the end to help companies in assessing their own needs, using check lists and decision paths.

SUMMARY

Our wide treatment of the subject, both conceptually and in practical terms, is mainly to encourage wider discussion of credit insurance. Every financial director should understand the product range and be able to review, from time to time, how his company's changing needs are best served. Similarly, every provider of credit insurance should understand what buyers need and plan marketing promotions to meet those needs. The trade-receivables asset is very large, valuable and fragile – for any one company, and also nationally in total. Its vulnerability makes it a fertile growth area for risk management innovations, in which credit insurance must surely take the main role.

As we said at the outset, credit insurance is a product which protects companies against unplanned future losses at costs which can be established in advance.

2

The nature of trade credit

vwvwvwvwwvwvwvwvw

BASIC DEFINITION AND BACKGROUND

Trade credit is both the value transferred by a seller on trust and the time interval before the buyer's return of that value in the form of payment. The definition sounds pedantic and old-fashioned, yet trade credit as we know it is fairly new. Perhaps the reason for its definition sounding unattractive is that it makes us feel uncomfortable because we do not give it the respect it demands. The most important word in the definition is trust. The value and the time allowed should depend upon the seller's trust of the customer.

For centuries, the basic nature of credit has not changed, because it cannot defy its definition. In the Middle Ages, substantial fortunes were risked for long periods of time – especially risky, one might think, without the benefit of modern communications – but invariably the seller had a personal knowledge of the debtor. Today, credit remains the same but business volumes deny the same degree of personal knowledge. Thus, that ingredient of 'trust' has faded from its original clarity as a decision to the blurred greyness of either a hope or an oversight! What has really changed are business attitudes to dealing with credit – sellers giving credit freely to obtain business whilst neglecting to assess the chances of being paid, and buyers evolving from taking credit with some regret as a temporary expedient to demanding it as a standard feature of buying anything. The late Lord Franks, in the 1950s, described trade credit as 'easily the most accessible source of additional funds'.

Selling on credit creates receivables, or debtors, as a balance-sheet asset. It is important to regard receivables as the vital transitional stage between sales and cash. In accounting procedures, debtors are entered on to the balance sheet at the same time that sales are booked to the profit and loss account (P & L). But there is no usable profit until there is cash. The many costs during the life of a debt, including accounting, administration, collection and financing, all reduce its value before it actually becomes cash. And some sales, through dispute or bad debt, are doomed never to become cash, that is, profit, at all.

In the ever-changing world of contemporary commerce, it seems to me essential that management should realise the vital importance of employing experienced and skilled credit managers.[1]

As the well-known insolvency practitioner who handled most of the famous failures of the '60s and '70s, it is not surprising that Sir Kenneth Cork wrote this.

Most of the 80,000 businesses that failed in 1984–87 (that is, one every ten minutes!) had adequate sales but they ran out of both money and the ability to borrow any more. The most common reason was the need to finance excessive stocks and uncollected debts. Were the failed businesses just unlucky? Or did they, perhaps, make and sell without bothering to check their customers' ability to generate payment? Or perhaps senior management did not give enough attention to collections?

There is no 'standard customer'. The financial strength of each of the 1,400,000 limited companies in the UK is as unique as a fingerprint. Any company's customer list is almost certainly a complex mixture of large, medium and small firms – every seller seems to attract a surprising number of newly formed or owner-managed buyers. The size of account balances will be from huge to uneconomically small. The 80/20 ratio is found almost universally, and most sellers are surprised at their volume of unplanned small orders, not necessarily from small firms. Some customers are growing and some in decline, all at different rates. Some are very liquid while others have poor cash flow. Some are profitable, others not so. Some have smart managements, others are sleepy, and so on. Yet credit is allowed to all and sundry, so a company should not be surprised if they cannot all make payment on time. Or be willing to.

Even those companies who manage their trade credit well, by checking creditworthiness and systematically collecting accounts, know that market pressures often lead them to 'over-sell': that is, to sell more to a customer than he has the capacity to pay for. How much greater the risk to profits or indeed survival, for companies that oversell and do not control the credit they allow! This, perhaps, is what Sir Kenneth really had in mind. Enlightened companies know the value of managing their working capital. They try to plan the minimum credit necessary to get orders and do not regard 'accounts' as just an accident of selling.

1. See Edwards, H., *Credit Management Handbook*, 2nd edn (Gower Publishing, Aldershot, 1985), pp. xxiii.

The treasurer of a multinational group of companies with receivables of over £500 million once told its annual sales convention: 'I regard our receivables as the failure of salesmen to sell for cash.' He was, of course, exaggerating to make a point – that business takes credit for granted, when it sometimes has a choice – cash! After all, cash was once the norm. When ancient man realised that business was getting nowhere by bartering sheep for axes, he invented money instead. His business decisions were simple – only those with the means to pay could have his goods. Traders probably always knew they could get more orders by supplying those lacking cash, but knew it was for the money-lenders to decide whether to put those customers in funds or not. As early banks, money-lenders lent only to customers they trusted (the very word 'credit' comes from the Latin for 'trust').

Nowadays, the distinction between bank lending and trade credit has become very blurred. Disreputable customers avoid borrowing more (at a cost) from their bank to meet essential obligations by delaying payment (free) to other suppliers. Trade credit is seen as just another flexible source of funds.

The attitude of being able to afford purchases has long gone. The modern world would grind to a halt if 'time to pay' was not available. When the Industrial Revolution set off the boom in manufacturing businesses, it ended the stable economic system of the agricultural society that existed up to then. During the twentieth century, the world moved rapidly to the attitude of 'buy now pay later' for everybody. The moral stance of 'don't buy it until you can afford it' has been replaced by 'get it now if you think you can pay for it in the future'. We have reached the position where the expectation of future income matters more than the certainty of actual money.

Credit, or the ability to acquire value without payment, has become normal for individuals, firms and nations. The abnormal increase in risk to sellers has not yet been fully realised, but is the sole reason why the job of 'credit manager' is important today, when it didn't even exist 50 years ago. It is also why trade credit must surely not remain as under-insured as it has been.

THE RISK IN ACCOUNTS RECEIVABLES

Most credit managers would probably vote for a return to cash accounting – counting profit only when payment is received. As the executives responsible for turning sales into cash, they know this would expose the true value of sales. Today, sales mean accounts receivable. The realised profit depends on the ability and willingness of customers to pay. The vital 'bottom line', or net margin, is reduced by the interest expense on the borrowings between invoice and payment.

The whole month's sales value which a company puts to P & L as a precise total represents a transfer of wealth to a number of unconnected customers. The receipt of profit in the form of cash depends upon the gamut of customer attitudes. The more customers a firm has, the more human resources have to be applied to controlling those attitudes and the exposure to delay and loss.

Most sales eventually get paid. The cash for a month's sales by manufacturing companies comes in on average about 72 days later – a mixture of prompt and late payments. A tiny proportion never arrives, due either to bad debts or unsolved invoice problems. The risk of bad debt loss increases the longer that accounts remain unpaid. Not only are overdue accounts the ones most likely to fail, but their amounts are greater because further sales have been made in the meantime.

So, a major pointer to the scope for saving profits is the list of overdue accounts – because of the interest expense of waiting to be paid, the non-use of the money, and the extra chance of bad debts.

Tables 2.1 and 2.2 illustrate the effect of overdues on profits and the sales needed to replace bad debt losses.

Table 2.1 How the age of overdue debts erodes profits

Cost of borrowing p.a. (%)	Net profit on sales				
	10%	8%	5%	4%	1%
8	15.0	12.0	7.5	6.0	1.5
10	12.0	9.6	6.0	4.8	1.2
12	10.0	8.0	5.0	4.0	1.0
15	8.0	6.4	4.0	3.2	0.8
18	6.7	5.3	3.3	2.6	0.6

Number of months after which a loss is caused

Table 2.2 The effect of bad debt on sales (for each £1,000 of bad debts)

Margin of net profit	New sales required to recover loss
1%	100,000
2%	50,000
4%	25,000
8%	12,500
10%	10,000

TRADE CREDIT AND CASH FLOW

To some companies 'cash management' means collecting money in quickly and paying it out slowly. Worse still is the practice of neglecting collections in the belief that sales will benefit, but keeping the bank happy by delaying payment to suppliers. The most efficient policy by far is to collect and pay on the agreed terms.

As credit is essential for modern business and its cost is a significant expense, it would undoubtedly aid trade (particularly for smaller firms) and the planning of funding, if companies complied with contracted terms and left the job of providing finance to the banks.

Monthly credit has become the most common trade term in the UK. The national 'norm' varies throughout western Europe, even in countries next to each other. In general, shorter credit is given in the north than the south. Sweden has a standard of 30 days, while Belgium has 60, France 90, and Italy 120 days. Credit seems to have evolved over the years within national boundaries, not internationally, despite intensive trading between members of, say, the EEC or EFTA.

Trade invoices usually represent separate contracts, each with its legally binding conditions, including the payment obligation. The abuse of credit in the UK can be traced to the growth of 'monthly account' terms, i.e., the grouping together by customers of several invoices payable individually on 30-day terms. The burden of settling invoices every day is such that it has become acceptable to make a single payment at the end of the following month. This gives an average of 45 days' credit for sales made between the 1st and the 30th of a month. The tolerance by sellers of the extra investment is stretched by then having to follow up overdues as a large monthly lump, rather than individually overdue invoices. The risk of loss is enormously increased when it attaches to a total debt for supplies made between 30 and 60 days earlier, rather than the contracted separate and smaller obligations of exactly 30 days ago in each case. In the USA, companies manage to operate successfully on terms of 30 days from invoice date which mean just that.

The problem with a general acceptance of credit abuse is that payment may depend more on company muscle than contract terms. Small firms are the least able to afford cash delays, yet depend for business on larger firms, who may be the slowest to pay their bills. The irresponsibility of ignoring agreed terms is compounded when the debtor company is itself being paid sooner by its own customers. Consider a petrol company which takes two months to pay its suppliers on monthly terms yet demands cash in seven or fourteen days from its garage outlets. Or supermarkets which retail for cash but delay payment to suppliers for up to three months.

The credit period agreed in a contract, usually through the seller's standard conditions, is usually regarded as unimportant compared to other obligations such as price and delivery. Many managers seem to believe that anything to do with money is a formality for the 'office', and not part of their commercial cut and thrust. Yet a sales manager in West Germany discusses payment as earnestly as he pursues price increases. It is not surprising that his country enjoys more buoyant trade, cheaper money and, perhaps significantly, has a slower development of the separate credit manager job than in the UK.

For sellers, the ideal cash-flow and profit situation would be sales on agreed terms, with credit costs allowed for in prices and invoices paid on time. The worst kind of buyers (including some famous names) would prefer goods on time at agreed prices but paying whenever it suited, without any interest charge for lateness. Unfortunately, in the competition for orders, sellers tolerate this attitude and it is this weakness which mainly accounts for the different ratios of receivables to sales in the same industry. It is also the root cause of illiquidity and why banks, fearing that companies are collecting too slowly to pay creditors, appoint a receiver.

So, trade credit is both a valuable donation to a customer who also enjoys the benefit of the goods, and a risky investment for a seller, whose profit varies with the date of payment.

PROFITS AND CREDIT

The Second World War seems to have been a watershed for credit and working capital. Before it, a firm might have made profits of 15% before tax, and paid about 5% p.a. on its overdraft. Thus the cost of extra trade credit could easily be afforded. From 1945, business changed significantly. Volumes shot up, including imports from newly developing countries. Competition became much tougher, and material and labour costs put pressure on margins. At the same time, the cost of bank borrowing increased, with the result that net profits of 5% are now quite respectable but money can cost 15% – a complete reversal of 50 years ago. Many companies were slow to realise that the cost of late-paying accounts could not be afforded as in the past. The drastic events of recent years – recession, cost-cutting, and record failure rates – have created a new awareness of cash and its cost.

Whereas companies previously looked for technical and marketing excellence, financial skills now have a higher profile. Almost every company is a net borrower. The debtors' asset represents a large concentration of borrowings and we have already mentioned its vulnerability to attack from costs. The effect of payment delays on margins – not gross margins, but what is left after all expenses are deducted – can be easily measured. In simple terms, a 4% net profit before tax is lost after four months' payment delay, if money costs 1% per month. An aged analysis of receivables may show debts up to twelve months overdue. By referring again to Table 2.1, it is possible to see the point in time when their profit disappeared.

THE NEED TO ASSESS CREDITWORTHINESS

By definition, a seller should trust every credit buyer but as the business grows, it becomes impossible to know all customers, let alone trust them. So the credit trust has to be standardised. Credit has to be expressed in money and time, e.g. '£5,000 can be allowed to customer A on 30-day terms, but customer B is only good for £500 and we require payment in seven days.' Those different decisions are based on information, but somebody has to obtain and evaluate it.

Personal knowledge of customers sometimes takes a fatal twist when a lack of objectivity means that a customer's limited liability is ignored because someone has a personal relationship with the customer. Most credit managers in their careers will have been told something like, 'Don't worry, they're OK; I've known the owner for years.' Whilst personal friendship is useful in selling, it has little to do with financial ability. Sadly, at meetings of creditors, there are always some people with long faces who have 'known the owner for years'.

> Let's put all this into an example: Adams Engineering Ltd manufactures plastic components. It has annual sales of £25 million, receivables of £5 million, profits before tax of £750,000, and borrows at 12% p.a. There are 1,000 accounts which owe between £50 and £100,000. Sales are on standard terms of 'Payment by end of month following date of invoice'. The receivables balance of £5 million is the equivalent of all sales for the last 73 days. Some accounts pay promptly, others are overdue for one, two or three months, with some residues up to twelve months old. All customers pay the same price. No interest is charged on overdue amounts. In the preceding twelve months £150,000 has been lost in bad debts.

Without any more detail one can see that Adams's credit control is fairly slack. Customers probably pay when it suits them, yet are still supplied when they reorder. Excess debtors hurt profits (only 3% on sales), and when customers go bust, the high overdues cause the amount owing to Adams to be high. To improve its profitability, the Adams company could assess the payment ability of customers; keep sales to risky customers within the assessed amounts; hold back deliveries to customers who cannot pay for previous supplies; and apply sales efforts to get more orders from creditworthy customers.

THE DSO, OR COLLECTION PERIOD

In the example, the Adams company has a ratio of receivables to sales of 73 DSO (days sales outstanding). This is its average collection period. Sales are converted into cash every 73 days. An invoice today will be paid in 73 days' time on average. By expressing receivables in relation to sales, the investment of funds in credit to support sales can be seen more clearly and improved if desired. Sales increases or reductions do not affect the ratio. It is only affected by the time taken by customers to pay, or by longer or shorter credit terms or better or worse collection actions.

Table 2.3 Collection periods (DSO) for various industries in 1986

Industry	No. of companies	DSO		
		Upper quartile	Median	Lower quartile
Agricultural services	187	24.2	43.2	72.7
Industrial building contractors	680	15.3	33.8	52.4
Electrical contractors	1,119	38.4	62.3	86.4
Dairy product manufacturers	125	26.5	32.6	42.8
Office furniture manufacturers	107	52.2	68.8	87.2
Publishers	408	48.5	73.4	98.5
Plastics manufacturers	155	56.3	71.4	86.8
Pottery manufacturers	117	54.0	65.5	78.8
Metal forgings	333	61.3	77.0	91.1
Construction machinery manufacturers	105	39.9	62.5	86.1
Household appliance manufacturers	138	44.3	57.7	73.5
Electronic components manufacturers	669	59.3	77.9	98.2
Motor vehicle manufacturers	156	34.7	54.9	85.0
Local hauliers	1,525	51.3	65.8	83.1
Freight forwarders	687	39.9	60.6	81.3
Electrical wholesalers	723	58.1	77.5	97.4
Industrial machinery wholesalers	1,551	49.8	73.0	95.3
Chemist wholesalers	334	29.4	49.2	73.9
Advertising	705	47.8	67.0	95.3
Food retailers	585	1.1	4.0	13.9

Seventy-two DSO is the estimated average credit for UK manufacturing industry. (Note: official statistics are notoriously defective in regard to trade credit – the authors rely more on commercial surveys and personal experience in consultancies.) In several industries, such as electronics and textiles, the average for twenty or so representative companies is also about 72 days, but is made up of the better firms with about 50 days and the worse performers with 125 days or so. Table 5.2 (see page 66) gives examples of how the DSO is calculated and Table 2.3 gives typical DSO performances in various industries.

THE CREDIT TERM

As a key contract condition, the credit term reflects (or should) the following:

1. The seller's wish to sell.
2. His margin and need for funds.
3. The buyer's ability to pay.
4. Competition from other suppliers.

In practical terms, it fixes the date when value is to be received for the goods or services supplied. For these points to be meaningful, the credit term should be a policy decision by top management, with the intention of enforcing compliance in case of default.

What factors influence the choice of credit terms?

1. The availability of working capital.
2. Traditional terms for the market.
3. Competitive offers.
4. Whether it is a buyers' or sellers' market.
5. How much scope there is in the profit margin.
6. The risk of the customer's failure.
7. The life of the product or service (customers may lose interest in paying for something that no longer exists).
8. The customer's own need for support – not strictly the seller's problem, but often a commercial reality.
9. Seasonal factors.
10. The availability of security from a third party.
11. The guidance available from a credit insurer.

For any seller, there is a mixture of factors. A well-managed company is likely to have a range of terms for different situations, rather than a crude policy of 'our terms are monthly – take it or leave it'.

It is important that terms are clear to both parties. For example, '30 days after receipt of invoice' may be attractive to a buyer, but outside the control of the seller to prove when the buyer receives the invoice. However, '30 days from invoice date' makes the payment date clear to both parties.

The seller must be careful not to establish a payment term by default, by failing to enforce the terms yet continuing to supply, or by not rejecting different terms stated on a buyer's order. A court may rule that the seller condoned the buyer's behaviour.

In domestic UK business, the vast majority of transactions are conducted on 'open account', whereby settlement is made at the instigation of the buyer. It is also used for some 60% of UK exports, particularly to western Europe and North America, the remainder involving bills of exchange, letters of credit or bank financing schemes. In these cases the seller, not the buyer, begins the payment process with documents to the bank.

Here is a representative selection of credit terms.

Home trade

Payment related to delivery

CWO:	cash with order (i.e., no credit allowed)
CIA:	cash in advance of delivery
COD:	cash on delivery
Load on load:	payment for this delivery before next delivery

Payment related to time

Net 7, 10 etc.:	payment of an invoice seven, ten days etc., after date
Weekly:	payment of a week's invoices by a date next week
Half-monthly:	payment of all invoices dated 1st to 15th by 30th, and all dated 16th to 30th by the next 15th
Net monthly, or monthly account:	payment of all invoices in one month by the end of the following month
30 days from invoice:	payment of an invoice exactly 30 days later
2% 14, net 30:	a cash discount of 2% for settlement within fourteen days of invoice date, or payment in full 30 days

Contra (offset):	settlement by offsetting debts to customer
Instalments or progress payments:	contracts for capital equipment, long-term manufacturing processes and construction projects usually require payment at specified stages, and sometimes verified by certificates from independent third parties.
Retentions:	major projects may specify that the buyer will keep back a percentage, usually from 5% to 15% of the total, for a warranty period, or a specified date, e.g., twelve months after commissioning of plant.

Notes:

1. The risk of loss increases with time.
2. The most usual UK payment term is monthly account.
3. Customers should not treat terms of '30 days from invoice' as 'net monthly' by paying all invoices at the end of the following month. Where there are many invoices in a month, customers can be asked to make weekly bulk payments.
4. Net monthly account means an average of 45 days' credit where there are deliveries through the month.
5. Cash discounts are an expensive way to get paid but bad debts are reduced because less is outstanding.
6. Contra, or offset, terms are not legally binding, unless a formal agreement is made. The contracts to sell and to buy are separately enforceable, e.g., a receiver can demand payment for goods supplied by the insolvent customer.
7. On major capital contracts, the credit period is invariably in instalments and the total related to when the end product becomes useful. For example, a supplier of flexible tubing might give twelve months for a factory project but 36 months for identical goods to an oil refinery. Prices include the different waiting costs.

Export trade

The factors that make export credit different are as follows:

1. Time scales are longer: for shipping time, transfer of funds across borders, and the credit period itself.
2. The extra time and distance imply that terms should also provide security if needed.
3. The usual terms in the buyers' market are expected.
4. Competitive offers are from different countries with differing money costs, and governmental policies.
5. International standard credit terminology applies.

The range of export credit terms is as follows:

CWO:	cash with order, or before shipment
CILC:	confirmed, irrevocable letter of credit
ILC:	irrevocable letter of credit
RLC:	revocable letter of credit
CAD:	cash against documents through a bank
Sight draft (D/P):	documents (access to goods) released by bank to buyer only against payment
Term draft (D/A):	bill of exchange payable at specified date, with documents released only against acceptance. Due date is a number of days after a particular event (e.g., invoice, bill of lading, arrival, etc.).
Open account *n* days after arrival:	direct payment required at a number of days after arrival of goods
Open account *n* days after date:	direct payment required at a number of days after a known date (e.g., invoice or bill of lading)
Open account:	direct payment required – no date or credit period shown (this is dangerous to use as it has no contractual payment date obligation).

Notes:

1. The seller's risk increases down the list.
2. A 'letter of credit' is normally an irrevocable letter of credit issued by the buyer's bank in favour of the seller usually advised and payable through a UK bank. It cannot be revoked or amended without the exporter's agreement but its 'no risk' value depends on the exporter's strict compliance with its conditions.
3. The CILC carries the added guarantee of a first-class UK bank.
4. The revocable L/C has all the benefits of a letter of credit but can be revoked or amended by the buyer at any time prior to payment.
5. In CAD or sight draft transactions, the seller retains ownership of the goods until payment, since the bank may only release the documents against payment. This works with sea shipments since the bill of lading is a document of title. The carrier will only release the goods to the holder of the original bill of lading (i.e., the customer, after he has paid the bank, or the exporter's agent if things go wrong). For exports by air, road or rail, no document of title exists, so the goods must be consigned to a bank or a representative of the exporter, for release to the customer only after payment.
6. With term drafts, the security position is the same as for sight drafts,

except that the collecting bank releases the goods against a legally binding obligation of payment later.

7. With both term drafts and open account, it is better for the exporter to apply a credit period from a fixed and indisputable event, such as shipment, rather than 'arrival' of the goods – which may be difficult to prove.

THE COST OF CREDIT

Trade credit involves a seller in several kinds of costs. They can all be quantified and thus could all be passed on to the buyer, although it may not be commercially sensible to do so. Some, such as the basic interest expense of the credit period, can be established in advance. Others, such as the interest incurred on delayed payments or collection costs can only be known after the event. Bad debts and all general expenses are usually spread over future prices in costings.

Even when debts are discounted or sold to a bank, credit costs are incurred in the finance charges. And a cash–discount inducement to the buyer for early payment only means the substitution of that cost for the interest cost of waiting for full payment.

Credit costs should never be ignored. They are substantial busines expenses and the price of goods and services directly or indirectly include them.

It is interesting to examine the costs of:

(a) the credit period and payment delays;
(b) bad debts and reserves;
(c) disputed or neglected accounts; and
(d) management and control;

and see their effect on profits and their risk to the business.

The credit period can be costed at the seller's overdraft rate and even a company with no overdraft (perhaps with net deposits at the bank) has the opportunity costs of reduced interest receivable.

For simplicity, assume that borrowings cost 12% p.a. That 1% per month means that the standard 30 days' credit costs 1% of the invoice value. Properly costed, prices should reflect this so that margins are not reduced. But realistically, prices should also take account of the full time that customers take to pay (the collection period, or DSO). A company with 75 DSO should be including a 2.5% interest cost in its prices.

Firstly, a company has to recognise this cost. Then it should decide whether its prices can stand the true credit expense, spread over all customers. It is usually unwieldy to load prices to individual customers according to payment delays. Some companies, but not many yet in the UK, recover credit costs by charging interest selectively to late-paying accounts (a commercial judgement and only possible if the right exists in the conditions of sale). If no method of passing on the expense is possible, a seller should at least measure the dilution of its P & L by the cost of the credit period and payment delays.

Bad debts are usually measured as a percentage of sales, e.g., losses of £30,000 = 0.2% of sales of £15 million. This seems insignificant, but it can be educational within a company to proclaim the extra sales needed to restore the losses. In the example, if net profit on sales is 5%, then fresh sales of £600,000 are needed on which 5% profit would replenish the lost amounts.

In practice, prudent companies reserve a part of profits for specifically doubtful accounts, with general reserves for a percentage of total receivables, in case of the unexpected. Having taken the pain in advance, it is then relatively easy to write off actual bad debts as they occur. Since reserves can be withdrawn for other needs at any time, credit managers usually prefer actual bad debt levels to be the basis for reserves or any other operating measurement. It is in this area of bad debt provisions that credit insurance protection can have a dramatically beneficial effect. Depending on audit policy, P & L account expense can be slashed to the minimum required for non-insured debts and the co-insurance percentages.

Uncollectable debts also arise from neglecting the administration of perfectly good accounts. It is bad practice to bracket these write-offs with real bad debts since it clouds the judgement of true credit control performance with that of collections and sales-ledger administration. The writing-off of residues of active accounts, whether minor disputes or unsolved queries, is invariably the fault of the seller.

When assets are being valued on a going-concern basis, e.g. in an acquisition proposal, it is usual to reduce the value of receivables according to their age. The following values are typical:

Current debts, not yet due	100%
1 month overdue	90%
3 months overdue	75%
6 months overdue	50%
12 months overdue	25%

This reduction of the book asset is an indication, based on experience, of the chances of collecting sales once they get old. The cost to profits already booked can be considerable and good credit systems are needed to avoid the decline.

The final credit cost area is that of management control. Whatever a company's degree of commitment to the credit task, it should somehow measure the cost of staff, computer, credit reports, credit insurance, and all other identifiable credit expenses. They should not be just mixed in with other general accounting items. Receivables should be measured on a DSO basis. Since interest expense can be measured from the DSO, it is possible to see whether spending more on credit systems would save a lot more in credit costs. Deciding how much to spend can benefit from first calculating the payback, e.g:

> sales are £20 million, so daily sales average £55,000;
> receivables are £5 million, so the DSO is 90;
> overdraft rate is 12% p.a., so bank interest is £600,000;
> a 10% DSO improvement would save £60,000;
> a reduction to 75 days would save £100,000.

Now the company can decide what it can afford to do to achieve the level of, say, 75 DSO and the saving of £100,000.

USING MANAGED CREDIT TO SELL TO RISKY ACCOUNTS

Apart from a very few overnight surprises, bad debts arise from slow-paying accounts, which usually exhibit signs of financial strain long before the crash. If companies were able to see the current financial status of all their customers at once, they could well find they had:

'A' accounts – very strong, negligible risk	10%
'B' accounts – average strength, some risk	60%
'C' accounts – undercapitalised, significant risk	30%

This is a typical pattern that has emerged from credit surveys. It means that, nationally, a lot of sales credit is allowed to customers who then fail. But how long elapses before 'then'? An aged debt analysis will probably show varying payment performance in all three classes, but *bad debts nearly always occur in 'C' type accounts that pay late*. Prompt-paying, well-capitalised accounts rarely go bust. The 'A', 'B' and 'C' codes can be allocated from available information or an analysis which then makes the management of the few really risky accounts much easier.

Good credit managers watch their 'marginal risk' accounts closely, so that maximum business is done while they live and not much remains unpaid when they eventually fail. It is a poor credit manager who loses available profit by refusing credit or closing high-risk accounts, unless he is certain that failure is imminent. It is important to put credit risk into the profit context, namely, most risky accounts will survive for some time; during that time they will buy things; profit is available in the short term; with good control, the unpaid debt will be small when they do go; and, of course, credit insurance cover puts a lot more confidence into the approach.

SUMMARY

Trade credit is essential for volume growth and to compete effectively. The range of business available to any one seller includes high-risk, average and low-risk customers. These can be identified from available information. Selling on credit presents a risky investment of borrowings or shareholders' funds in the receivables asset. The return on that investment is the profit margin expected from paid sales. That return is eroded by the interest expense of unplanned delays and completely lost when bad debts are incurred.

Competent management of trade credit requires positive action in several areas of the business and, in case the unexpected does still happen, protecting the asset with suitable credit insurance.

Credit means trust, after all.

3

Commercial credit risks

vwvwvwvwvwvwvwvw

The two key questions to probe credit risk are as follows:

1. 'Are they going bust?'
2. 'Can they pay our sales value on time?'

The information needed to answer these questions can also help sales staff, by dealing with the question, 'Are they growing or declining in their ability to buy from us in the future?'

Thus the main risks concern the *solvency*, *liquidity* and *growth* of customers.

Companies are free to sell or not to any customer, and since the risks all exist in the range of available customers, it is important to get answers to the risk questions before investing company funds in trade credit. Combined with the seller's freedom to allow credit or not is the need to organise a pause, in the rush for orders, to consider if the return justifies the risk. Not every seller pauses.

Earlier, we described the present-day atmosphere of volume risk in trade credit, created by a complex mixture of events which are not always allowed for by sellers. We went into more detail on specific features of credit, defining it as a separate entity in the sales contract, and said that the differing financial strengths of customers imply a number of risky situations.

There are usually financial or commercial pressures which tempt companies to accept risky orders. It is perhaps understandable when a seller decides to go ahead and supply, for special reasons, despite bad information he holds on a customer. There is no excuse, though, when a seller claims to be surprised by a bad debt loss without ever having checked on the ability of the customer to pay. Too many companies still put their managerial skills into production and selling, with little resource applied at the order-taking stage to controlling the risks.

Few insolvencies are total surprises. The build-up of warning signs are there, in payment behaviour, in balance-sheet information, and in personal comments and observations. But somebody must have the responsibility for watching for the signs and acting on them to protect sales and collections. Fortunately, because of today's high money cost and slimmer net margins, companies are applying more effort to asset control. Just as inventory had more attention in the 1970s era of cutbacks and cost reductions, so debtors took on more significance in the 1980s. But in some firms, credit control still only means collecting debts coming onto the sales ledger, rather than assessing the prospects of being paid before orders are delivered. Credit control should mean being on top of risk problems, not being taken by surprise. The mature position in credit management means being able to point sales staff towards the more worthwhile customers and away from the risky ones, who have less potential buying ability.

So, as sellers have a choice, there is a clear inference that insolvency losses are created largely by sellers themselves, in selling to customers without the ability to pay.

WHAT ARE THE RISKS?

Commercial credit risks are those which cause nonpayment by the default of trade and non-governmental buyers. They exist in both home and export sales. Political risks such as defaults by governments or actions by them which prevent payment by trade buyers, are found only in export sales. (See Table 3.1.)

Table 3.1 Credit risk in home and export sales

	Home sales	Export sales
Commercial risks:		
Buyer's insolvency	X	X
Buyer's payment default at due date	X	X
Buyer's repudiation of contract	X	X
Political risks:		
Non transfer of hard currency to UK		X
Moratorium on external debt by buyer's country		X
Import or export licence regulations		X
War preventing contract performance		X
Other governmental actions		X

Note: a fuller list of political risks is given in chapter 4.

PAYMENT BEHAVIOUR

In commercial credit risks, we are really focussing on buyers' insolvencies because the others – payment default and repudiation of contract
– are due, usually, to buyers' actual or near state of insolvency. There is
also a great deal of commercial breach of contract by companies from
day to day. Business language is full of euphemisms for undesirable
activities. 'Cash management' is typical, when it really means delaying
payment for 'as long as we can get away with it', regardless of agreed
terms.

The range of excuses for delaying payment is as wide as man's
ingenuity and excuses are only used because people know they are in the
wrong. Credit managers soon learn during routine collection action that
payment delays produce highly improbable excuses, such as the
following:

1. 'The cheque is in the post/on its way to you/being prepared.'
2. 'The computer run is in two week's time.'
3. 'Mr (important name) has to approve all payments.'
4. 'One of the signatories is on holiday/off sick/not here.'
5. 'We need proof of delivery.' (Again!)
6. 'We've run out of cheques.'
7. 'We have a temporary cash-flow problem.' (This slick excuse, meant
   to put off a creditor, has legal implications of insolvency. A
   company either can or cannot meet its liabilities as they fall due. No
   director should ever make this excuse.)

Then there are the debtors that refuse to pay until they feel good and
ready, blatantly in breach of agreed contract terms, with responses such
as, 'We pay everyone at 60 days – if you don't like it, we'll buy from
someone else.' These sinister threats are very worrying to smaller
businesses, who also suffer damage from the lack of major cash receipts.
Other off-putting threats from larger to smaller firms are, 'We'll cancel
the contract unless you agree to . . .', and, 'We know other suppliers
who are willing to give us longer credit.'

Customers' reactions to payment requests in daily collection activity
are an underrated source of credit intelligence. All put-offs represent
risks of loss because sellers cannot be sure when, if ever, payment will be
made. Because most orders have a payment condition, nonpayment at
the precise date is a breach of contract, technically actionable in law. In
practice, payment delays tend to be resolved within days or weeks.
Those overdue customers who play games for a long time with no
genuine excuse are frequently found to be the insolvencies of the near
future.

A genuine total inability to pay, for more than a few days, is rare. If a customer wants to pay, it will find the money, even if this means borrowing extra from the bank. However, when its borrowing powers are fully stretched, the bank starts to take a close interest, with receivership a strong possibility. It is during this critical period, usually unknown in detail by supplier–creditors, that the excuses offered by a customer are the first signals of an insolvency cover-up. The task for credit managers is to segregate the real insolvencies from the day to day delaying tactics.

Some sellers, especially those not employing skilled credit managers, make life difficult for themselves by being unwilling even to ask for overdues, to avoid 'upsetting' customers. Not only do such weak firms fail to take the right collection steps to compete for their cash, but they also tend to have larger bad debts. Any supposed sales advantage in not pressing for due payments is far outweighed by the interest and bad debt effects on profits. Sadly, it is the companies that do not apply the required effort to credit and collection management that complain loudest to press and government about their bad treatment by large customers.

THE LAW OF 10:1

This states that 'an average company incurs ten times more expense in interest on the extra borrowings needed to finance overdue debtors than it loses in bad debts each year.' A sweeping generalisation? Every company can work out its own ratio. But what are the implications? One might be that the obsession of top management with bad debt risk should be replaced immediately by an investigation of their slow-paying customers. This would improve bad debt performance anyway, since insolvencies come from slow-paying accounts rather than good payers. This is precisely why credit insurance companies prefer policy-holders with good credit systems.

STANDARD OR SPECIAL GOODS

A major factor in granting credit is whether products are standard, and thus resaleable elsewhere, or specially tailored ones which would be dead stock if credit were restricted. This consideration helps to decide whether to assess the risks at the order stage or only when delivery is due.

For example, a manufacturer of electric light bulbs would not suffer undue loss if an order were frustrated before delivery. The goods could still be sent to the next buyer. Exposure to credit loss would only begin once goods were delivered. On the other hand, a company which had made electronic controls to operate a specific customer's machinery would certainly suffer loss if orders were cancelled, because their particular output would not be saleable to others.

Some businesses are able to deliver their products almost immediately orders are received, i.e., with no significant lead time. When the order date and the date of sale are almost the same, all credit risks begin at that point.

CREDIT RISK AND MARKETING

Credit risk should obviously influence sales planning and expense. Considerable time and money is spent on activities such as product design, market research, production planning and, not least, customer cultivation. When customers go into decline, let alone go bust, there is invariably a setback to marketing plans and a write-off of advance expense. It is always sensible for sales and credit people to work closely together in identifying good, average and time-wasting sales prospects. And to know more about each other's activities.

How can all this be brought together for simple practical application? The evaluation and control of risks is dealt with in detail in chapter 5, but at this stage we can say that sellers should look at each major customer and ask themselves the following questions:

1. Is the buyer about to go bust? If so, when? If not:
2. How much can the buyer comfortably pay at the due date? And if the answers so far are positive:
3. Will the buyer still exist next year, to justify marketing expense and further planning?

It does not matter whether buyers are in this country or abroad – the judgement is equally necessary.

USING CREDIT INFORMATION

A buyer's financial situation obviously influences his ability to purchase and to pay. As it is possible to find out how much a buyer can pay comfortably within a certain period, it seems pointless to discuss order values that can never materialise or will be far less than the salesman anticipates.

When getting information on buyers, sellers usually want to find out something like, 'Are they good for £x?', meaning 'If we sell them £x, will they be able to pay us?' A seller is volunteering for a slow or bad debt if he sells £100,000 to a buyer known by others to be good for only

£1,000. And he is doubly guilty if he does not even bother to find out the buyer's capability.

Credit reports and the opinions of others, including credit insurers, are available as aids to a seller's business decisions. They should never dictate how he runs his business. The seller's own credit management function must aim at approving every possible piece of profitable business, and the key word 'profitable' means identifying any risks and doing something about them. A bad debt in a controlled situation is rarely as serious or as large as a surprise one.

CREDIT RATINGS

There is no exact way of calculating how much a customer can find to pay on time – it depends on his liquidity, obligations to other creditors and attitudes to particular suppliers. But it certainly is possible to allocate credit ratings within broad bands, e.g., customers good for £1,000 but not £10,000, or those easily good for over half a million pounds (i.e., more than enough for most businesses), and so on. For example, if a customer's cash flow intake is only £1,000 a month, it is very unlikely that he can settle a £50,000 bill on time. And if his own DSO is 76 and his creditors' total is equivalent to 92 days, it would need a very special arrangement to be sure of getting monthly payments from him on time.

Having obtained reports and opinions, it is a pity to restrict conclusions to just a credit rating. The same data also gives indications of customers' growth and activity. It can be useful to sales and marketing staff to know that customer 'A', whether a prompt or a slow payer, is growing steadily and worth cultivating, whereas customer 'B' shows a stagnating or failing trend, so that further marketing would be a poor investment. As more firms tighten up on sales cost per order, and salesmen are motivated to get better ratios of orders to visits, it is well worth identifying the better prospects in advance.

COLLECTIONS

Financial resources indicate ability to pay but this is not the same as willingness to pay, which is why substantial efforts have to be made to collect accounts. The money does not just turn up, even from rich customers. Collection of debts needs some planning – how to use limited resources; the right approach for different kinds of debts; the constant training of staff; the support of top management; but, above all, a company-wide approach to the importance of the task. The secret of maximising cash intake is to be willing and able to ask every customer to pay. The willingness must not be clouded by some vague fear of losing sales – the customer has, after all, had the benefit from the goods, and has contracted to pay for them on a defined date, even if he intends to stretch the credit a little. There is no genuine risk to relationships. The ability to ask for every single debt at the right time requires enough resources to send letters and make telephone calls or personal visits. Rarely can companies afford enough staff to achieve full coverage and cut-backs in this area of expertise are certainly a false economy.

WHY DO COMPANIES FAIL?

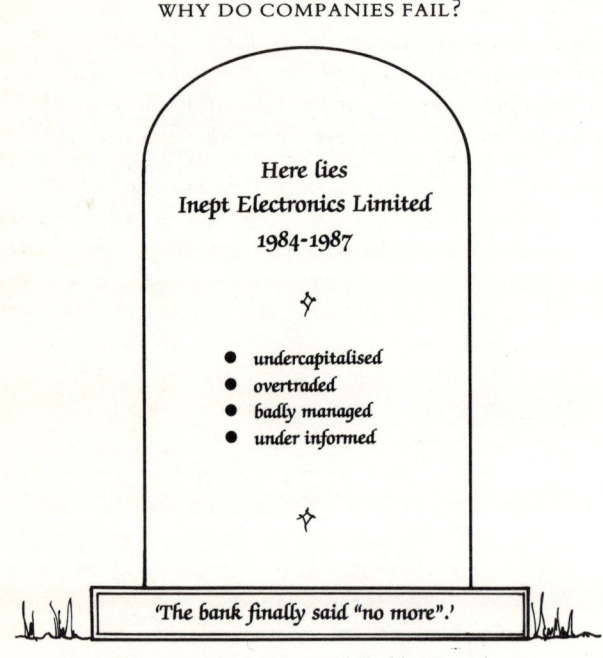

Fig. 3.1 'Epitaph to a failed business'

Just as humans always die from lack of breath, for which there are many reasons, so do companies always die from lack of funds, with many different reasons for that occurring. (See Fig. 3.1.)

In the unprecedented UK business scene of 1984–7, with record insolvency numbers, millions of jobs gone, much technical skill lost and thousands of buyers looking for new suppliers, there were two common denominators.

Firstly, the failed businesses often had enough orders, but had too much money tied up in over-manufactured stocks and overdue debtors so that they were unable to repay their creditors. At some point, their banks refused to lend any more, because they could not see the possibility of repayment, even of interest. So, lack of liquid funds is the prime indicator of impending doom. Even when a balance sheet shows an excess of assets over liabilities (i.e., solvency), the 'going-concern' position no longer obtains when a creditor forces a winding-up. The break-up value when assets have to be sold off is always far less than the balance sheet showed and thus there is even less ability to pay creditors, whose claims do not reduce. That is why companies should not just demonstrate solvency to their banks and creditors – they must also be liquid enough to meet commitments. The preventative medicine for insolvency is liquidity, not solvency, or even profit.

The second common feature in business failures is the lack of management information. In a well-run company, operating data is produced at frequent intervals, at least monthly. It gives visibility and warning of problems such as excess costs, loss-making activities, slow-paying customers, and so on, early enough to correct them. There are some successful companies who have less frequent data but excellent communication all the way from shop-floor right up to the Board. But companies get into trouble when they do not produce timely data. Or choose to ignore it.

One kind of company at risk is that driven by an autocrat who has consistently suppressed the views of his functional experts. Another is where strong personal relationships with suppliers have created a false sense of well-being, which means nothing when the bank calls in the overdraft. Yet another occurs when large corporations develop too many levels of management and supervision over the years; the Board becomes isolated from the daily hurly-burly and if data is slow to reach them because of too many levels, or if bad news is disguised by creative accounting, even a company with a good asset base can become sluggish and highly geared, and usually vulnerable to acquisition – a more respectable form of failure.

Most UK businesses are small, with less than 50 employees or £1 million turnover. Very few can employ specialist managers. They have usually grown because of technical or sales excellence. Growth gradually makes it more difficult for the owners to keep a personal watch on everything, and there is often a mistaken belief that the bank or the auditors will keep them on the right financial lines. Many a small businessman is shocked to find that banks and auditors have no such obligation. Auditors perform only their legal duty and do not, unasked or unpaid, sit down with owners to discuss ratios and trends. Banks are too busy to manage clients' finances and concern themselves with ensuring there is adequate security for the lending (usually a ratio of one and a half or two times). When the crash occurs, the plaintive cry, often, is, 'Why didn't anyone warn me?'

LIQUIDITY AND INFORMATION: LACK OF EITHER IS DANGEROUS
TO A BUSINESS; LACK OF BOTH IS ALMOST CERTAINLY FATAL

That being so obvious, why do companies still fail? If the signs are there, why don't managements take corrective actions? There is a disease of myopic business optimism, by no means the same as genuine business confidence. Right up to the end, some owners do not believe their bank will enforce closure of the company because, 'We are different.'

Financial analysis of a cross-section of companies in various industries shows that solvency, liquidity and growth ratios rise or fall gradually over a short period of years, rather than steeply. And they rarely zigzag. For companies going down, it is the angle of decline which usually dictates whether rescue is possible or not.

WARNING SIGNS OF INSOLVENCY

'Receivers have been called in to the troubled De Lorean company in Belfast, where losses are expected to reach several millions.' So stated the TV newsreader one evening in our living rooms. Other business failures are given varying degrees of prominence in the daily media. To the uninvolved, there is usually an element of surprise ('Gosh! Who'd have thought that Rolls Royce would ever go bust!'). Some businessmen even have a kind of blind faith that their particular customers are somehow insulated from the national insolvency statistics. But for alert creditors, there is almost always plenty of warning. It is one thing to see the signs, but quite another to take the steps necessary to reducing the exposure.

Credit managers, bank lending officers and City analysts all have their own ways of spotting potential failures. The main methods are the following:

1.   Account behaviour and responses to payment requests.
2.   Trends in financial ratios.
3.   Behaviour of key personalities.
4.   Computerised failure-forecasting services.

John Argenti, writing on corporate collapse,[1] stated that the final stages of a company's dive to failure are not reversible (for failure, include acquisition or merger). Instead of measuring balance-sheet factors, he observed that external symptoms show in three phases over a short period of years. The initial defect is a serious imbalance of senior

1. See Edwards, H., *Credit Management Handbook*, 2nd edn (Gower Publishing, Aldershot, 1985), pp. 108–12.

management, either in skills or personalities, which results in the second phase of major mistakes in funding and handling debt obligations; then come the final acts of desperation with creative accounting, cut-backs in premises or operations, resignations and so on to the end.

No supplier could watch for those features in all his customers but it is possible for selected accounts, where any debt or loss of outlet would seriously damage the business.

In specific industries, credit analysts have developed balance-sheet profiles of firms that have failed and compared them with those that have succeeded over a given period, say, five years. The features and year-to-year trends are weighted and given scores, so that comparisons can be made with existing or new customers.

Some commercial organisations sell insolvency forecasting services. From a large database of company-performance ratios, usually by industry sector, they make comparative analyses and have a vital pass-mark level, and companies scoring above it are expected to survive and those below it to fail. Critics point to the lack of a predicted date of failure but agree that the warning itself is valuable. In *Credit Management Handbook*[2] Howard Tisshaw shows how the PAS-score of his company, Performance Analysis Services Ltd, is a UK refinement of the original Z-score model of Altman in the USA. Tisshaw states boldly, 'No company has failed without warning since 1972 and there has usually been three years' notice.'

In a lighter vein, but based on solid professional experience, a well-known receiver, William Mackey, has written that any company exhibiting four or more of the following fifteen non-financial factors is doomed to fail:

1. A fish tank or fountain in reception.
2. A Rolls-Royce with personalised number plates.
3. A flag-pole.
4. The Queen's Award for Industry (not exports).
5. A chairman knighted for services to industry.
6. A salesman or engineer as chief executive.
7. A recent move into a prestigious new office block.
8. An elderly chief accountant.
9. Market leaders.
10. Recently changed main bankers.
11. Auditors that grew up with the company.
12. A chairman who is an MP.
13. A recently announced huge order from Afghanistan.

2. *Ibid.*, pp. 103–7.

14. Satisfied staff with no strike record.
15. A recently publicised major technological breakthrough.

People managing credit risk from day to day look first to payment behaviour and the way customers respond to collection requests. In Dick Bass's book *Credit Management*[3] he warns particularly of cheques returned by the bank marked 'refer to drawer' rather than 'please represent' as a reliable warning of near insolvency. Suppliers unaware of this may treat them as routine for cashiers to handle, rather than risk indicators.

Every day, salesman talk to customers about orders and credit staff telephone for payments. Both activities are strong opportunities to detect insolvency signals. A customer's employee may say, too freely, 'We've got problems, I've heard the bank is cracking the whip.' Or, 'Can't do anything right now, we've been told to freeze orders (or payments, etc.)' Other comments may be less direct, and sales and credit staff must be trained to listen for signals.

DISPUTED DEBTS AS A RISK

Most companies experience a level of disputed billings, where customers refuse to pay until mistakes have been rectified. Ideally, sellers would rectify errors immediately and satisfy customers for good commercial reasons, apart from their liability to do so. But in practice, chasing new orders means that customer claims are deferred as less urgent. It is then not long before claims accumulate and delays in settling them become the norm.

What kind of disputes? In many manufacturing industries there is a pattern of credit notes issued of between 1% and 5% of sales billed, mostly for wrong price charged; goods defective; delivery too late; shortages; goods not received; proof of delivery needed, and so on.

Because few sellers rectify errors straightaway, customers have learned that it pays to generate formal claim documents, or debit notes. These are sent to suppliers for action and payments are reduced in one of the following ways:

1. The error value is deducted from the next payment.
2. Payment is withheld for the value of the entire invoice on which the error occurred.
3. Payment is withheld for the entire account.

Credit departments usually refer the claims to sales staff for action and

3. Bass, Dick, *Credit Management* (Business Books, London, 1979).

this can take time. The delay has already been aggravated by the error detail only becoming known when an amount is deducted from a payment. This may be well after the due date, and a long time after the original sales error. A customer in financial difficulty is able to play the system and delay payments or make deductions by alleging faults and defects. The time lapse before his true motive is detected depends on the efficiency of the supplier in handling claims. It is to be hoped that the customer does not go bust meanwhile.

Apart from the interest cost of supporting receivables inflated by excessive disputed amounts, some suppliers lose more than they need to in insolvencies, if they have been slack in resolving claims so that properly due balances may be collected.

EVENTS PRECEDING RECEIVERSHIP

We have said that there is usually an observable behaviour by a customer before a receiver is appointed. Thus it pays a creditor to keep in close touch with his customers, especially those in the high-risk category.

The major credit reporting agencies provide a service to 'watch' specified account names. In addition to obtaining standard reports on customers when opening accounts, a supplier can nominate accounts on which he would like a flash notice of problems, including county court judgements, adverse press reports or trade rumours, and deteriorations seen at Companies House.

Prior to a receivership, the debtor has probably had his assets secured by a bank by means of a debenture or charge. This document, legally registered at Companies House, gives the lender the right to appoint someone to take charge of the business if he feels justified (usually if he cannot see a good prospect of recovering his investment). The debtor receives one or more dire warnings to reduce or repay the loan and this creates frantic activity by the debtor to (a) ask for more time, or (b) try to raise capital elsewhere and (c) delay payment to other creditors so as to conserve funds for its prime lender. There may be a series of meetings, where the bank looks for a solution to avoid receivership. Quite often, banks are persuaded to put further good money after bad, while the directors try to complete a sale, sell off plant or stock, or perhaps the entire business. At the other extreme, banks are sometimes accused of doing nothing for years because they hold security, then deciding in haste that the overdraft must be reduced within hours.

The warnings of a debenture holder to its debtor are usually in confidence since any publicity could cause a panic by other creditors. Sometimes a debtor takes major suppliers into his confidence to reduce pressure for payment. But most ordinary suppliers are unaware of the critical events just prior to a receivership, so the possibility of any constructive collaborative action to save the customer is lost. Contrast the hectic, last-throes situation within a company with the unaware view from the outside. Several trade creditors are owed money by one particular company which is about to go bust. With many other overdue accounts and no special knowledge of this crisis, a creditor regards the debtor as just an overdue account in the sales ledger. One day, a number of suppliers get a standard letter from a receiver telling them of his appointment. Despite the importance of their product to the customer, or the years of business relationship, they will have been totally excluded from the final discussions.

THE INSOLVENCY ACT 1986

The Act has changed several aspects of receivership, not the least being to change his title to 'administrative receiver'. Recognising that the average unsecured creditor is excluded from the decision to appoint him, the Act requires him to provide a lot more information to creditors.

The Act was based on the report of the Insolvency Law Review Committee, under Sir Kenneth Cork (President of the Institute of Credit Management), which worked diligently over a long period to rationalise the peculiar morass of insolvency and bankruptcy drills then in force. Parliament duly took some years to debate the Report and the new Insolvency Act finally came into force in January 1987.

Sir Kenneth had emphasised that insolvent businesses should be given more help to survive. The credit world was, however, generally surprised that his committee recommended continuation of the floating charge, stating that it had become central to commercial life in the UK and had actually helped company survival by allowing debenture holders to appoint receivers. This conclusion went against the view of all other EEC countries where a floating charge to secure lending is either illegal or not practised.

Experienced credit managers generally took the view that a chance had been missed to force banks to lend more expertly, and improve the day to day management of companies by taking a charge only on specific assets, or taking up shares or joining the boards of major borrowers. A charge on floating stocks and debtors is not only too easy for a dominant lender to force onto a dependent borrower, but it also reduces the break-up value of assets available to unsecured trade suppliers. Floating charges, whilst of help to the banks, reduce the confidence level for trade credit.

Nor did the Cork Committee do anything to strengthen unsecured creditors' rights with Retention of Title (ROT). Since the Romalpa case in the 1970s, suppliers have tried to achieve an effective clause in their conditions of contract to keep ownership of goods until the customer has paid. If this practice were reliably in everyday use (as in Germany and some other EEC countries), it would help to equalise the position of trade creditors and banks. If unpaid stocks could be recovered from receivers, it is possible that trade credit would be more adventurously granted in marginal cases – that is, to the very companies that need credit when liquidity is tight.

Various court cases since Romalpa have shown the difficulty of trying to apply ROT. The result is that trade creditors cannot be confident of recovery and banks can be confident that their floating charges include goods contractually stated to belong to trade suppliers.

At a European credit management conference in Madrid in 1982, a German credit analyst expressed astonishment that UK trade creditors labour under the double handicap of having no effective ROT rights and losing their own property to banks holding floating charges over customers' assets well in excess of their loans. He believed that the German post-war economic miracle had benefited from the extra confidence in granting credit that the German ROT (*Eigentumsvorbehalt*) had provided to unsecured creditors.

The new Insolvency Act can be summarised as follows:

1. *Insolvency practitioners* need authorisation to practise as receivers, liquidators, administrators or trustees in bankruptcy. Authority is given by recognised professional bodies or the Department of Trade and Industry.
2. *Company directors* can be disqualified from office if unfit for the job. Receivers and the like have to report any such unfitness. Where insolvent companies have traded wrongfully, directors may be ordered to contribute personally to the assets. Directors are not allowed to use the names of failed companies within five years of liquidation.
3. *Administrators* can be appointed by courts at the request of company directors or creditors, to help companies in difficulty. Between petition and appointment the company is protected by the court from being wound up. The administrator can try to get creditors' support for a rescue plan within three months, then manage the company back to health or increase the realisable assets.
4. *Receivers* are now called administrative receivers (*not* the same as administrators) and the Act sets out their powers over the company's

property. It also requires them to notify all creditors of their appointment and to provide them with more information and progress reports.

5. *Company winding-up* is simpler, for creditors' benefit. The two kinds are by court order, or voluntary. Winding-up by the courts helps the official receiver to concentrate on investigating fraud or the right to disqualify directors. Statements of affairs and dividend forecasts have to be given to creditors within three months. Voluntary winding-up requires the company to give more information to creditors and not to sell assets until creditors have met to discuss the situation. In a members' voluntary winding-up (where the shareholders believe the creditors can all be paid in full) the liquidator has to inform the creditors if he disagrees.

6. *Common provisions* include the reduction of governmental preference in tax debts and the abolition of preference for local authority rates. Utility suppliers, such as gas and electricity, are no longer able to demand payment of overdues as a condition of further supply. Courts have more power to recover debts due to insolvent companies and recent credit transactions on unusual terms can be reviewed by the courts. Other transactions during or just before the insolvency can be set aside.

7. *Company voluntary arrangements* with creditors by small firms in temporary difficulty are made easier by the concept of nominees and supervisors. The nominee works with the directors to propose arrangements with creditors. Then the supervisor (usually the ex-nominee) is responsible for implementing the final agreements.

8. *Bankruptcy* for individuals is simplified and aligned as far as possible with insolvency drills applying to companies. Personal voluntary arrangements are now allowed more time and encouragement to succeed and thus avoid actual bankruptcy.

Michael Howard, the Government minister responsible at the time of the Act said:

Perhaps the most significant sections of the Act are those that tackle the problems caused by the minority of company directors who fail in their duties and responsibilities. They not only harm their own businesses but also damage others, consumers, and the economy as a whole.

I believe the new Act will offer much greater protection for creditors; it will encourage directors to take prompt action when their businesses experience financial difficulties; and it will deter directors from abusing the privileges of limited liability.

Cork Gully's *Guide to the Insolvency Act 1986*[4] states, 'We look forward to the enhanced opportunities it will provide to rehabilitate insolvent businesses.'

In summary, trade creditors should be encouraged by the Act – that directors are discouraged from taking credit when insolvent; that governmental preference is reduced; that receivers should consult creditors a lot more; and that more companies should be helped to survive.

LIQUIDATION AND BANKRUPTCY

Insolvent individuals (including sole traders and partnerships) can be made bankrupt but limited companies go into liquidation. Prior to liquidation, a receiver may be appointed to manage the business with a view to recovering the lender's investment. In a very few cases, the receiver does succeed in turning a company round, or he sells it on to another company, so that it continues to operate in some form. But otherwise it is liquidated.

We can look at what happens to available funds when a company closes. In chapter 5, we look in detail at the different forms of winding up a company. Whether it is instigated by shareholders, courts or creditors, a liquidator is appointed to sell off assets and pay out proceeds in a certain sequence:

1. Secured creditors with fixed charges.
2. Liquidator's costs and fees.
3. Preferential debts (pro-rated if proceeds are inadequate):
   (a) wages for the previous four months;
   (b) accrued holiday pay;
   (c) social security contributions for twelve months;
   (d) PAYE for twelve months;
   (e) VAT for six months.
   NB If a bank has specifically advanced extra money for wages it takes the place of (a).
4. Secured creditors with floating charges.
5. *Unsecured creditors.*
6. Debts due to shareholders, (e.g., unpaid dividends).
7. Capital of shareholders.
8. Surplus to shareholders.

4. Cork Gully's *Guide to the Insolvency Act 1986* (Coopers & Lybrand, London, 1987).

Precedence is given to security, governmental dictate and staff protection. Whereas it may be right that shareholders come last (after all, they voluntarily risked their money, had control of the business and could pay themselves dividends) it is baffling that the largest debt, i.e., ordinary trade credit, should rank next to last.

It is usually found that the money from assets sold does not go very far down the list. In the 1960s, a credit manager had a rule of thumb of recovering 10% from insolvencies. In the 1980s it is usually zero.

In other countries, notably Scandinavian, attempts are made to avoid company closure by arranging compromise settlements with all creditors, secured or not. It is quite common for all creditors, including banks, to agree to scale down their claims to 30% or 40%. Apart from the social and technical advantages, this gives creditors the chance to offset their losses with profits from continued sales. Such compromises are perfectly possible in the UK, but are rare, due to the fervency of secured lenders to achieve full recovery.

An important feature of the 1986 Act is the intention to rescue more companies by the use of 'administrators' appointed by the courts. Once an order is made, actions to exercise securities or wind up a company are effectively blocked. A court will grant an order if it believes that one of the following could be achieved:

1. Survival of the company as a going concern.
2. Approval of a voluntary arrangement.
3. Sanctioning of a scheme of arrangement under section 425 of the Companies Act 1985.
4. A much better realisation of assets than in a liquidation.

In a personal insolvency (formerly, bankruptcy), the prospects of recovery by trade creditors are minimal. After all, if a debtor has a surplus of net assets, prior collection measures would probably have worked. If the deficit is considerable, there is no point in going for a bankruptcy just for vengeance. For the evasive debtor with funds who is determined to delay until the last minute, whatever is threatened, a seller should be really certain that only a Notice of Bankruptcy would produce payment, otherwise it would be uneconomic to incur the costs required by the process.

In both insolvency and bankruptcy, voluntary agreements with creditors are encouraged, so that official closure can be stayed whilst attempts are made to agree alternative arrangements.

The experience of other countries, who achieved the UK's intentions on insolvency law many years ago, has been that generally it is better for all creditors to accept a compromise settlement, lick their wounds, and allow a debtor company to continue its life, with improved management and financial reorganisation, than for secured creditors to be allowed to force the death of a company without even being certain of recovering their debts.

In managing his companies' investments in trade credit over the last 30 years, the author has found that legal action and the insolvency routines that may follow are negative, futile and never cost-effective. The time and expense devoted to killing off customers is much better spent at the front end of transactions, so that sales efforts can be concentrated on good and growing customers. The poor risks can be left to competitors, who may take today's profit of 5% and tomorrow's write-off of 100%!

4

Political credit risks

vwvwvwvwvwvwvwvwvw

INTRODUCTION: COUNTRY RISK BEFORE CUSTOMER RISK

'If the country risk is not acceptable there is no point in examining the buyer.'[1] That concise observation pinpoints the problem of the dramatic increase in the 1980s of country credit risks. The most careful credit assessment of export customers and their cultivation by sales staff is of little use if their local payments of pesos, kwachas or other soft currencies cannot be converted into dollars or pounds. The situation is that nearly half the nations of the world have almost zero foreign currency to spend on imports. And, for a variety of reasons, governments impose restrictive conditions to prevent the intended performance of contracts between willing commercial parties.

Political risks apply only to international business. The two main kinds are:

(a) the *transfer* risk, where a shortage of foreign exchange in the buyer's country delays payment to the UK; and
(b) the risk of *political events* which prevent or delay payment even if there is enough currency available.

The risks are defined by the state credit insurance agencies such as ECGD (Export Credits Guarantee Department) as follows:

1. A general moratorium on external debt decreed by the government of the buyer's country or of a third country through which payment must be made.
2. Any other action by the government of the buyer's country which prevents performance of the contract in whole or in part.
3. Political events, economic difficulties, legislative or administrative measures arising outside the UK which prevent or delay the transfer of payments or deposits made in respect of the contract.
4. Legal discharge of a debt (not being legal discharge under the proper law of the contract) in a foreign currency, which results in a shortfall at the date of transfer.

5. War and certain other events preventing performance of the contract provided that the event is not one normally insured with commercial insurers.

6. Cancellation or nonrenewal of a UK export licence or the prohibition or restriction on export from the UK by law.

Political risks arise from events which are outside the control of the exporter and the buyer. The most common one is the transfer risk where the buyer's government has insufficient foreign currency to enable him to meet his obligations in the currency of the contract, even though he can pay in full in his local currency. Even in a continuing situation of currency shortage, the buyer should still deposit his local payment at the prevailing rate of exchange on the due date and be contractually obliged to make up any shortfall to achieve the necessary hard currency total at the date of the eventual transfer.

There is serious country risk in most South American countries, much of Africa and parts of Asia. Even a person not remotely interested in exporting sees frequent press and TV reports of 'debt rescheduling' and the 'world debt crisis'. In 1987, over 60 of the world's 208 countries were under the strict influence of the IMF (International Monetary Fund) to help them to reschedule their foreign debt obligations. Some had reapplied for the second or third time in less than five years, because they had failed to keep to stretched out instalment plans. Compare this to a trade debtor who cannot pay, agrees an instalment plan, then fails to keep to it. Should he get more credit?

ECGD and their OECD (Organisation for Economic Cooperation and Development) equivalents (which exist, after all, to encourage exports) were restricting cover for about 70 markets in 1987 because of past defaults and claims experience.

Countertrade is an anachronistic device which is officially frowned upon by OECD governments and makes no long-term economic sense, yet it is demanded by some 90 countries as a condition of ordering from strong countries, so as to offset the outflow of hard currency. These countries include major nations such as Canada and Australia when really large import contracts are involved, such as defence equipment and telecommunications systems.

Of great potential significance is the influence of population growth on political risk situations. About two-thirds of the world's nations are already net importers from the other one-third. As continuing net importers they will remain net debtors. The importer-debtor nations are

1. Bass, Dick, *Credit Management* (Business Books, London, 1979).

those with large and growing populations while the strong exporter–creditor nations tend to have stable populations. This people-driven economic timebomb must be a bigger threat than even the present vast debt crisis. The demand for food and basic requirements is growing enormously in the very countries that cannot afford to buy them, whilst the rich nations, with negligible domestic growth in demand, must somehow export their over-abundance of production. The prospects for exporters and their banks of being paid in traditional ways seem very uncertain. For many markets, we are surely entering an era of innovative funding within political and regional groupings, which will involve official institutions, banks, and governments, as well as very long-term pay-back periods for equity and investment schemes. The average exporter of ordinary products will either have to compete harder in the few, strong markets available or get involved in complicated ways of getting paid for sales to the mass of soft-currency markets. The risk management task would appear to be increasing in difficulty.

It has been said by the pundits that the large Third World debts will never actually be repaid to creditor banks and governmental agencies. Continued rescheduling plus occasional new lending enables interest payments and sometimes a little principal debt to be repaid. But the enforced hardship and reduced spending needed to find the repayments is extreme and unending.

The risk situation in all over-borrowed countries must be a major concern to all exporters, since it not only delays payment of old sales, but severely restricts the scope for new business.

Apart from those countries lacking foreign currency resources, there is also political credit risk in the ones that are hostile to, or who create trade difficulties with, established supplying nations.

WHAT CAUSES COUNTRIES TO BECOME CREDIT RISKS?

It is simply their inability to earn surpluses from foreign trade and repay instalments on foreign loans as they fall due. A country can only pay for imported goods and services with currencies earned by exporting at least as much, i.e., having a good balance of trade. To supplement FX (foreign exchange) earnings during occasional periods of deficit, nations borrow from foreign banks on fairly long terms. These governmental loans are known by the banks as 'sovereign risk debts'. Countries also have specific medium-term loans for capital projects such as roads, factories and waterworks. These projects take some years to become useful, either by earning foreign income themselves or by saving import payments. But all the borrowings have to be repaid on the terms contracted with the foreign banks or governments. When lending, banks assume that foreign governmental borrowers have tied in repayment obligations with their national planning of foreign earnings, spending and reserves. But this is not necessarily so. The rapid boom of the 1970s in capital lending by western banks to the LDCs (less developed countries) took little or no account of their abilities to repay, mainly because nobody kept the score on behalf of all lenders. Thus, whilst the export industry was notching up record sales figures and pleasing shareholders in the 1970s, the banks and export credit agencies began to worry about the loan repayments due in the 1980s.

Oil prices increased fourfold in the '70s and the producers banked their wealth with western banks, who lent on to Third World countries to finance huge imported infrastructure projects. Then the boom collapsed, interest rates, and thus country debts, increased, whilst demand reduced for LDC exports. So their repayment obligations increased just when their earnings reduced. Payments began to be delayed to trade creditors, many of whom were not credit insured. Banks began to express concern about repayment of sovereign loans and instalments of trade-related loans. Further lending was drastically cut.

Mexico started the slide in August 1982 when it officially declared its inability to repay that year's instalments on $90,000 million due to some 400 US, European and Japanese banks. Then followed Brazil and thirty or so other nations and the IMF were required to be central organisers of many rescue plans. Their actions included insisting that debtor governments restricted imports, devalued their local currency against the dollar, and froze wage levels. All these actions increased the hardships of already poor citizens and caused civil disorder and riots in places such as Brazil and Argentina.

The Latin American debts are the highest in world history, a testament to the neglect of good credit management principles by the banks. Brazil and Mexico together owe $200,000 million. The rest of South America owes a further $150,000 million. Nearer to home, Poland has been cut adrift from normal Comecon support, and owes $25,000 million, whilst oil-rich Nigeria is the leading African debtor nation with over $20,000 million.

If any of the major debtor nations ever declare that they will cease repayments, especially of interest amounts, the consequences for several creditor banks could be fatal. The probability is that the banks will reschedule again and again so that the debts can be kept alive with interest payments, whilst the banks earn money elsewhere.

THE TRANSFER RISK

Almost all payments for exports are made by international transfer of funds between banks, i.e., from those representing customers to those acting for exporters. Every bank handling foreign business holds accounts with major banks in most other countries. When a UK exporter has to be paid say, £5,000 by a customer in West Germany, the payment should arrive rapidly and without difficulty, because West Germany is a net exporter to the UK. The customer's bank in West Germany will almost certainly have ample sterling funds in its London branch or owed to it by a UK correspondent bank. It will simply credit a tiny part of those funds to the exporter's bank and the exporter should receive his £5,000 within a few days.

But now consider a payment to be made by a customer in Zambia or Peru. Poor countries such as these have little or no pools of foreign currency, simply because they are net importers and also have borrowed so much from abroad in recent years that most foreign earnings are already pledged in loan repayments. The customer's bank would not have any surplus sterling funds in London as the German bank did. When countries have serious foreign currency shortages, their central banks impose various forms of rationing of payments with systems involving import licences and special approvals, prone to delays and errors within the massive bureaucracy required.

Priority lists usually operate so that hard currency can be allocated as it becomes available to certain classes of goods depending on national need. Defence items, food and medical goods normally have preference over luxuries and consumer equipment, whilst payment of royalties and dividends, and remittances of subsidiaries' profits come very low on the list.

Customers and subsidiaries may be blameless, with local payments made on due dates in an orderly manner. But the time taken for their conversion into the hard currencies of contracts depends on the country's store of FX and the priority given to transactions.

The length of delays in hard currency transfers also depends on the organisational efficiency of the less well-off countries. Bureaucracy, corruption and political preferences all play their part, as does the efficiency and paperwork of the exporter. For example, UK exporters find that transfer delays can vary between one month to perhaps twelve months from the same market. When they look into the reasons for the differences, they find them to be a mixture of the priorities for their goods, the efforts made by local agents to influence officials, mistakes on their invoices, and the country's untidy mass of FX applications awaiting attention.

Import licences are the commonest and most effective mechanism used by countries to control their foreign currency priorities. In the better planned systems, governments decide the priorities before orders can be placed by importers, so that the granting of import licences means that hard currency is available to meet payment dates, possibly with slight delays while the system matches documents. But if no licence exists, foreign currency will certainly not be provided. This is why exporters must always check on the licence position before they commit themselves.

Experienced exporters know that in all markets where transfer delays are prevalent, they must put extra effort into nursing the payment back home. For example, an exporter should always carry out the following measures:

1. Check that local payment has been deposited with the bank.
2. Obtain a local certificate showing the FX reference number.
3. Establish locally (e.g., via the agent) the current system for allocating FX for imports.
4. Ensure that the invoice has been matched locally with the import licence and FX approval document.

In other words, make sure that everything has been done locally to enable the transfer to be made and that the only step left is the actual transfer. Sadly many exporters who suffer the non-arrival of funds from risky markets relax in the complacent belief that 'everyone else is in the same boat'. Only months later when they check do they discover that their particular invoices are not even in the queue for payment. It is the experience of ECGD, for example, that several claims have to be rejected because insured exporters have not ensured that the debt has been paid locally.

LOCAL CURRENCY SHORTFALL

Consider the stages in a payment of £10,000 from Mexico to the UK (see Table 4.1). The non-transfer situation breeds an increased risk of buyer default or insolvency. Due to his country's situation but through no fault of his own, the buyer has to find a further four million pesos some nineteen months after he thought he had paid in full. He has long since used his import, yet he still has an obligation to pay an unknown extra amount of pesos when FX becomes available. The high Mexican inflation rate in that period may have given the importer extra sales profits from which to find the extra requirement, but on the other hand, many of his local customers may have gone to the wall. The Mexican bank would only transfer to the UK the sterling equivalent of what it has received from the importer.

Table 4.1 Stages in a payment of £10,000 from Mexico to the UK

Date	Pesos: £1 rate	Action	Local currency needed to settle
15.6.86		Importer requests bank to pay £10,000 to exporter	
16.6.86	300	Bank debits importer's a/c at current official rate	3,000,000
16.6.86		Bank requests central bank approval to remit sterling to UK. Importer notified.	
10.1.88	700	Central bank approves transfer at current official rate	7,000,000
		Local currency shortfall to be paid by importer	4,000,000
		Increase of original cost to importer	+ 134%
31.1.88		Exporter receives £10,000. Interest cost of waiting 19 months at 1% per month = £1,900	
		Reduction of £10,000 by UK inflation rate of average 6% from 15.6.86 to 31.1.88 = £950	
		Total reduced = £7,150	

In contractual and legal terms, the illustrated delay of nineteen months is a political risk event. The buyer has not defaulted but the risk was always there and it increased when he had to find the extra four million pesos. Contract, invoice and bill of exchange clausing should make it clear that the customer is responsible for depositing enough local currency to produce the contracted hard currency total at the date of transfer.

The transfer risk concerns the cost of delays rather than total loss, because most payments are eventually transferred. Exporters with credit insurance should receive payment of claims for transfer delays after a few months, whereas uninsured exporters are hostages to the fortunes of the foreign countries concerned. Their waiting times can be from a few weeks in some markets such as Jamaica to six years, at time of writing, from Zambia.

When debts are rescheduled by foreign governments during the delay period, uninsured creditors become unable to do anything but wait – up to twelve years has been known.

There is also the question of the exporter's net profit and the value of money to consider. We have explained earlier in the book how profit is eroded by the interest cost of waiting for customers' payments. When debts are officially rescheduled, interest is paid by the foreign governments, but the very low rates, perhaps 4% or 5% p.a., never cover exporters' actual costs.

The inflation-reduced value of £5,000 received five years later, when originally priced on, say, 60 days' terms, is a significant loss. In these highly competitive times, it is difficult for exporters to pass on even the cost of 60 days' credit, let alone build in the cost of possible transfer delays.

The prime task of the governments of countries experiencing severe FX shortage is to take care of their populations, rather than give priority to the claims of foreign banks and suppliers. However, they know that new foreign loans and goods will dry up if they default. They cannot afford to be too off-hand about debt obligations, since they have millions of people to feed and govern. So, some resources have to be used to keep banks and creditors happy, at least with interest payments on rescheduled instalments stretching years into the future. Banks and major credit institutions are usually only willing to reschedule if the IMF exercises strong control of the debtor nation's economy. IMF officials supervise debt negotiations, and influence import priorities and government spending. Their wisdom rarely has popular support, since IMF rules impose hardships and shortages on populations already suffering. For this reason, even the framework of official debt rescheduling will always be fragile.

Countries experiencing IMF intervention are well documented in bank and official bulletins, so exporters can clearly see the risks before they get involved.

Some countries reduce import volume by requiring 'prior' or 'import' deposits of local currency. Importers who wish to spend the nation's meagre FX funds then not only have to get import licences but also pay the central bank in advance. The requirement can be flexed at the government's will, and ranges of 5% to 100% have been seen for different product priorities, and even 200% or 300%. Local importers are thus forced to think hard about their need for the goods, their profitability and their market's willingness to pay enhanced prices. Evidence from official reports on import deposit schemes is that they (a) restrict imports, but often due to the financial state of buyers, and (b) they are inflationary, since importers' costs of tying up money are recovered in resale prices.

Some poor countries allow a two-tier, or even a three-tier system of exchange rates to operate, to deter excessive spending of FX. A few years ago, the government of Costa Rica decreed that only the central bank could issue foreign exchange, not the usual commercial banks. Essential imports were approved for payment at a controlled rate of colones to the dollar. For less essential goods, a secondary market was allowed to develop freely with banks and importers agreeing much higher rates of exchange, according to supply and demand, usually between two and three times the controlled rate.

With three-tier systems, in addition to the official or controlled rate, and the free market or commercial rate, a third level is used for officially approved profit remittance, salary transfers of expatriates, and other specific financing.

With multi-rate systems, the commercial or uncontrolled rate is the one which most accurately reflects the international market opinion. It is that factor which governments have to grapple with in sorting out their economies. This applies even in the EEC where the EMS (European monetary system) 'snake' is a form of control within agreed limits. If free market forces were allowed to apply, supply and demand would force the weaker EEC countries to impose many restrictions on imports. If that is true for some of the so-called strong countries, the problem is that much worse for the poorer nations of the world.

OTHER POLITICAL RISK EVENTS

After orders have been booked there is the risk that a government body, outside the control of both exporter and customer, will take some action that nullifies the contract. It may prevent or interrupt shipment or local performance, or prevent payment being made.

When this happens, the government involved is usually the customer's. But it could be the exporter's government, for example, imposing an export licence on hi-tech equipment. It could be the government of another country, for example, a South American one refusing to allow UK goods to be off-loaded *en route* to the buyer's country because of a stance against the UK over the Falklands.

To a certain extent, an exporter can try to foresee political risks for important contracts. He can ask himself the following questions, in relation to a particular market:

1. Is the government likely to impose any restrictions before we are finally paid in full?
2. Are we sure there will be no interference by our own government, for any reason?
3. Is there likely to be any dispute (or war) between its government and ours?
4. While the goods are in transit, is any other government likely to interfere?

If there is anything other than clear *NOs* to these, the exporter can take some action to clear the hurdles, if possible, in good time and not just hope that the problems will go away.

Not all political events can be foreseen, and many export contracts have suffered from sudden overnight pronouncements by governments. It is this risk of the unexpected which often leads exporters to the credit insurance market – at least on major contracts, where losses would be painful.

Political risks are not confined to countries trying to conserve FX. For example, there is the East–West cold war, protectionist quotas which flare up suddenly, various alliances in Central America, the Middle East and North Africa and, in early 1988, some seventeen wars going on in the world. Wars certainly cause blacklists and embargoes, as well as redefined priorities for imports.

Governments of all political flavours justify their intervention in international commerce as 'acting in the public interest'. They have the power to make statutory regulations concerning the following:

1. New or increased taxes or duties.
2. Technical approvals and standards.
3. Quotas and tariffs.
4. Health-related inspections.
5. New, amended or cancelled import or export licences.
6. Any feature of specific individual contracts.

Major export contracts usually contain 'conditions precedent' which must be met after a contract is signed but before it becomes legally effective. Typically, a capital goods contract might require the following:

1. An advance payment.
2. Approvals or tests by an official body.
3. Sample signatures for financing arrangements.
4. Cross-guarantees by the exporter for payments due before work is approved.

Some of these conditions may even be passed on to sub-contractors with relatively small shares of the business.

We often see large export orders announced with a flurry of publicity with photographs of important people smiling as they sign. But behind the scenes, there then follows a frantic period for subordinates to achieve all the pre-conditions before there really is an export order. There have been notable cases, particularly in Africa during the early days of the debt crisis, when governments simply changed their minds on spending priorities and nullified contracts by not complying with the conditions precedent, leaving exporters with much expense but no contract.

The most common pre-condition, even in everyday exports on short-term credit, is the need for an import licence. In the UK, exporters may simply need to know that the buyer has an import licence, so that No. BW876325/87, or whatever, can be shown on the invoice. But in the buying country there could be weeks of activity on form filling, FX approval drills, and possibly commissions being paid. Licensing is very serious to the countries practising it, and without a licence, a buyer is unable to land goods and process them. If the goods have somehow got into the country without a licence, for example in a salesman's briefcase, payment will not be approved.

The risks with import licensing are:

(a) that existing licences are cancelled, either before shipment or before importation; or

(b) that new licence requirements are imposed after an order has been manufactured or shipped.

If goods are specially made and cannot be sold elsewhere, the risk is a major consideration which should be investigated and protected against, most obviously through credit insurance. If goods are standard, it may be possible to resell them elsewhere, and even retrieve and redirect a shipment *en route*.

The most usual danger signal for exporters is a change of the buyer's government, sometimes brought about by civil disorder or foreign debt restrictions. It is only to be expected that a new regime will announce restrictive measures to conserve resources. Such measures may involve the cancellation of contracts or their renegotiation on less favourable terms.

The world debt crisis will restrict trade with many countries for years to come and the only safe assumption is that more governments will exercise their muscle to interfere in commercial contracts, both before and after contracts are signed.

FORCE MAJEURE

It is important not to confuse acts by governments, just discussed, with *force-majeure* events which may prevent contract performance. Dictionaries vary in their definitions of *force majeure* and major exporters know from painful experience that buyers and contractual partners have differing opinions on what constitutes a *force-majeure* event, when there is a significant liability to be settled.

Theoretically, *force majeure* refers to acts of God, wars, strikes and other events totally outside the control of the contracting parties who should not be blamed if such events interfere with performance.

The exporter has a risk if his contract makes him perform despite such events. He also has a risk if *force-majeure* events stop the customer from importing the goods or paying for them.

It makes sense, therefore, to negotiate contract terms which free an exporter from obligations if *force majeure*, as a particular contract defines it, occurs. The risk of the buyer not importing or paying for goods because of *force majeure* can be covered by credit insurance, provided contract terms are properly worded.

PUBLIC BUYER RISK

Whereas firms may not do very much of their total business with public sector customers in the UK, those that export find that a goodly proportion of their customers are government bodies or are officially acting on behalf of them.

A public sector buyer can be any of the following:

1. A department or ministry of a foreign government.
2. A local, state or regional authority.
3. A public service funded by government, e.g., transport, power, water, hospitals, etc.
4. A nationalised industry operating commercially.

If an exporter does not know that his customer is a public buyer, he may not have a valid contract, or be able to receive payment.

Examples of this include an eastern European hospital which obtained Ministry of Health approval to purchase UK equipment, but neglected to mention that the Ministry of Finance had to co-sign orders before foreign spending was allowed; and a Latin American state oil refinery which was in conflict with its minister about over-spending yet placed further large orders. This led to the dismissal of top men and cancellation of orders they had placed.

The main risk with public sector buyers is that they cannot be sued for non-performance. Can an exporter effectively sue a government? It is doubtful. Exporters should discover for certain whether their contract is with a commercial buyer who can negotiate and be sued if necessary, or with a truly public sector buyer, who cannot. If the latter, there are usually detailed, bureaucratic procedures which have to be followed diligently to lead to payment. There are some countries with a reputation for lethargic public sector performance and erratic payments. This can be found out in advance from credit reports and trade information, so an exporter is able to choose whether to risk default or not.

THE 'ON-DEMAND' RISK IN BONDS AND GUARANTEES

Another political risk concerns the unfair claiming by a foreign buyer under a guarantee given by the exporter. Claims are unfair when the exporter has properly performed his part of the contract, or where he is prevented from doing so by the buyer's government. The risky feature of the 'on-demand' type of bond is that it can be called by the beneficiary at any time he chooses. For this reason, exporters are encouraged by the International Chamber of Commerce to resist requests for such bonds. Unfortunately, the readiness of competitors to comply coerces even unwilling exporters to do so.

Public authorities in many developing countries, particularly in the Middle East, have had the power ever since the surge in oil wealth to award massive contracts to western suppliers. Having little experience of negotiating such contracts, or not knowing the efficiency of the contractors, the newly important buyers wanted a simple kind of protection so that if they were taken advantage of, they could easily get their money back without having to go through western courts they did not trust. On-demand bonds gave them this comfort. Unfortunately, the justice they sought also allows the less scrupulous to claim repayment without justification. Even if an exporter's contractual buyer is well-trusted, the bond may have a validity period which extends to a change of government when hostile acts may include demands under bonds.

A bond is issued by a financially strong third party, usually a bank or an insurance company, to guarantee the exporter's performance.

For many years before the boom in Middle East construction work, bonds were issued by specialised insurance companies, known as surety companies, who were usually subsidiaries of major insurance companies. They still issue bonds into many markets and their 'surety bonds' are perfectly fair to buyers. Indeed, they actually help buyers because the surety company, to protect its own position, actively checks contract performance. It may exert pressure on the exporter, inject funds into a project, or even find new managers, if that would solve a problem. If the guaranteed customer still needs to claim, the insurer will check the alleged nonperformance before paying out.

Thus, a customer asks an exporter for a bond; a surety company provides it; premium is paid by the exporter (who may charge it on to the customer); the exporter duly performs or not; if not, the buyer proves default to the surety company, who pays or not after checking.

Surety bonds are therefore 'conditional' and fit the bill eminently well for all concerned. The only cost is the insurance premium and it will be apparent that this method of bonding does not tie up the exporter's bank facilities in any way.

Compare that with the 'on-demand' guarantee given by a bank. Without being at all concerned about the performance of a contract, a bank will lend its name to the exporter by issuing an unconditional guarantee that it will pay the buyer an amount on first demand without requiring proof of the exporter's nonperformance. Apart from the fee for the guarantee, the bank requires the exporter to be worthy of recourse in case of a claim and his credit line is charged with all outstanding bonds.

There are different kinds of on-demand bonds. The most usual are the following:

1. Tender bonds: commonly for between 5% and 25% of a tender value, to show the serious intent of the exporter. If the tender is successful but the exporter decides not to go ahead, the customer can claim under the bond for wasted expense.
2. Advance payment bonds: commonly for up to 15% of the contract value paid in advance of performance. The amount can then be reclaimed by the customer if the exporter fails to perform this amount of work.
3. Performance bonds: commonly for up to 25% of the contract price, but have been seen for 100%. They enable the buyer to recover amounts paid if the exporter fails to complete.
4. Retention bonds: offered by exporters rather than demanded by buyers, to enable 100% payment to be received instead of, e.g., '10% to be retained for eighteen months after completion'.

If an on-demand bond is called by the customer, the procedure is as follows:

1. The buyer claims payment under the bond from the bank which issued it on behalf of the UK bank.
2. The foreign bank pays out without quibbling.
3. It reclaims the amount paid from its UK principal bank.
4. The UK bank takes recourse to the exporter's account.

Because the on-demand bond is a full-strength bank guarantee, the first, single demand from the bona-fide holder will be met in full. In the past, exporters have asked their banks to withhold payments until complaints have been checked. However, banks have not been able to do so, and British courts have ordered them to honour their guarantees to foreign beneficiaries, regardless of the innocence of their clients, or the impact on their fortunes. However, courts in Germany and Austria have begun to order investigations into the rights of debatable claims, before payment.

How realistic are the risks that the buyer will call the bond when the exporter is not in breach of the contract, or when he has been prevented from performing by a political risk event? The much-quoted example of unfair calling is when the Libyan government hostilely called bonds they were holding from foreign contractors in 1953. It is said that Italian construction firms went bust as a result, including some who had completed their work successfully some time earlier. The Iranian revolution also produced several anti-western threats of bond-calling. Looking forward, the real risk to exporters and contractors is that foreign governments may change, or the balance of the Middle East power game will cause new national leaders to call in bonds from innocent firms. Exporters should regularly review their outstanding 'on-demand' or 'suicide' bonds and do all they can to reduce exposure.

There are some contractual points worth observing:

1. Contracts should stipulate an expiry date for bonds, to make it easier to recall and cancel them. However, the law in some countries, such as Syria, requires bonds to stay alive for a specific time after a contract is complete.
2. Contracts which require bonds should be carefully worded and checked, to avoid later disputes which may result in calling.
3. By negotiating to have standard international arbitration procedures in contract conditions, the exporter may be able to influence the buyer against the later use of unfair calling as a 'gun to the head' approach.
4. *Force-majeure* clauses should allow the exporter to be innocent of delays and expenses beyond his control which might otherwise tempt a buyer to call a bond.

5

The management of trade credit

vwvwvwvwvwvwvwvw

Chapter 2 described credit as a dynamic entity in commercial life and touched on the measures needed to control its costs and effects. The credit risks described in chapters 3 and 4 are the events which may prevent sales turning into cash. Companies need cash. The profit from sales is the means to that cash but, between booking invoices to sales and receiving cash from customers, the waiting period is fraught with risks and costs. It is strange, in a way, that it is customary for a balance sheet to value unpaid sales in full as an actual asset called debtors (or receivables), owned by the seller. It is certainly a weak asset, constantly under pressure. Until it is paid, a sale loses its cash value from the following:

1. The passage of time: interest expense on borrowings and inflation effect.
2. Administration costs: ledgering and collection actions.

The sale's profit has to pay for two other major selling costs:

1. Credit assessment: reports and information administration and checking.
2. Insolvency loss: if written off as uncollectable.

Thus, compared to retail sales over the counter, or any other sales on cash or prepayment terms, the business decision to give customers time to pay attracts both *cost* and *risk* to the P & L account.

These cost and risk factors indicate two sensible requirements:

1. Prices must properly allow for the real costs of credit.
2. Credit sales must be managed at a senior level.

When companies realise the need to manage their trade credit better, they begin to see the complex nature of the credit manager's job. It cannot be performed at too junior a level, because it needs daily decisions affecting the business; the credit manager has to be able to influence other managers without having control of them. Also, it is one of the few company jobs with a genuine conflict of loyalties – the need to control risky sales *yet* increase total sales. To achieve those requirements, the person managing the credit investment has to be multi-skilled: salesman/ analyst/accountant/lawyer/economist/psychologist/trouble-shooter and persuader, as well as having normal management skills with staff and resources.

In an era when credit is readily available, even expected, and insolvencies running at record high levels, it is extraordinary that companies do not apply the same resources and training to managing credit as they do to selling and production.

Most companies borrow working funds. They pay between, say, 10% and 18% p.a. for money when net profit averages only between 2% and 5% of sales, in most industries. Although payment terms are usually monthly, receivables often represent between two and three months' sales value. Excessive debtors clog up company performance, whereas slim debtor/sales ratios enable companies to be much more competitive. They can reuse their cash to carry more stock or bring forward other plans, or just increase profits with the interest saved; and, in any event, have a 'fitter' balance sheet. Astute investors know that accounts receivable are a vital indicator of the health of any company they are looking at.

See Table 5.1 for an example of the effect of a company's improvement in credit performance.

INVESTMENT AND RISK IN SALES CREDIT

Companies tend to improve their profitability when they treat credit as an investment, instead of just selling and trying to collect the proceeds. For investments in capital plant, companies produce all kinds of data for approval, and have to be convinced that spending now will earn more over a period. The cost and risk has to be justified by the payback. The parameters should be exactly the same for credit decisions. Whilst nobody should over-sophisticate them, they do need information and calculations to be confident of bringing in the planned return by means of a well-paid account.

Credit limits for customer accounts are now widely in use, with a varying degree of determination. They are nothing less than high-volume specific investment decisions – 'We will risk £*n* of our money as a

Table 5.1 The effect of a company's improvement in
credit performance

| | £000s | | 1986 |
	March '85	March '86	Restated at 65 DSO
Sales	16,135	18,220	18,220
Profit before interest	711	725	725
Interest expense	437	470	369
Pre-tax profit	274	255	356
as % of sales	1.7	1.4	2
Borrowings	3,364	3,922	3,074
Interest as % of profit	62	65	51
Receivables	3,360	4,093	3,245
Collection period (DSO)	76	82	65

Note: A collection period of 65 instead of 82 days would have reduced borrowings by £848,000 and increased profit by £102,000. This seventeen-day reduction was actually achieved in 1987, after reorganisation. The DSO-ratio improvement was the key focal point in the changes.

loan to a customer, based on what we know, in the belief that he will pay us back, including our profit.'

Every company with excessive debtors should examine the controls they apply before and after a sale, to see if enough effort goes into assessing how much customers can pay, and whether collection methods are good enough.

The treasury departments of large companies obtain funding from banks at the finest rates, yet they may not be getting their own money back from customers because of weak credit controls. They are putting managerial skills into negotiating with banks to finance, *inter alia*, an excessive asset and all such companies should review the case for switching senior human resources into the credit management area, to make sure that everything possible is being done to turn credit sales into cash quickly to minimise the need to borrow externally.

Companies without the luxury of a treasurer should put the same responsibility on to a financial executive.

The two main risks to the investment in trade credit are:

(a) profit erosion by the interest expense of late payments; and
(b) bad debt loss from insolvent customers.

For example, a company sells £10 million p.a. and makes pre-tax profits of £400,000, or 4% on sales. Its overdraft costs 12% p.a. Prices include credit for one month at 1%. If a customer's account is overdue two months, the net profit is halved. If an account for £5000 goes bust, extra sales of £125,000 are required to recover the profit lost.

RECEIVABLES STATISTICS

The investment in debtors should always be related to sales because debtors originate in sales. The quality of the asset cannot be assessed simply by its total. If a company's debtors are normally £3 million but are now £2 million or £4 million, we cannot know if they are being collected faster or slower without comparing the total to the most recent sales included.

The most widely used ratio is the DSO or days sales outstanding. This is also known as the debtor days or the collection period. It shows the debtors' total as the *equivalent of all sales made* for a certain number of days (or weeks or months instead).

With the briefest of data, just total sales for a period and the debtors at the end of that period, a rough idea of an average DSO can be calculated. For example, if a company's annual sales were £10 million and their year-end debtors totalled £1,800,000, their DSO or collection period would be approximately 66 days; i.e., £10 million divided by 365 = 27,400 sales per day; £1,800,000 divided by £27,400 = 66 days of sales (66 DSO).

However, most companies these days calculate the ratio each month end, by counting back through the most recent sales month by month, as being the most likely to have influenced performance. (See Table 5.2.)

Table 5.2 Days sales outstanding using the 'count-back' method

September debtors' total		£6,250,000	
Equivalent to sales for:	September	£2,950,000	30 days
	leaving	£3,300,000	
	August	£3,050,000	31 days
	leaving	£ 250,000	
	July (total		
	£3,875,000)	£ 250,000	2 days
		000	63 days

The debtors at the end of September can be said to be the equivalent of 63 days of sales, or 63 DSO. It means that sales turn into cash, on average, every 63 days (compare this to the terms!). A DSO usually varies only slightly from month to month, unless payment terms or collection methods change significantly. Sales fluctuations hardly affect it, since debtors fluctuate in sympathy.

Some companies count back by averaging sales for a quarter, or other period, to level out major monthly sales fluctuations.

Within an industry, the DSO ratio varies considerably between companies, indicating different corporate attitudes to the importance of cash. In surveys of competitors selling similar products to the same broad range of customers, one sees totally different credit performances. For example, in electronic components, DSOs varied from 52 to 130 in 1986, with an industry average of 78. Companies allowing customers to take too long to pay (compared with the shorter DSO achieved by competitors) generally incur more and larger bad debts. By collecting faster, companies selling to customers that go bust have less, or even nothing, owing to them.

The DSO is ideal for calculating achievable cash targets. Because past DSO performance is known, it can be maintained or improved by working out how much cash is needed in a particular month to end with the required ratio.

Similarly, a financial director can reliably budget debtors for the balance sheet, and therefore borrowings, by applying the DSO to planned sales figures.

And, of course, DSO ratios can be calculated for each customer, especially by computer, and for groupings if needed. It usually makes sense, for example, to produce separate ratios for home and export debtors, because the terms and risks are so different.

ORGANISATION OF CREDIT MANAGEMENT

Every company regardless of size should decide at board level how to manage its investment in credit.

Should it be a sales or a finance function?

It is common to have senior financial control of credit to balance the ability of salespeople to commit the company. But the credit manager must always think and act commercially to find ways of accommodating all possible orders.

What should be the relative weight given to the front-end task of risk assessment, compared to the collection activity?

Most companies think of credit control as debt collection which starts at the sales ledger. In those cases, the unknown mix of quality in debts taken on will need much more collection resource to achieve good cash inflow. On the other hand, excessive credit checking of orders may produce very collectable accounts, but will frustrate sales efforts and probably reject business that could be profitable. Professionals try to create the right mix of credit assessment and collection effort.

How should credit management be organised to protect the asset?

Decisions have to be made on how customer evaluation should be done; how credit limits and risk categories should be used; which collection methods to use for customers of different size and importance; when to demand security from customers; which management reports will best give visibility of exposures; and how credit insurance disciplines should influence everything else.

How should credit management accelerate cash intake?

Decisions have to be made about methods and resources to achieve planned DSO levels; involvement in budgets; who should calculate cash targets; the use of letters, fax, telexes, telephone and visits; clearance of claims and disputes; and reports to highlight key action areas.

How should credit management help to increase profits?

Apart from the interest-saving benefits of faster cash intake; collaboration with sales to identify priorities; using non-standard credit to get profitable business; techniques for covering the risk with marginal customers; customer visits to demonstrate a united sales/credit team; high visibility in company meetings; and good communication and reports, so that the credit influences on profits are not overlooked.

The duties of a typically well-organised credit management department can be summarised thus:

1. Planning/budgeting/forecasting/reporting for receivables.
2. The same for functional expense levels.
3. Maintaining the vital customer data file.
4. Opening new customer accounts.
5. Assessment of customer risk and communicating it.

6. Setting credit limits for all or significant accounts.
7. Deciding credit risk categories for daily use.
8. Checking daily orders and shipments.
9. Handling over-limit situations.
10. Dealing with orders from unsatisfactory accounts.
11. Administration of credit insurance.
12. Taking correct action on bad debts.
13. Processing selective legal action.
14. Meetings with customers.
15. Collecting all accounts.
16. In-putting cash accurately to the computer system.
17. Resolving all customer claims and disputes.

Any good credit manager could add several more, but the list shows that the job is somewhat more than collecting debts.

Since the credit manager's job is a lively, extrovert one, it may be appropriate to reproduce some job slogans seen on the desk of senior practitioners in recent years. (See Fig. 5.1.)

Fig. 5.1 Credit management slogans

'The credit decision is part of the total business decision'

'Anybody can say no to an order – our job is to find a way of saying Yes!'

'A sale is not complete until it is paid for'

'No profit is made from business we turn away'

'There is profit to be made from risky customers before they go bust'

'Net income is depleted more by slow-paying accounts than by bad debts'

'Credit insurance means a good night's sleep'

CREDIT RISK ASSESSMENT

The risk in granting credit depends on the status of the customer, the type of profit margin and the business sector. There may be a single sale or a continuing regular supply; a high margin with some 'fat' in it to absorb a loss; a loss-reducing sale of obsolete stock; a high-volume scattering of low-value accounts; or there may be some company reason for doing the business regardless of risk.

A reliable approach is to ask three questions of each customer account or new prospect:

1. Will he go bust before payment is due?
2. Can he generate the cash needed to pay us in time?
3. Is he viable to spend time and expense on for the future?

These decisions may have to be restricted to customers above a certain value, for reasons of time or expense.

Ways of assessing risk vary from a 'seat of the pants' opinion to computerised calculations. At the other extreme, some credit checking is so bureaucratic that it is not cost-effective.

A sales force normally acquires valuable data on a customer's financial condition but often lacks a system for channelling it to the credit decision makers. This can be remedied by the checklist approach, listing items such as the condition of premises, owned or leased, morale of employees, condition of plant and equipment, names of other suppliers, key contacts and so on. It can be extended to details of the customer's recent sales and, if possible, to append the latest balance sheet.

A seller's ledger is a mine of underused information. For the total pool of customers it shows sales trends and history, payment ability, attitudes to payment requests and tendencies to 'be difficult' or make claims.

The main external sources of information are practically all free of charge: bank reports, trade references, industry contacts, balance-sheet analysis, trade journals, the financial press and, by no means least, the customer himself. Only the credit registers and agency reports are commercial purchases.

Why does risk assessment matter? Well, if by magic, a company knew the latest exact financial status of each of its 1,000 customers, there would be general surprise, if not disappointment, at the variation in customers' ability to buy, to pay and to survive. Of the outlets on whom the seller depends, only ten may be undoubted no-risk accounts, possibly 300 very poorly regarded and the other 690 a mixture of average performance. The three key credit questions could be answered perfectly and ideal decisions could be made on sales priorities, payment terms, credit limits, security needed and collection methods.

But such perfect visibility is not available on all customers at once and most systems are used imperfectly as needs arise. Certainly credit dossiers should be kept on all regular customers and all accounts given credit limits and even risk categories, of say, 'A', 'B' or 'C'. Some risk-coding systems run to many more subdivisions.

A credit limit should be the maximum value it is believed that a customer can safely be allowed to owe. This can be roughly assessed from the opinions of banks, trade references or credit agencies or, ideally, from the balance sheet. A rule of thumb taken by some credit managers is a maximum of 20% of working capital or 10% of net worth. It is pointless just to set a credit limit equal to current sales needs because it will require frequent up-dating when it could have been higher in the first place. Not many sellers would want to be more than, say, 25% of a customer's total creditor value. The customer's own DSO period will tell if he can generate enough cash to pay, and his ratio of creditors to purchases will show how quickly he pays others on average.

Credit limits cannot be precise but are certainly useful as general guides. If a customer's correct limit is about £1,000 and a seller delivers £10,000, it is highly unlikely that enough cash can be generated to pay promptly. That would be a self-inflicted overdue account and the customer may even have been encouraged to over-trade so much that he cannot meet his commitments at all. On the other hand, no credit manager will worry about delivering £2,000 to a £1,000 credit limit account where payments have been immaculate to date.

Dun and Bradstreet's set of registers covers the UK and gives a quick indication of credit rating. Fuller reports are available in text form or on-line from several credit agencies but may take a few days if data is not on file.

Companies House provide a microfiche of filed accounts. Although many companies are delinquent in lodging accounts, three-year trends can compensate for lateness. The most useful ratios divined from balance sheets are as follows:

1. Liquidity, showing how cash and debtors cover current liabilities.
2. DSO, showing how quickly the customer collects his sales.
3. Stocks/sales ratio, showing how quickly he sells his product.
4. Debt/equity, showing the relative burden of interest to be serviced out of profits.
5. Net worth/current liabilities, comparting the customer's own investment in his business with that of outside creditors.

The percentage growth net profits should parallel or better that of sales and any decline is a warning to check further. A three-year trend provides a good financial picture of customers and gives more confidence in the credit decision.

Credit risk categories are extremely useful and can be allocated to accounts on a basis such as:

A = no risk
B = average risk
C = high risk

The rating and risk codes can be used for priorities in delivery dates and collection actions. For example a 'C £500' account should get less sales attention than an 'A £20,000' account. If a product is being quoted at four weeks' delivery, it can help to increase orders and goodwill of 'A' and 'B' accounts if, say, two weeks are quoted to them and six weeks to 'C' risks. Supplies can be stopped to a slow-paying 'C' account very soon after due date, whereas more collection effort is justified on a 'B' type before blocking deliveries. The word 'urgent' for orders and customer service can be redefined for 'A' accounts compared to 'B', and again for 'C' types. There are several innovative opportunities for improving results in sales and credit areas through the use of credit risk categories.

There is no real reason why risk assessments and credit limits should not be discussed openly with customers. If one does not like what he hears, he may well offer new information to justify a change. But if he gets upset about an external view of his business, he is forgetting that banks and market analysts apply appraisals just as critically, so a risktaking creditor is certainly entitled to do so. Many firms, particularly smaller ones, make little or no analysis of their own business, relying on outside accountants to 'do the books'. A discussion, for credit purposes, of a customer's situation is often welcomed by owners who never seem to find the time to stand back and look at where their business is going. Some credit managers even have customers who send them the latest balance sheet, and ask, 'How do you see our progress?' The subsequent analysis of trends and ratios is a first-class basis for bringing seller and buyer closer.

Having investigated customers and obtained a good idea of risks, how should assessments be used from day to day?

New customers can be given a small 'quickstart' credit rating with no expensive checking. The amount should be one which would not hurt the business if lost and a proper assessment can be made before the second order arrives.

Computer systems make it easy to enter the value of a proposed delivery, add it to the existing debt and compare the total with the credit rating. If it creates an unhealthy excess, the shipment can be held back while the exposure is sorted out – the rating may be revised, a special payment obtained, or the order split into phases which fit the rating.

Opening a credit account

It is good practice to have a standardised form for prospective customers to complete before they can have credit facilities. By requiring customers actually to request credit, the procedure helps to equalise any assumption (by customers or salesmen) that credit is freely available. If eager sales staff fill in the form to save the customer time, it is important that the customer is required to sign it, and that key points are explained – especially the payment terms. A sample credit application form is given in Fig. 5.2. Note: whilst it is good practice to ask for two trade referees who can speak for the required amount, it is better if the sales person supplies the names. This overcomes the risk that a customer selects names cultivated specially for the purpose.

It is a good idea to standardise the request to the referees for information, to something like that shown in Fig. 5.3.

Trade references

Most credit managers place little faith in trade references, which should never be the sole source of information. Even those supplied honestly may be answered in a hurry, or may be for products with different payment priorities. Their value is in comparing them with other reports, with any mismatch signalling a further check.

Bank references

These are similarly of limited value because of the banks' brevity and first loyalty to their customers. Surprisingly, a bank report is all that some sellers bother to obtain. They are simply opinions of how customers conduct their bank accounts and are coded into five or six standard replies. The only worthwhile one is, 'undoubted', and the worst a bank will say is, 'We cannot speak for your figure.' Banks only give reports to other banks, so time should be saved by phoning to start the process.

Credit registers

These cover a tremendous range and volume of traders and are worth having readily available in the office, unless the incidence of new customers is small. If many orders are obtained from new customers and credit decision speed is important, registers are indispensable. The registers indicate an average transaction value which is a good guide but

Fig. 5.2 Example of a credit application form

Request for credit facilities

To: (name and address of seller)

_____

We request you to open a credit account for:

Name _____

Address _____
_____
_____

We confirm our agreement to comply with the payment terms set out in your conditions of sale – clause 4: '30 days from invoice date'.

Expected value of   Signature _____
monthly purchases £ _____   _____
         (position) _____

Bankers
Name of bank _____   Adress _____
   _____
   _____

Trade referees   Adress _____
(1) Name _____   Address _____
   _____
   _____

(2) Name _____   Address _____
   _____
   _____

(NB Trade referees should be able to speak for at least the credit required for the expected purchases)

---

is certainly not a credit limit. Generally, the figures are conservative so if the credit required is within the value shown a quick decision can be made. Registers have to be up-dated and most issue amendments at frequent intervals.

Fig. 5.3 Request for trade reference: example of form letter

Please reply in the column below, deleting where necessary.

1. How long has the credit applicant been known to you?

_____ months
_____ years
many years

2. What amount do you customarily allow on credit?

£ _____

3. On what terms?

Cash only
Monthly credit
On _____ terms

4. Are payments made regularly and in accordance with your terms?

Prompt
Slow (up to 1 month o/due)
Very slow (more than 1 month overdue)

5. Please add any other useful information below:

The above information is given in strict confidence and without responsibility on my/our part.

Date _____ 198 __   (Signature) _____

We thank you for your help in supplying this information and we will always be pleased to reciprocate at any time.

(Signature _____ Credit Manager)

Credit agency reports

These are available on printed pages, on-line through dedicated terminals, or called down from Prestel-type services. Standards of accuracy and up-to-dateness vary enormously. It is best to shop around and find out which sources give the best value for a company's needs. Reports are issued quite quickly from a file but are frequently out of date. More expensive ones are specially written but take a little longer. Some agencies provide a credit rating, while others leave it to the reader to decide – which is the preference of many credit analysts. Most reports are reliable, but the cost must be assessed against the value involved in the decision.

Balance sheets

All limited companies must file their accounts annually at Companies House but some are so late that they are a poor guide to the present position. It is more useful to obtain a series of three balance sheets to see trends. A weak company growing stronger is a better risk than one which is stronger but in decline. A single balance sheet would not reveal this. Financial analysis is not every credit manager's strong point; it takes time and the results are sometimes unpopular. Where a seller is a major creditor, the customer's financial status should be clearly identified. It is also a good policy to make a regular analysis of the few customers who provide most of the sales on the 80/20 basis which so often applies.

Representatives' reports

A standard information form can be very educational for increasing the awareness of the sales force of the need to assess creditworthiness. It is a useful complement to the data file and can do much to reduce the worries of granting credit on urgent small orders.

Forms such as the example in Fig. 5.4 are frequently used to give early warning of prospective business to the credit department.

Trade rumours

Although they should not always be believed, they may be useful for checking further when important or marginal risk customers are involved. A good credit manager always cultivates trade contacts and regular confidential meetings to exchange credit information between those in the same trade is a valuable credit tool.

Telephone and trade directories

Credit departments of companies who sell over a wide area should have readily available all relevant telephone directories plus the 'yellow page' types and whatever trade directories apply. When goods are sent to a new customer before credit is approved, directories at least provide a check that the customer exists and that the name and address are correct. If a new account can't even make the directory the initial order may need cash terms.

MARGINAL RISK ACCOUNTS

A company's customers, both current and potential, are all potential sources of income, regardless of their financial condition. What differs is the period of time that business is available to the seller, which in turn

Fig. 5.4 Sales representative's report

1. Date _____

1. Rep's name _____
2. New customer's full name _____
4. Address _____
   _____
5. Telephone number _____
6. How long in present business _____
7. Size (number of employees) _____
8. Nature of business _____
9. Situation _____
10. Competitors' lines carried _____
    _____
11. Nature/value of initial order _____
    _____
12. Estimated capacity (How much of our   (week)
    product could be reasonably buy?)   £ _____ per (month)
                                                       (year)
13. Whether branch or subsidiary of a larger firm (state name) _____
    _____
14. Accounts to be rendered to _____
15. Terms of sale _____
16. General remarks _____
    _____
17. Other suppliers (a) _____
    _____
    (b) _____
    _____

depends on creditworthiness. Although sellers would prefer only strong companies who pay on time and will still be alive next year, competition forces them to sell to a wider range than that. This highlights where credit management can help company sales; i.e., 'Let's consider every order, but let's check out potential problems. Then we can sell to the risky accounts with some control, or at least knowing how much we might lose, and we can get some useful profit before things turn sour.'

Marginal accounts are for customers with the following:

1. High probability of going out of business (insolvency).
2. Excessive slowness in meeting agreed payment dates (illiquidity).

Having a simple, standard credit system may result not only in profitable business being rejected, but overdues and bad debts would occur anyway, because of lack of priorities.

A business-like approach, which earns respect from sales colleagues, as well as extra profit for the company, is to say, 'We'll build information on customers, identify the risky ones, communicate well with sales-people and encourage them to sell up to the limits set; but they must understand and support our controls, because of the chances we are taking.'

The indirect advantage of segregating marginal risks is that orders from all other less risky customers can flow through quickly. Far from being accused of losing orders through credit stringency, a marginal risk approach allows credit managers to measure the extra sales and profit obtained. There should be a board level decision that the receivables asset may contain a certain percentage or value of high-risk accounts, accepting that these will pay more slowly, that some may go bust, and that extra cost and 'noise' will occur.

A reasonable policy may be to allow 20% of the asset value to be of high risk 'C' accounts. Whatever the percentage decided, it must be limited to that. The policy must not be an open door to uncontrolled credit.

Controls for risky accounts can be divided between pre-shipment; collection; and risk reduction.

Pre-shipment controls include scrutiny of all incoming orders to compare them to the existing debt, payment performance and credit rating. Credit data on file should be updated at short intervals.

Collection controls depend on size, but require telephone or rapid sales contact to judge customers' attitudes and intentions. After one unsatis-factory collection attempt, further supplies must be held until the account is in order.

Risk reduction steps include the following:

1. Guarantees from creditworthy third parties.
2. Credit insurance.
3. Pre-payment (all or part-value).
4. Special short payment terms, e.g., seven or fourteen days.
5. Cash discounts, allowed for in prices.
6. Retention of title, where products are suitably identifiable.
7. Bills of exchange, for acceptance and collection via the banks.
8. Offsetting any payables, by prior written agreement.

BAD DEBT RESERVE POLICIES

Categorisation of accounts also helps savings to be made in bad debt provisions since it is only necessary to reserve for risky accounts. The three main methods are as follows:

1. One hundred per cent with reversal: each month, reserve the total of all 'C' category accounts. As debts are paid, transfer income back to P & L. In practice, all that is needed is to keep a bad debt reserve (BDR) equal to the total of high risk accounts.
2. Reserve according to age: this matches the risk that increases with age on 'C'-type accounts. A percentage of 'C' accounts is reserved from the aged debt analysis, e.g., 25% of balances in the one-month overdue column, 50% of the two-months column, 75% of the three months and 100% of the four or more months.
3. Annual write-off experience: this method is related to a company's experience of bad debts each year. It may traditionally reserve 1% of all sales, but finds that all its bad debts occur in the 'C' category accounts, of whose sales the bad debt losses may be 5%. So there are considerable profit savings in having a BDR of 5% of sales only to 'C' accounts.

Where credit insurance is held, bad debt reserve expense can be greatly reduced, since it needs to apply only to the uninsured portion of 'C' accounts. The saving reduces the net premium cost.

COLLECTION TECHNIQUES

Collection of debts begins long before payment is due. Firstly careful assessment of creditworthiness helps avoid selling a higher value than the customer is capable of paying on time. Payment terms and credit ratings should be clearly communicated to the buyer. If the assessment is correct and the customer blusters, it would be unwise to ignore this warning signal. Prompt or slow collections are partly decided at this early stage of setting up payment arrangements.

Every business, large or small, should produce a brief instruction to all staff, not just those engaged in credit work. It should state the importance of cash to the business and remind everyone that slow payments reduce profits, that the company prefers customers who pay promptly and that sales efforts should be concentrated on the more liquid customers.

GOOD COLLECTIONS DEPEND ON TIMING, COVERAGE AND METHODS

On timing, an amazingly effective basic principle is, 'The sooner you ask, the sooner you are paid.' Sellers should not be afraid to ask for payment: it is their money; the customer has only borrowed it. He has had the benefit of the goods and contractually agreed to pay on time. A worthwhile customer will not be offended by a firm but polite payment request.

Statistics show that the older a debt becomes, the less chance there is of it ever being paid. So, if the first prompt request does not succeed, it must be followed up soon after, say at seven-day intervals. Reminders by monthly statements alone are dreadfully inadequate in today's expensive money climate.

The overall time to complete standard follow-ups should not exceed six weeks from due date. If a previous, unsuccessful demand is followed up at the right interval, everything that can be said will have been said within that time. For example, a statement sent within three days, a first reminder seven days later, another after fourteen days and a final demand after another fourteen days would all occur within six weeks of the due date. Fourteen days is long enough for a message to reach a delinquent and achieve a response. If there is no reply, there is no point in just waiting hopefully for longer.

Full coverage of accounts is important. Inspection of a ledger often reveals that the first half is in better condition than the rest, simply because collectors always run out of time each month. All available time should be spent first on high value or older debts, and secondly on smaller and newer ones.

If credit clerks currently handle both collection and cash entry, it is usually better to split them into specialists. The methodical accuracy needed for cash allocation is not normally found in the more extrovert collector, and vice versa. If the same person must do both tasks, specific times should be allocated for each. For example, cash can be applied early and late in the day, leaving the hard-core time for customer contact. Whatever the split of time or task, the manager must ensure that all overdue accounts are followed up at the prescribed intervals. Collection is labour-intensive and staff cuts in this area are normally false economies.

The most effective ways to collect are by visit, telephone, telex and letter, in that order. It is pointless to send a polite no. 2 reminder letter to a vast bureaucratic corporation. An expensive visit, or a long-distance telephone call are very cost-effective in interest saved.

It is well worth the effort to target the collectable cash each month by using a 'who owes what?' analysis. List the individual accounts that owe 80% of the cash needed to achieve the DSO budget level. It is frequently found that only 5% of customers provide 50% of cash, a further 15% or so another 30% and then 80% the rest. The 80/20 ratio applies in cash collection because debtors are the result of the same 80/20 principle for sales.

Very few customers can refuse a personal request for payment, but time and expense restrict the visits possible. All key accounts should be collected in person and a strong personal relationship developed. Next best is to telephone all accounts down to the value permitted by time available. A phone call avoids the uncertainty when a letter is ignored. Collecting by telephone can be improved by professional training in call preparation, persuasion skills and 'closing', much the same as in telephone selling.

Below the economic value for visits and telephoning, letters must be sent. The first should be brief, polite, but firm. It should refer to the undisputed overdue amount and request payment by return. The second reminder should express disappointment at the lack of response to the first and conclude with a threat of what will happen next, if payment is not made by return. There is no point in letters stating 'within fourteen days', or 'by the end of the month', otherwise payment terms become meaningless. There is no point in threatening steps which cannot be implemented. The most effective ones are either to cut off supplies or to take third-party action. Collectors operate more effectively when they are clear on their 'threat power'. To avoid getting to the end of a relationship too soon, creditors should improve their initial collection actions.

Any final reminder should be *very final*. What else is left to say? It should refer to the lack of response to previous requests and formally notify that the prior threat has been (not will be) carried out but will be cancelled on receipt of payment.

Any debts still not paid should be transferred from the collector, whose skills can be better spent on high-volume cash, to a senior person for specialised action such as telephoning the managing director, getting a salesman to speak to a buyer, instructing collection agents or solicitors, or even writing off small values if further pursuit is uneconomic.

Visual aids help collection but should only ever be working tools and not works of art. Useful aids are a collection progress sheet (CPS) for each collector and a cash graph for the total. The CPS should list individually the accounts providing 80% of cash, with a single total for the rest. Two columns on the right should record 'cash promised' and 'cash in'. As the month progresses, attention can concentrate on the visible gaps, either in promises or receipts.

A cash graph can highlight key actions at certain dates, e.g., 'phone 60-day overdues', 'stop supplies' or 'review with manager'. Promises and receipts are plotted each day, so that two 'snakes' creep across the chart. The graph is a vivid reminder of progress and what still needs to be done.

Almost any collection system will obtain 75% of a target. The real success is achieving 100%, reliably every month, without hurting the sales effort.

Non-standard collection techniques include direct debiting, inland bills of exchange, cash discounts and settlement rebates, whenever appropriate to the business.

Better than cash discounts are settlement rebate schemes where customers are guaranteed an annual sales rebate, if they exceed a certain purchase value and pay accounts promptly. A typical agreement stipulates that invoices paid late will be excluded from the qualifying turnover for rebate.

A relatively small number of firms charge interest on overdues. The purpose must always be to get the account paid on time, not to earn income from interest. The penalty rate should be at least 2% per month, the customer notified in advance, and the right to charge clearly stated in conditions of sale.

The fund of cash in the marketplace is reducing as competition for it increases. To prosper, companies need commitment and training to get their share of the cash available.

THIRD PARTIES AND LEGAL ACTION

When standard collection efforts have failed, the effect of a third party can be stirring. A seller can resort to three main kinds:

1. A solicitor.
2. The in-house legal department.
3. A collection agency.

Not many solicitors specialise in debt collection although most will attempt it. The less successful ones either neglect timely follow-ups or crash on to court action too soon. The successful ones send effective letters, followed if necessary by a well-timed phone call prior to legal action. The threat of action is implied anyway to the debtor in the seller's use of a solicitor. In addition, the debtor who has played games with a creditor (perhaps the contempt from familiarity) realises that a third party also knows about the default. An effective solicitor's letter which produces payment within days is an economic step to take.

Collection agencies operate independently and depend for income on the percentage they charge on amounts collected. No fees are charged for non-collection, so there is every incentive for them to succeed. The better ones claim to collect over 90% in the first month the debts are put to them. Published fees are generally negotiable and depend on the age of debts, their volume, and the frequency agreed for reporting results and remitting collections.

The ultimate in third-party collection of debts is the use of the courts: the county court up to £5,000 and the High Court above that.

Resorting to court action for recovery should always be seen as failure on the part of the seller, not as a standard option. Sellers who frequently have to take legal action should attempt to remedy the real cause. Assuming that the best attempts have been made to collect, the uncollectability of too many sales may be due to over-zealous selling or the authorising of too many high-risk orders.

Customers fall into three main divisions:

1. Sole traders.
2. Partnerships.
3. Limited companies.

The first two types have unlimited liability, so if claims cannot be satisfied from business assets there is the right to claim private assets such as house, car, shares, paintings and jewellery.

A limited company has only its net assets to meet creditors' claims and the directors cannot be compelled to give up private assets except where they have committed personal liability.

When a seller decides to instruct a solicitor to start legal action to recover a debt, the solicitor will write to the debtor:

I have been instructed by _____ of _____ to apply to you for payment of £540, for goods supplied.

If I do not have your remittance by noon on Friday next, the 28th February, then I am instructed to commence proceedings.

It is accepted wisdom not to issue proceedings without prior notice from the solicitor. If a seller deals directly with a county court, he should similarly notify the debtor.

If there is no satisfactory reply, action commences with a form called a *praecipe*, which is a request to the county court to issue a summons. The seller/creditor becomes the plaintiff and receives from the court a 'plaint note'. The plaint is entered in a minute book, and a summons served on the defendant by post or a court official.

When the defendant receives the summons he may do any one of the following:

1. Ignore it, which means judgement for the seller/plaintiff who then applies for execution. This results in the bailiff visiting the defendant to confiscate goods to be sold to settle the debt.
2. Admit the debt and offer to pay in instalments, whereby the defendant has to detail his income and expenses. If the instalments are acceptable, judgement is given. If instalments are missed, execution can be levied. If the instalment offer is refused, a court hearing will fix a level of repayment that is believed to be reasonable.
3. Deny the debt and give reasons for non-payment, whereby the court fixes a hearing date. If the plaintiff does not settle privately, it will hear both sides and make an award.
4. Deny the debt and counter-claim for damages, whereby the court fixes a hearing to decide the merits of both claims.
5. Pay the money into court – success!

If execution is unsuccessful, the plaintiff can require the debtor to appear in court for an examination as to his means. This enables the court to see what resources are available to satisfy the debt.

If the defendant is owed money by third parties, a garnishee order can be issued, requiring the bank or institution holding assets or funds to pay the sum due into court.

A county court may make an attachment of earnings order, requiring the debtor's employer to pay regular deductions from his earnings into court.

The High Court must be used for debts above £5,000, and smaller amounts can also be pursued there. But remember, High Court:

(a) costs on claims below £5,000 are not always recoverable;
(b) fees are higher than in the county court;
(c) writs have to be served personally;
(d) execution of judgements can be issued straight away;
(e) jurisdiction is wider than that of a county court;
(f) machinery for hearing a defended case is more complex;

and the High Court does not have pre-trial reviews to eliminate flimsy defences.

High Court proceedings begin with a writ, requiring the defendant to appear within fourteen days. As there is no bailiff in the High Court, execution warrants are handled by sheriffs, on a 'first-issued, first-executed' basis. The law supports the vigilant, not the sleepy!

A limited company is created very easily, it has a fragile life, and can be killed off rather easily by legal process – liquidation.

The two methods of winding-up or liquidating a company are as follows:

1. Winding-up by the court – i.e., compulsory liquidation.
2. Voluntary winding-up, either:
   (a) the members' (shareholders') decision – stating the company is solvent and able to settle its liabilities within twelve months;
   (b) a creditor's decision – when a company cannot pay its debts.

COLLECTING EXPORT DEBTS

Even if export risks are assessed and payment terms properly managed there is still a jungle of payment difficulties caused, for example, by the following:

1. Excessive shipping delays.
2. Goods not wanted on arrival.
3. Drafts not accepted.
4. Deliberate default at due date.
5. Delays in bank transfers of funds.
6. Shortage of hard currency.
7. Insolvency.

Collections can be considerably improved by:

(a) choosing the correct terms to suit customer and country risks;
(b) processing the order accurately from quotation to shipment;
(c) getting the documentation right first time;
(d) using rapid (i.e., telephone or telex) means of contact;
(e) involving useful aids and other resources when appropriate.

The key rules for export collections are *immediacy* and *local contact*. Collection delays mostly reflect poor handling of problem situations:

1. Shipping delays: the customer expects his goods to arrive on time. Unplanned delays can cause havoc and he may retaliate by not paying, as leverage to get better service. Delays may invalidate letters of credit, import licences or currency authorisations.
2. Goods not wanted: there may be late shipment, or a customer may change his mind or run out of funds. Problems of storage, insurance, customs or demurrage charges arise, as well as reselling, reshipping or scrapping the goods.
3. Drafts not accepted: is the delay temporary? Can the local agent solve it quickly? Should the drafts be protested?
4. Deliberate default at due date: is the customer insolvent? Has a dispute not been resolved? Is the default only temporary?
5. Delays in bank transfer: there may be documentation errors or buyers may delay inadvertently by not completing local formalities.

6. Shortage of hard currency: the customer's country may lack foreign currency, or a sudden decree may affect existing contracts.
7. Insolvency of the buyer: in many countries, customer insolvency results in compromise arrangements with creditors. Or a total loss may occur.
8. Disputes and misunderstandings: caused by distance, time differences, language and attitude. Few exporters can negotiate in the language of customers, who may wrongly answer 'yes' or 'no' in what they believe are the right places. Local attitudes need interpretation by a local aide. It takes time to learn to think internationally.

Documentation controls

The credit manager should check documents for accuracy and be responsible for passing them on to the customer or bank. He has to be sure the right payment terms are used, and he has the motivation to get paid quickly.

For letter of credit shipments, the documents must be supplied precisely as listed. For bills of exchange there will be standard documents required for each country plus any specified in the order. With open account terms a copy invoice should always be sent to the local agent in case he needs it to clear disputes on the spot.

Use of the banking system

Collectors can reduce bank 'float time' if they do the following:

1. Tell customers the exact name, address and code number of the bank to which payment should be sent.
2. Put payment details on every invoice on open account terms.
3. Ask customers to use the telegraphic transfer (TT) method, agreeing who should pay the extra charges.
4. Ask customers to notify them by telex of every payment made, quoting the bank reference number and date of transfer.
5. Allow two days for a TT and ten days for a mail transfer (MT) to arrive in their account, then follow up with their own bank for any lateness, quoting bank reference details.
6. Establish where delays occur and demand interest from the bank.

Protest of bills

In some countries, bills of exchange have to be 'protested' for dishonour if legal action is to be taken. The exporter should give protest instructions when sending the bill for collection because no time is allowed for discussion after the bill is dishonoured. As a check do the following:

1. Decide in which countries protest action is required.
2. Decide which customers you are willing to upset by protesting.
3. Instruct the bank not to protest on all other bills.

Order acknowledgement – the first useful collecting tool

1. Show conditions of sale and eliminate any unsatisfactory conditions of the customer.
2. Stress payment terms and any financial clauses.
3. Notify customer of bank to be used.
4. Tell customer who to contact locally (agent).
5. Where L/C (letter of credit) terms apply, notify manageable requirements.

Invoice

The sole purpose of the invoice is to obtain payment. Exporters should not use home trade invoices, simply adding extra 'bits', nor clutter the invoice with advertising or technical data.

Local currency release

Drafts are paid by the customer in his own currency. If local currency devalues before the bank transfer, the exporter will be short-paid. Banks should be instructed only to release documents against a 'shortfall undertaking', whereby the customer agrees to pay enough local currency to meet the hard currency total invoiced.

Letters

Collection by letter is too slow. Immediacy is essential. This means telephone, telex, cable or a personal visit. If letters are sent the following will help:

1. Address the letter to an individual.
2. Avoid English jargon.
3. Be extremely polite, however firm, and observe courtesies.
4. Best of all, correspond in the buyer's language.
5. Copy the local agent.

Telexes and cables

The customer file should always hold any telex number. Cables should only be used for high-value debts but even an expensive cable is cheaper than the interest cost of late payments.

Telephone

Rapid contact by telephone is better than waiting for a letter reply and not even knowing whether it has been sent. Time differences require pre-planning calls. Avoid asking questions that can be answered with a 'yes' or 'no'. Get details of when and how a payment was made or else a promise of a specific amount by a particular date. Confirm by letter or telex the points agreed.

Personal visits

Airfares are justified if the debt is large enough and a collection visit can also be used to solve problems, make contacts and build relationships. A sales person can help with introductions and a local agent or subsidiary with translations. It can be worthwhile to go with a customer to his bank to discuss transfer delays.

Follow-up systems

Check the ledger at short intervals for past–due items. List accounts for action, e.g., telex below £5,000 and phone above £5,001. Telex lists to agents in each country. Ask for a telex reply by return. Follow up unpaid and unaccepted bills jointly with banks. *Do not rush into legal action.*

Use of sales staff

Sales staff should never neglect to tackle customers about payment problems when discussing other matters. They should also feed back any intelligence affecting risk or payment. Travelling staff should carry details of overdue debts and take any chance of action on them.

Use of agents and associates

Collection of overdue accounts should be an essential part of an agent's agreement, with commission credited but not paid until funds are in. Bill instructions to the bank should show the agent as 'case of need'. Overseas associated companies or subsidiaries should always get involved in local unpaid accounts.

The following checklist will improve export collections:

1.   Order acknowledged, showing terms? Bank to be used? L/C needs?
2.   Agent or representation in customer's area?
3.   Valid L/C received before shipment and checked and amended?
4.   Import licence obtained?
5.   Customer still creditworthy at shipment date?
6.   Credit department checked shipping documents?
7.   If open account, copy invoice to local agent?
8.   Most effective banks used for bill collections?
9.   Bank instructed on protest, interest, exchange, case of need?
10. Bank chased for advice on non-acceptance/non-payment?
11. Funds to be TT or cabled at own expense?
12. Overdue customers contacted by telex, phone or visit?
13. Local agent active on overdue debts?
14. Legal action avoided?

SUMMARY

Credit management begins long before debts have to be collected. The wise trader manages credit from the time that potential customers are prospected for orders. By checking out their creditworthiness he has the chance of putting energy and expense where there is likely to be increasing profit, not just volume orders that cause emotion and loss when payments do not arrive. Selectivity and professionalism have to be applied to the daily credit routines with good collaboration between sales and credit staff. Interest at board level is usually necessary to achieve good policies and cooperation between affected departments. The ratio of debtors to sales, or DSO, is the most effective management control tool for credit – resources and job responsibilities tend to be allocated properly when senior people are aware of the DSO performance, and its effect on profits and cash flow. Export credit is extremely different from the home trade and needs separate records and measurement. The risks and credit and collection techniques for export sales need handling with experience reinforced by appropriate payment terms and speedy methods of settlement. For all forms of trade credit, home or export, it is sensible to assess the costs and benefits of credit insurance to reinforce the credit job being performed in-house.

Part Two

Credit insurance facilities

vwvwvwvwvwvwvwvw

6

General principles of credit insurance

vwvwvwvwvwvwvwvw

Credit insurance is a speciality. It is concerned with a subject matter unlike that of any other class of insurance; so much so that few underwriters, brokers or managers in the general insurance field claim any acquaintance with it. We relate elsewhere how Cuthbert Heath, 'father of Lloyds', saw the credit risk as a promising opportunity for the exercise of his underwriting flair. Yet the business only prospered when it was separated from the general insurance market. Before we examine the principles which have evolved in the underwriting of trade credit, we should look briefly at those general insurance principles which are most relevant to our study.

A high court judge once defined insurance as 'the creation of a fund from the contributions of the many to compensate the misfortunes of the few'. That knowledgeable and romantic layman Sir Winston Churchill described it as 'the magic of averages'. Insurance enables us to share risk with others while we continue to enjoy ownership of an asset or the reward for an enterprise. Modern insurance calls for much technical and legal knowledge and a clear grasp of many of the complexities of other people's business and affairs.

CONTINGENCY V. INDEMNITY

There are two broad classes of insurance:

1. A *contingency insurance* pays a predetermined sum on the happening of an insured event. Life insurance and sickness and accident benefit schemes are typical contingency insurances.
2. An *indemnity insurance* compensates the insured for the defined financial loss which he has suffered as a direct result of an insured event.

    All credit insurance is indemnity insurance.

THE ESSENTIAL FEATURES OF THE INSURANCE CONTRACT

Insurable interest

The event insured against must be fortuitous, that is, there must be uncertainty as to whether it will happen. It must also be an event which, on the face of it, would adversely affect the insured. These two factors are said to give the insured an *insurable interest* in the event. A curious aspect of credit insurance is that there is often a likelihood of a particular buyer becoming insolvent. The uncertainty as to whether he will fail is derived from different readings of events and different opinions of his ability to survive. The justification for insurable interest in the credit risk is that, in theory at least, any trading concern of any size or nature might be unable to pay its debts on the due date and cause its creditors to suffer loss.

Utmost good faith

A contract of insurance is a contract *uberrimae fidei*, that is, a contract in which each party owes a duty of utmost good faith to the other. The fullest disclosure of all facts material to the risk is a condition precedent to any liability under a contract of insurance and this has special significance in credit insurance. There is a wide variety of financial and commercial information which, in the hands of a discerning creditor, would affect his view of a buyer and might therefore be taken to affect the view of a credit insurer. The creditor who is at risk for a large amount on a particular buyer might reasonably be expected to have an intimate knowledge of that buyer's affairs. Unfortunately, there are still far too many instances of the creditor failing to make elementary inquiries or, having acquired information, failing to convey it. Failures of communication between departments and lack of appreciation of the corporate significance of an event are commonplace in the business world. They can be very costly when the company owes a duty of utmost good faith to an insurer and we cannot stress too strongly the need for the fullest disclosure of all material facts to a credit insurer.

Indemnity

The principle of indemnity applies to all credit insurance. It is the principle that the insured may only recover the amount of his loss, that is, the value of the asset or property which has been lost or, in the case of liability insurances, the amount of the liability which has been incurred. In credit insurance he may not, by being insured, gain more than he bargained for in the underlying contract of sale or service. It follows, too, that any factor which has in any way mitigated the financial loss must be taken into account in determining the amount of indemnity to which the insured is entitled. This will be significant when we come to consider the amount of loss payable under a credit insurance policy.

Insurance v. guarantee

The distinction between an indemnity insurance and a guarantee is relevant to credit insurance, but for the practical purposes of this work the following simple comparison will be sufficient. The characteristics of a contract of guarantee are as follows:

1. There are three parties, each of whom is aware of the involvement of the others.
2. The primary liability to pay rests with the debtor and the guarantor's liability is secondary – he is only liable if the debtor does not pay.
3. The guarantor has no interest in the underlying contract other than in his role as surety for the buyer.

The corresponding characteristics of a contract of indemnity insurance are the following:

1. There are only two parties, the insurer and the insured, each of whom is inevitably aware of the other's involvement.
2. The primary, and only, liability rests with the insurer – there is no secondary liability.
3. The insurer is directly concerned with the underlying contract and is entitled to make stipulations about it.

These three characteristics are clearly evident in the credit insurance contract.

Proximate cause

An insurer is only liable when the insured event is the direct, active, effective and dominant cause of the loss for which indemnity is claimed. Where there is only one cause, no problem arises but where there are a number of causes prevailing at the time of the loss, some of them may be excluded from the insurance or they may be subject to limitations on the cover. The insurer is then only liable to the extent that the insured cause can be separated and the insured loss quantified. The burden of proof rests with the insured and it is for him to demonstrate that the insured event has occurred as the proximate cause of the loss for which he claims indemnity. There is usually no difficulty in domestic (or 'commercial') credit insurance because the cause of loss is insolvency and this is clearly recorded, while the amount of indemnity is based on the debt admitted by a liquidator or receiver.

The proximate cause principle can be more significant in export credit insurance where, for example, the conditions of cover for insolvency or default may be different from those for the political causes of loss. Again, there may be cover if an import licence is withdrawn but no cover if the buyer has simply neglected to obtain a licence which was necessary at the time the risk commenced.

Premium

The consideration in a contract of insurance is known as the *premium*. It is a consideration for the insurer's commitment to share the risk and not a payment for services rendered although it is sometimes adjusted pro rata to the amount of risk subsequently entailed – and this adjustment is usually upward. It is not usually the intention to refund premium for a shortfall between the amount of cover bought and the amount of risk actually run. In some forms of credit insurance, a non-refundable lump sum is payable on inception of the cover while in others a deposit premium is held by the insurer (as explained in chapter 8).

Subrogation

An insurer who has paid a claim under an indemnity insurance enjoys the common law right to 'receive the benefit of all the rights of the Assured against third parties which, if satisfied, will extinguish or diminish the ultimate loss sustained'. This doctrine upholds the principle of indemnity because it prevents the insured whose claim has been paid from recovering from other parties more than he has lost. Some policies give the insurer the additional right to receive these benefits even before he has met a claim.

The most obvious remedies open to the insured creditor would be against the debtor, any guarantor and the liquidator or receiver of the insolvent estate. Even for political causes of loss, the insured's only contractual rights are usually against the debtor. It follows, therefore, that he must not, either by act or omission, prejudice any line of recovery to which the insurer is subrogated.

Assignment

An insurance can only be assigned if the subject matter can be assigned because the assignee must acquire an insurable interest. The title to a marine cargo is transferred by the passing of a bill of lading to the buyer and if a separate insurance policy has been issued it can properly be assigned to the buyer under the Marine Insurance Act. Insurances of property and of liabilities are regarded as personal to the insured and can only be assigned with the formal consent of the insurer and only provided the insured has not already parted with his insurable interest.

Credit insurance policies are not generally suitable for assignment. The benefits of a policy (as distinct from the title to the policy) can, however, be assigned as, for example, when a bank advances money against an insured debt.

The proposal in credit insurance

The status of the proposal varies between different classes of insurance. It is customary for marine insurance to be written without any proposal and on the basis of a 'slip' prepared by the broker and initialled by the underwriter. In some simple property insurances, the proposals submitted by the prospective insured with the appropriate premium constitutes an offer which the insurer accepts by issuing the policy. In others, the so-called 'coupon' insurances, an open offer is made to a wide audience any of whom may accept it by lodging the coupon and premium with the insurer or his agent. In most credit insurance the proposal is an invitation to the insurer to treat by offering terms and the contract is made on acceptance and payment of the premium by the proposer.

The underwriter's perception of the risk

In later chapters we shall compare 'commercial credit insurance' with 'export credit insurance' and 'whole turnover' and 'spread' cover with 'specific risk' cover. Despite these comparisons, there is a wide area of common understanding and if we examine a typical whole turnover proposition, the underwriter's perception of the credit risk becomes clear. There are five governing factors:

1. The nature of the business.
2. The buyers.
3. The number and size of accounts.
4. The loss experience.
5. Credit policy and practice.

The nature of the business

Experience in most countries suggests that, in general, manufacturing industry has the best credit record and merchanting the worst. Insurers have come to expect a degree of stability from the manufacturing sector whereas many forms of merchanting are prone to the temptations of high turnover on low margins and a reluctance to limit credit exposures. In the middle ground lies a wide range of commercial, service and supporting activities all with their own credit patterns and characteristics. Some show a continuity in their customers with whom they often have long trading relationships. Others, like builders' merchants and suppliers of engineering sundries, expect a larger percentage of casual buyers. Advertising agencies face a particular problem because companies change their agencies frequently and often abruptly.

The buyers

An insurer like Trade Indemnity has a unique knowledge of trade credit patterns: the names of principal buyers and the credit limits required on them show where the company fits into its own trade, whether it is at the 'top' or 'bottom' end, the high-quality wholesale sector perhaps or the high-risk retail sector. In some trades a 'domino' pattern can be seen in which the credit given by one supplier rests on the quality of his buyer's own debtors. Any company in the pattern is both creditor and debtor at the same time and a significant loss anywhere down the line can cause a run of losses right back to the original supplier. This risk has long been recognised in trades such as timber, paper, pulp, textiles and carpet manufacture. Many companies can be exposed to risk on one debtor or class of debtor and, in practice, insurers often take an active role in risk management and loss prevention on behalf of many policyholders. Their vantage point gives them a more comprehensive view of the trade than most individual creditors can hope to gain.

Number and size of accounts

These figures can best be displayed as a 'pyramid of risk' (shown in Fig. 6.1). This clearly shows where the major risks lie and indicates the appropriate style of credit control and level of discretionary trading, which we discuss later.

Loss experience

If a company has made a practice of writing off a certain level of debt, it presumably expects and provides for those losses. To the insurer they are predictable, not fortuitous, losses and ought not to be insured. How they can be excluded is discussed later under 'first loss' provisions.

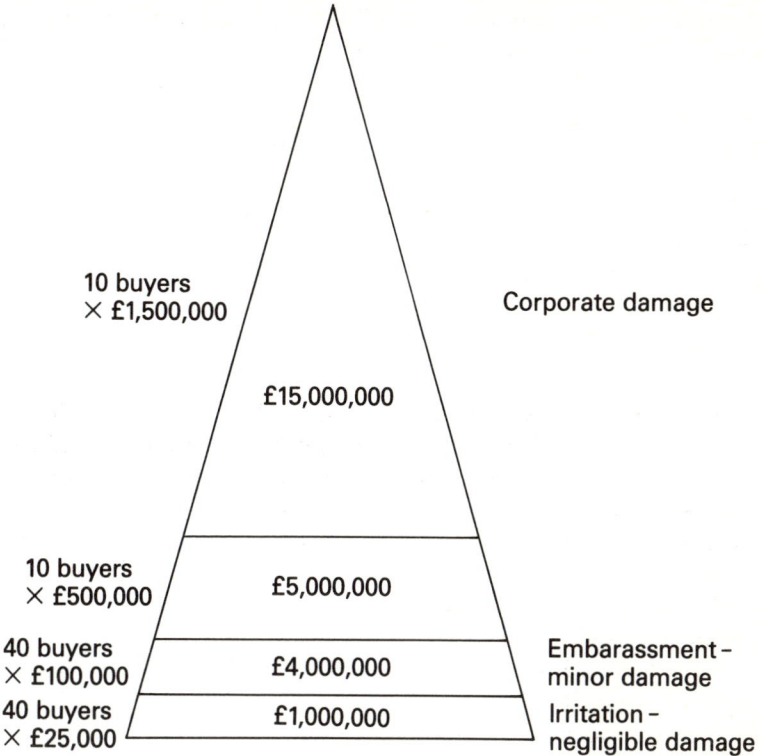

Fig. 6.1 Pyramid of risk on average outstandings and the likely effect of one buyer in ten of each group becoming insolvent

Credit policy and practice

A credit insurance policy is a long-term risk-sharing partnership between underwriter and insured. The underwriter relies on the insured to act in their best mutual interest at all times and, in giving cover, he will assume that the company will pursue a sound credit policy and practise effective credit control on the lines set out in chapter 5. The first question on Trade Indemnity's credit management questionnaire, 'Please state name and position of person responsible for credit management', could well be rephrased, 'How seriously does your company take the risks it wants us to share?' We have discussed a typical aspect of this in chapter 1 when we questioned the wisdom of simply tacking credit management onto the job specification of the sales manager or the chief accountant.

Risk control

In most classes of insurance underwriting is related to practices and yardsticks which are acceptable to policyholders and which can be justified as criteria for admission of liability. Marine and aircraft insurers, for example, draw heavily on the certification of ships and aircraft and their crews, while fire insurers follow well-known practices and regulations. The credit insurer has no such reference frame. Credit control depends on subjective judgements of the likelihood of insolvency and the amount which it is reasonable for a company to put at risk on a buyer.

The credit limit

Most credit insurers still control their risks by setting credit limits on individual buyers although, as we explain in chapter 8, when we discuss credit limit practice, much of this control may now be delegated to the insured. The insurer's problem is that, unlike the credit reporting agency, he is not simply giving an opinion or offering a recommendation but committing himself firmly to share any loss and he may not know whether the risk has even been run until the buyer becomes insolvent and the policyholder gives notice of a claim.

Special credit limit conditions

Most trade credit risks are taken unsecured and most credit limits are agreed by credit insurers on that basis. If an insurer believes that the figure he is asked to cover is too high for the buyer's resources, he may only agree a lower figure. It is up to the policyholder to restrict outstandings to this level or take a conscious decision to exceed the limit knowing that any excess loss will be for his account and not the insurer's. In a few cases, a higher limit cannot be avoided and the insurer must call for some additional safeguard as a condition of cover. The most common is that the insured must obtain a guarantee of payment from a creditworthy third party.

Third-party guarantees

We must dispel some misconceptions often held about third-party guarantees, for example, 'If you call for a guarantee, you're not taking any risk'. This statement is based on two false assumptions. The first is that the underwriter expects the buyer to default. He actually expects the opposite because it will be in the guarantor's direct interest to make sure that the buyer pays on time and thus avoids the calling of the guarantee. The guarantor has a strong incentive to keep a close watch on the buyer and take appropriate action if things go wrong. It is for him to decide whether to secure himself with any kind of charge on the buyer's assets and this decision is no concern of the seller or his insurer.

The second assumption is that the seller invariably recovers from the guarantor. Claims experience proves otherwise. There is a risk on any name, be it 'high', 'low' or 'normal' and the insurer has merely substituted an acceptable name for an unacceptable one which must surely be sound risk management.

Personal guarantees

Many distressing bankruptcies result from businessmen giving their personal guarantees too freely and putting the whole of their personal wealth at the disposal of creditors, only to find that their faith in the buyer or borrower was misplaced. A few years ago, a London financier well known for his property fortune was bankrupted having given personal guarantees for more than £40 million.

Credit insurers have learned the folly of trying to transfer a trade credit risk on to even the wealthiest personal guarantor. Occasionally a personal guarantee can serve not so much as an enforceable line of recovery but as an assurance that the guarantor will continue to be personally involved in the business.

Parent company guarantees

When the buyer is a subsidiary, the guarantee of the parent is a sensible precaution because if a parent has insufficient control over the commitments of its subsidiaries, there is the risk of the whole group being brought down by the failure of one or more of its members. Giving its guarantee may make the parent company more aware of that danger. There is always, too, the possibility of a change of ownership of the subsidiary and the creditor has the opportunity of holding the original parent to the guarantee obligation. Under some systems of law, the parent may have a *prima facie* liability but it may still be prudent to formalise it by, for example, the endorsement of accepted bills of exchange.

Other special conditions

Other special conditions applied by insurers to control exposures include the following:

1. A retention of title clause or similar reservation of property rights by the insured.
2. A restrictive covenant on borrowings.
3. An undertaking to maintain a particular source of funds such as a parent company loan or special bank facility.

4.   The continued interest of a named shareholder.
5.   Withdrawal or restriction of the insured's right to extend due dates.
6.   Temporary limits to cover peak exposures only.

Any guarantee or security condition imposed by a credit insurer is intended to be a condition precedent to his liability and if it is not fulfilled to the letter he can disclaim liability.

It is fair to say that most insurers prefer not to impose special conditions if they can be avoided. They almost always involve expense and they may complicate the settlement of claims. The policyholder must decide whether, on balance, the importance of the business, or the additional turnover, outweighs the limitation on the insurance cover.

Other conditions which may be necessary in export credit insurance and political risk insurance are discussed in chapter 9.

The uninsured percentage

Credit insurance is not so much a product as a partnership. Historically, an uninsured percentage was imposed at a level intended to be not less than the policyholder's profit margin so that he would never find it more profitable to bear the uninsured percentage on claims than to collect his debts and protect his profit. It would also remove any temptation to engage in poor quality business under the umbrella of the policy.

Cuthbert Heath recommended that the insured should bear not less than 25% of the loss and even today some German insurers require him to carry 30%. In the United Kingdom, indemnities of 80% and 85% have been the norm for many years but in the growing services sector operating on much finer margins, lower uninsured percentages are common. Advertising agents, for example, often budget for margins of less than 10% and can expect a 90% indemnity.

On the other hand, regardless of margins, a business with a very quick turnround of orders may sacrifice the quality of its credit control in favour of turnover. It is reasonable, then, for a larger share of the loss to be left with the policyholder as an incentive to him not to let standards fall too far. Considerable losses among confirming houses, for instance, have persuaded Trade Indemnity to reduce indemnities for some of this business to 75%, and even 50%.

We shall see later that a high uninsured percentage may be treated as a 'first loss deductible' and bargained against a saving in premium cost.

Cover for work in progress

Credit insurers normally only admit liability for debts which have been admitted to rank against an insolvent estate. In the usual course of events, a liquidator or receiver will admit an unpaid invoice only when he has evidence that the goods or services have been accepted and he will not usually admit liability for work done on goods or services which are incomplete.*

If he hopes to sell the business as a going concern, he may pay for essential supplies and services to keep it 'ticking over' until the new owners can negotiate fresh contracts. This does not, however, solve the dilemma of the creditor who supplies a product or service specially for a buyer and incurs costs for which he cannot look to the buyer and commitments from which he cannot easily withdraw. The risk is greatest for the company which takes single contracts for large amounts.†

The export policyholder is more likely to be exposed to work-in-progress risk because many goods are made specially for overseas markets and because political causes of loss may prevent him shipping. All insurers, both home and export, only pay irrecoverable costs and irrevocable commitments and exclude the insured's profit margin altogether. They also place a finite limit on the amount of costs covered so that the policyholder cannot, in effect, insure excess costs and commitments. In the home market, they look for companies which can forecast their commitments and programme their expenditure accurately. Work-in-progress and preshipment risks are only written as an addition to credit risk cover and not in isolation.

Claims

Commercial credit insurance is predominantly concerned with the risk of insolvency, the great majority of claims arising from the appointment of a receiver, a creditors' voluntary liquidation or a compulsory liquidation. In export credit insurance the regulations and practice in the buyer's country may vary from the UK scene described in chapter 4 but the intention of most insurers is to admit liability if the policyholder is legally precluded from taking further direct action to recover the debt or if he can demonstrate conclusively that the buyer's assets would not cover the cost of such action. In other words, the action would simply result in a further loss without retrieving the original debt – sometimes spoken of as 'throwing good money after bad'.

* Rolls Royce was a notable exception in that the receiver (subsequently the liquidator) agreed to meet 'reasonable' work-in-progress claims.
† Advertising agents are invariably offered cover for work-in-progress because they commit themselves to forward bookings of media space and are liable for cancellation charges resulting from the insolvency of the advertiser.

It should be noted, however, that while the appointment of a receiver by a bank or debenture holder is a common occurrence in Britain and is listed as an insured risk by domestic insurers, it is much less common overseas and is not normally admitted by export credit insurers. At the same time, many foreign systems of law provide for a judicial administrator or 'caretaker' to be appointed to run a company and this may be admitted as a state of insolvency. (The 1986 Insolvency Act has created the 'administrator' to do this in the UK.)

Date for payment of claims

Most policies provide for insolvency claims to be paid as soon as insolvency can be formally evidenced and the insured debt has been admitted to rank against the insolvent estate.

Where the loss is due to 'protracted default', the loss only arises at the end of the period specified in the policy. Trade Indemnity's standard wording, for example, defines this as 'the end of a period of ninety days after the due date or if the original due date shall have been postponed at the end of a period of ninety days after the postponed due date'.

Claims documentation

The potential complexity of export credit claims arises from overseas legal requirements and commercial practices and from the supporting documents which are often needed to testify to the circumstances of the loss. The basic requirements of any indemnity insurer are to know the cause of loss, to confirm that he is liable under the policy conditions and to ascertain the amount of indemnity which he should pay. In credit insurance terms, some of the following, depending on the cause of loss, are essential:

1. Proof of insolvency.
2. Evidence that:
   (a) the debt is not disputed;
   (b) the credit limit on the buyer has not been exceeded;
   (c) any special conditions imposed on the buyer or his country have been complied with;
   (d) in any political claim, the insured event was the proximate cause of the loss;
   (e) in a transfer claim, the buyer has paid in full in local currency and completed all necessary formalities for transfer;
   (f) all reasonable steps have been taken to minimise the loss and preserve any lines of recovery (e.g., calling of guarantees, protesting of bills of exchange, realisation of securities).

Recoveries

The substance of credit insurance is money rather than money's worth. The insured matter is a trade debt – a financial obligation derived from a sale of goods (or services) and insurers do not, as a rule, wish to be involved in the goods themselves. Unlike insurers of tangible assets, credit insurers look only for recovery in money. In paying an insolvency claim, the insurer regards the policyholder's claim against the insolvent estate as his own first line of recovery.

The money recovered is divided between insurer and insured in the proportions in which the total loss was borne.

Recovery from guarantors

In addition to his contractual rights against the buyer, the insured may have a right to call on a guarantee of payment given by an independent third party. It might be desirable for this demand to be made by a lawyer, especially for an overseas guarantee, so that if legal proceedings eventually have to be commenced, the ground can have been professionally prepared.

Bills of exchange

The decision whether to protest a bill of exchange must be made by the seller as drawer of the bill and must have regard to local law and practice. If there is no other practical way to preserve the validity of the bill, any insurer will expect it to be protested so that recovery action can be taken on it for his benefit. That the buyer may be offended or that goodwill between the seller and the buyer may be damaged cannot influence the insurer. Having discharged his liability by paying the claim, he is entitled under the doctrine of subrogation to any rights which would have been available to the seller. Those rights must, therefore, be properly preserved.

We began this chapter by identifying some general insurance principles to show how the ground rules of credit insurance have evolved. Modern business activity entails a wide variety of financial risks presenting opportunities and challenges to the credit insurance fraternity. We shall return to this theme in the next chapter when we discuss the continuing development of the market.

7

The United Kingdom underwriting market

vwvwvwvwvwvwvwvw

The credit insurance market offers two distinct 'products':

1. *Commercial credit insurance* against insolvency and default (the 'credit' or 'buyer' risk) on buyers at home and abroad.
2. *Export credit insurance* against a range of 'buyer' and 'political' or 'country' risks.

The insurers in the market underwrite in the following three 'modes':

1. *Specific cover* on a single risk (a buyer, contract or country).
2. *Spread cover* on an agreed selection of risks.
3. *Catastrophe cover* on an agreed selection of risks but for an 'excess of loss' only.

These 'products' and 'modes' are explained in detail in the chapters which follow and from which the reader will appreciate the skill and knowledge needed to select the most suitable insurer and negotiate the most advantageous terms of cover. There are areas where insurers compete head-on and others where they complement each other. It is more than likely that since this book was published some new product or producer has arrived in the market. This will only serve to confirm the pace of change and the breadth of opportunity for the businessman and the credit insurance practitioner. Table 7.1 shows which insurers offer each product and mode of underwriting.

COMMERCIAL CREDIT INSURANCE

The short history of credit insurance in appendix A shows how new the craft is, when we remember that marine insurance is thought to have originated in thirteenth-century Europe, the first life insurances, the

Table 7.1 'Layout' of the United Kingdom underwriting market

Commercial credit insurance	Modes of underwriting		
	Spread	Specific	Catastrophe (Excess of loss)
Credit and Guarantee Insurance Company plc		★	
Insurances of Credit	★		
PanFinancial Insurance Company Limited			★
Trade Indemnity plc	★	★	★
Export credit insurance			
American International Underwriters (UK) Ltd	★	★¹	
Export Credits Guarantee Department	★	★	★
PanFinancial Insurance Company Limited		★¹	
Trade Indemnity plc	★	★²	★

1. For political risks only (see chapter 9).
2. Only for the holder of a 'spread' policy.

London underwriting market and large-scale fire insurance emerged in the seventeenth century and liability insurances were probably first written in the early 1800s. Until the end of the Second World War, more cover was written for insolvency and default than for the 'export credit package'. The United Kingdom was served exclusively by the Trade Indemnity Company Limited until the early 1950s and Trade Indemnity is still the foremost name in an expanding market place.

Commercial credit insurance in the 'spread' mode reinforces, but can never replace, sound credit control practice on the lines drawn in chapter 5. In chapter 8 we discuss the underwriter's perception of the risk involved in this reinforcing role and it will be clear that, where there is a case for insuring, the credit controller and the credit insurer, far from being incompatible, are mutually indispensable.

Specific risk cover is widely used by, for example, sub-contractors in the construction industry where the main contractor is increasingly the contract manager for an employer or where large sums are outstanding on 'pay when paid' terms. A few contracts can each take up a large part of a company's resources and expose it to significant insolvency risk. Its bankers are usually aware of these exposures and many specific covers are placed on the insistence of banks, often with an assignment of the benefits of the cover.

Component suppliers and subcontractors in the engineering industry often run similar risks. The company making special tooling relies on repeat orders from a few customers who look to it for quick delivery and known specifications of work. A subcontractor working on parts for a mass producer will inevitably commit a large part of his capacity to that customer.

In chapter 8 we explain the advanced concept of catastrophe cover to indemnify suitable companies against an excess of loss on their very large debtor ledgers.

EXPORT CREDIT INSURANCE

Insurance against the combined risks of insolvency, default and political losses has been provided largely by governments since the end of the First World War. It arose from the recognition that the revival of world trade was threatened not only by the risk of weakened buyers but by 'country' risks as well, and it soon became an accepted feature of the export promotion facilities of every industrial nation, a process markedly hastened by the ending of the 1939–45 hostilities.

Many of the government insurers have, like ECGD, relied on 'whole turnover' cover to achieve the maximum spread of risks, but attitudes are to some extent influenced by the relative importance of export earnings to their economies, and the percentages of their national exports which they insure vary widely. As will be seen from chapter 11, some of the official insurers are private companies acting as underwriting agents for governments and many of them also write commercial credit insurance on their own accounts. Others are semi-autonomous bodies and some share some risks with the private sector. There are few features common to them all.

ECGD remains, however, the doyen of export credit insurers and the brief review of its underwriting practice in chapter 9 will, we believe, provide a useful model for the reader to study the subject.

THE PROVIDERS

Trade Indemnity plc

Formed in 1918, Trade Indemnity is now substantially owned by composite insurance companies. Over 400 staff are employed in London and branches throughout Great Britain and in a wholly owned underwriting subsidiary in Australia. Insured turnover in commercial credit insurance is running at about £23 billion, while the new export department wrote £2 billion in 1987–8 and expects to reach £3 billion for 1988–9.

The Whole Turnover Credit Insurance Policy gives 'spread' cover for insolvency and default on United Kingdom buyers and a small export turnover can be included in acceptable markets. Policies are normally written for one year on a 'risks attaching' basis or as term agreements. Most insured business is on monthly account or similar terms but credit up to 360 days has been covered exceptionally. 'First loss deductibles' and no-claim bonuses are frequently negotiated.

The export credit policy is normally offered to companies with an export turnover of at least £2 million. A simplified small business policy is available for lower figures. Trade Indemnity expects 60% of the turnover to be with OECD countries and rates the business according to quality and spread with additional premiums for the separate political risk, transfer and public buyer endorsements which are entirely at the proposer's option. Terms of payment up to two years are covered, longer terms being written under specific policies, but only for the exporter who holds a 'spread' policy. Although most Trade Indemnity policyholders are United Kingdom companies, business originating overseas is written, as explained in chapter 11.

Trade Indemnity's special underwriting unit drafts individual policies to cover unusual insolvency risks arising from commercial transactions outside the trade credit field, such as major sales of assets.

The Export Credits Guarantee Department

ECGD is a self-accounting department of the Department of Trade charged with conducting its credit insurance function at no eventual net cost to the public. Its statutory authority (currently the Export Guarantees and Overseas Investments Act 1978) allows it to issue policies to 'persons carrying on business in the United Kingdom' which means that the policyholder must normally be registered under the Companies Act although other incorporated bodies may be eligible.

ECGD's credit insurance activities   The policies cover the full range of 'buyer' and 'political' risks outlined in chapters 3 and 4 and fall under four main headings:

1. Comprehensive Short Term Guarantee (the CST) to cover repetitive sales, mostly of consumable goods, on terms up to 180 days' credit. This policy is examined in detail in chapter 9. An additional Subsidiaries Guarantee can cover on-sales made by an overseas subsidiary of the policyholder.
2. Supplemental Extended Terms Guarantee (the CXT) to cover sales of capital and semi-capital goods, typically on two to five years' credit.
3. Comprehensive Services Guarantee drafted in similar terms to the CST but covering contracts for the performance of services.

These are all 'spread' policies and account for some 75% of ECGD's insured turnover which in 1986–7 totalled nearly £13.9 billion or 19.6% of non-oil exports.

4. Specific Guarantees for individual contracts for major sales of goods or project-type contracts involving both goods and services, such as engineering construction. Credit terms do not normally exceed seven years but a construction period of two or three years is common. Special variants of the Specific Guarantee cover a wide variety of services and civil engineering construction works.

ECGD's financial guarantee activities   In addition to its credit insurance function, ECGD is authorised to act as a unique financial guarantor, giving its unconditional guarantee to banks to enable them to finance insured sales of capital goods and project-type contracts on 'supplier credit' at favourable rates of interest and without recourse to the exporter. This combination of credit insurance and financial guarantee is explained in chapter 10 under the ECGD Specific Bank Guarantee.

Separately, under its Buyer Credits, the department gives similar unconditional guarantees to banks who finance export business by making direct loans to overseas borrowers/buyers, thus relieving the exporter of all responsibility for raising finance. Buyer Credits for major contracts involve the complex interlocking of a contract of sale on 'cash' terms, a bank loan agreement, ECGD's guarantee to the bank and a premium and recourse agreement between ECGD and the exporter/contractor. The department vets those features of the contract and the loan agreement which affect its position as guarantor. When more than one contractor is involved and the buyer acts as contract manager instead of appointing a main contractor, ECGD can guarantee a line of credit under which each contractor draws independently from the lending bank.

ECGD General Purpose Lines of Credit   This arrangement is offered as an inducement to overseas buyers, often in conjunction with a specific UK trade promotion.

With the benefit of ECGD's unconditional guarantee, a bank or group of banks makes a line of credit available to an overseas bank. Buyers apply to the borrowing bank for credit and the contracts are approved by the UK lending bank for financing. Buyer and seller conclude their contract on 'cash' terms, payment being made to the seller in the UK by the lending bank. It is for the borrowing bank to collect principal and interest from the buyers over the credit period and repay the UK lender.

Details of funds currently available under these lines of credit are published regularly in *British Business* yet the take-up rate is still very disappointing. Many export sales must be lost which could be closed quickly with these offers of ready-made credit. A wide range of manufactured goods qualify for inclusion and cover for pre-shipment risks can often be provided if needed.

Credit and Guarantee Insurance Company plc

Formed in 1957 to underwrite individual insolvency risks, Credit and Guarantee is now owned by leading Danish, Swedish and Dutch insurance and surety companies and its business is equally divided between commercial credit insurance and surety underwriting.

Credit insurance is written on buyers in the United Kingdom, Denmark, Finland, France, Holland, Norway, Portugal, Spain, Sweden and the USA. Individual contracts must be in excess of £100,000 and the company avoids random business in which the proposer seeks to select a single risk which by quantity or quality causes concern. There must be a sound reason for supporting the business as when, for example, one contract or customer accounts for a significant portion of total turnover. In 1971, Credit and Guarantee paid the largest commercial credit insurance claim on record to a policyholder who had committed some 75% of his turnover to Rolls Royce for special parts for the RB211 engine. C & G's cheque for over £1,076,000 saved him from certain insolvency.

By catering for a limited number of policyholders and buyers, the company can concentrate on rigorous investigation of the risks put to it and careful drafting of the cover which often alerts a proposer to dangers he has not appreciated. It makes no secret of its intention to underwrite realistically and with precision, which allows it to cover exposures which might otherwise be unacceptable and to offer personal service to its clients. The policyholder who takes proper note of the underwriting assessment and follows the conditions of cover can have expert advice, and sometimes direct intervention, in risk control throughout a contract or programme of contracts.

American International Underwriters (London) Limited

AIU, the third largest insurance company in the United States, has been in business in London for many years underwriting marine and political risks in competition both with other insurance companies and with Lloyd's. Its success in covering the political risks in export contracts led to the introduction of its Comprehensive Export Credit Policy – described in chapter 9 – covering buyer and political risks. AIU sees its market as among large companies, self-sufficient in credit management and prepared to accept high 'deductibles' and discretionary limits.

PanFinancial Insurance Company Limited

PanFinancial originated as the credit insurance operation of British National, a subsidiary of the US Armco financial services group. It was acquired in 1985 by Continental Casualty of the United States, Skandia of Sweden and Yasuda Fire and Marine of Japan. The mainstay of PanFinancial's business is its Insolvency Catastrophe Insurance which provides a strategic reserve for the policyholder rather than a tactical reinforcement of his credit control. Indeed, PanFinancial must first be satisfied with its own in-depth investigation of the proposer's credit procedures and capabilities.

For a single premium, it offers cover designed to limit potential damage to the balance sheet, borrowing capacity and perhaps even the share price, of an unforseeable run of insolvency losses.

The proposer must normally have an annual sales turnover of at least £10 million. The cover is worldwide, requires the minimum of administration and, following the initial investigation and agreement, there is no interference with credit management. The emphasis is on conservative underwriting of high-quality business on an excess of loss basis only and the company does not quote for all the inquiries put to it.

PanFinancial enjoys the distinction of insuring the International Commodities Clearing House under the largest commercial credit insurance risk yet placed in the London market with a liability of £70 million after a first loss deductible of £30 million. The resources of more than a dozen specialist and non-specialist insurance companies were marshalled round PanFinancial's lead for this unique 'catastrophe' cover. The policy also reflects the great flexibility of modern credit insurance. Although the commodity contracts under which the clearing house assumes liability are different from everyday contracts for the sale and delivery of goods, PanFinancial's simple policy wording responds well to this special individual need.

In the political risk field, PanFinancial covers single contracts with its Contract Completion Insurance while substantially the same cover is offered for the *purchase* of goods from a public sector seller. Separate policies are issued for the non-honouring of a letter of credit and for bond risks.

Insurances of Credit

'IOC' or 'Namur' is the United Kingdom branch of the very successful Les Assurances du Crédit SA of Namur. Since March 1988 United Kingdom risks have been written at the London office which previously collated information for underwriting in Belgium. A small staff runs about 200 policies with a premium income in excess of £2 million. Policies paying less than £2,000 p.a. are not encouraged.

The cover is for insolvency and default only and is written on a 'spread' basis. Credit terms do not normally exceed 180 days but 360 days has been agreed on occasion. Discretionary limits range from £2,500 to £10,000. Deductibles are negotiated, individual or aggregate first losses being preferred. Other features of Namur's operation are described in chapter 8.

With its origins in the steelmaking area of Belgium, the company is strong in the UK steel industry and has increased its general engineering portfolio, especially in the Midlands and north of England. Other trades include advertising agencies and some timber. Work-in-progress is covered on request but on stringent terms and at the same rate of premium as the corresponding credit risk. The company also covers long-term capital leases (for which it can arrange finance) and bond risks.

OTHER OPPORTUNITIES

Wherever, in a commercial situation, it can be shown that one party is at risk for the insolvency of another (or others) there is a case for credit insurers to consider. The following is a selection of covers which have been written.

Sales of assets

The great majority of bids and deals do not reach the headlines yet many have only been possible with the security of an insolvency guarantee on the purchaser. In sales by receivers and divestment through management buy-outs, the seller can share, and in some cases transfer, the nonpayment risk while, conversely, the purchaser can improve his (or their) offer by adding a credit insurance indemnity. This can have a special appeal to directors whose personal interests are at stake and almost any sale of tangible or intangible assets can be considered. Credit and Guarantee's Financial Indemnity and Trade Indemnity's Divestment Policy can cover deferred payment terms up to five years.

Rent Guarantees and Tenant Default Guarantees cover loss of rent and charges following insolvency of a tenant of a commercial or industrial property.

Deposit Insurance covers monies due from banks, assurance companies, unit trusts, building societies and other deposit-taking institutions.

Consequential loss

There is as yet no consequential loss cover generally available to complement trade credit insurance in the way that fire and 'interruption' insurances provide for loss of profits and expenses. There are, however, a number of specific indemnities which give contingency cover for certain losses arising as the direct result of an insolvency.

Insolvency of a supplier

The failure of a key supplier or subcontractor may result in the loss of an advance payment and this is covered by Trade Indemnity's Anticipatory Credit Cover. Credit and Guarantee's Supplier Default Guarantee is aimed at the net cost of replacing a key supplier or subcontractor including, for example, liquidated damages for delay in completion of a contract.

Property leases

Leases are frequently assigned on vacation of premises, leaving the original lessee still bound to the freeholder and the better his credit standing, the less willing the freeholder will be to release him from his covenant. A lease may be assigned several times and the freeholder is at liberty to act against any lessee in the chain if the current incumbent goes insolvent.

Any assignor may find that the loss of rent with dilapidations and other expenses exceeds the income achieved when the premises are eventually relet. He might, of course, actually show a profit but the present uncertainty is enough to steer many towards an insurance solution. On suitable names, Credit and Guarantee will write three years' cover with a roll-over under its Assignors' Consequential Loss Insurance.

Personal guarantors

Company directors often give their personal guarantees for the obligations of their companies under commercial and industrial property leases and unforseen external events can lead to these guarantees being 'called'. Under its Guarantors' Personal Liability Protection, Credit and Guarantee indemnifies the individual where the proximate cause of the call is a natural disaster or similar *force-majeure* event. Mismanagement and any cause within the control of the guarantor or the company is excluded. The application is made, and the premium paid, by the company but the indemnity is issued personally to the guarantor. If the ownership of the company changes or there is any other material change in the circumstances, the cover is suspended until Credit and Guarantee has approved the new risk.

Equipment leases (operating leases)

The insolvency of the hirer puts the owner at risk for unpaid rent, the cost of recovering (and perhaps refurbishing) the equipment and any loss incidental to the arranging of a new lease. These consequential losses arising from the insolvency of a lessee are insurable but there are clearly some inherently high-risk situations and underwriters are very selective. Credit and Guarantee, for example, prefers not to entertain a proposal if the anticipated total rent is less than £100,000.

There is now an almost unlimited capacity to cover the insolvency risks run by commercial and industrial concerns and an unparalleled opportunity for insurers and specialist brokers to find the needs and match the cover to them.

FINANCIAL INSURANCE

In addition to the 'retail' market underwriting individual risks in either the spread or specific modes, a very healthy 'wholesale' market is developing which applies the insurance principle to securitised debt in order to increase the lending capacity of financial institutions. A bank which needs to improve its ratios may be able to raise the status of some of its portfolio of debt by packaging and insuring it. The expanding commercial paper market in which companies borrow on the strength of their own acceptances offers opportunities for credit enhancement in the shape of insurance backing. The practice of selling blocks of commercial property mortgages has been extended to residential property with the support of insurers, some of whom take no part in trade credit insurance.

The selection of the risks and insurers and the negotiation of the cover calls for high-level broking skill not unlike large-scale reinsurance broking.

It is very likely that consumer credit such as hire purchase and credit cards will be reinforced in this way. Loss experience on credit cards is certainly low enough to justify a minimal stop-loss cover.

OTHER OPTIONS FOR THE CREDITOR

In surveying the market for credit insurance in this chapter and in assessing the need in chapter 12, we must not ignore other options which are sometimes available.

Factoring

A factor buys debts and if, in the agreement, he takes full responsibility for debt collection, he is offering an alternative to credit insurance. Under some agreements, unpaid debts revert to the seller. 'Full' factoring, however, combines finance and debt collection, the factor only having recourse to the seller for disputed debts. Factoring does not usually cater for the same degree of selection that insurers will accommodate, nor does it seem expedient to maintain a credit control facility for only part of the total debt. Most of the factors are owned by banks and some are themselves insured, especially for export business.

Some companies choose to confine themselves to manufacturing and supply and are happy to subcontract credit control and sales financing. Others regard these as inseparable functions of the body corporate.

Non-recourse finance

In the same way, any form of finance which removes recourse to the seller relieves him of the credit risk. London Bridge Finance Company acts as an undisclosed principal to provide finance at competitive rates against the security of 'blue chip' trade debt. It buys the goods (or the work-in-progress) from the seller but appoints him as its agent to deliver the goods to the buyer. As a secondary benefit, non-recourse finance provides a highly selective form of protection but it cannot be expected to cope with the same spread of risks as credit insurance.

Forfaiting

As a method of financing medium-term export credit, some international banks are willing to buy accepted bills of exchange or promissory notes for cash at a discount. The instruments must normally be guaranteed by an acceptable bank so that they become, in effect, bank debt. The cost to the exporter depends on the prevailing discount rates and he must pay a commitment fee for a rate in advance. He carries all risks until the forfaiter takes up the paper but there is no recourse thereafter. Although concentrated in the two to five-year field, the forfaiting market can now deal in any credit between six months and ten years.

Captive insurance companies

The classes of insurance which can properly be delegated to a 'captive' are limited, but a multinational company with first-class corporate credit management may already have the nucleus of a captive. It may be possible to offer the trading companies cover more in line with their requirements and at lower cost than in the open market because the insurers' profit element is clawed back. One interesting possibility is that a captive might use as its reinsurance vehicle the catastrophe-type cover described in chapter 8. Many believe that the market must move in this direction to satisfy some of the world's largest corporations.

Small business

Because credit insurance requires more servicing than most others, it is more difficult to maintain an acceptable standard for small-volume policies. The problem most concerns Trade Indemnity and ECGD with their preponderance of 'spread' cover. Both recognise the needs of 'small' business and are doubtless mindful of the growth potential of small companies. For an insurable turnover of less than about £1 million Trade Indemnity usually offers its Smaller Business Policy covering insolvency and default only. The discretionary limit facility is omitted but the policy needs only minimal administration.

The small exporter

A small *exporter* is not always a small *company* yet the administrative burden of running a policy may still take too much of its limited export resources. While not discouraging direct approaches, ECGD has enthusiastically supported banks and other financial institutions who can provide 'over the counter' service to the exporter seeking finance and insurance and use their own large policies to buy the cover 'wholesale' from ECGD. High discretionary limits reduce the use of the credit limit service and skilled staff ought to ensure compliance with policy conditions. These facilities are discussed in chapter 10.

The role of the brokers

The small group of specialist brokers are indispensable to the smooth functioning of the credit insurance market. Like all insurance brokers, they engage in selling, placing and servicing. Credit insurance almost always has to be *sold* intensively because few companies recognise their need until it has been demonstrated by an irrecoverable loss or by a convincing approach from a salesman. The selling process is often long and frustrating.

Placing means selling the prospect to the insurers. The broker must have understood the prospect's business sufficiently to be able to present the risk to the market in a favourable but truthful way. He often needs to obtain agreement on the principal credit limits to make a more meaningful offer to the prospect and it is his duty to produce as many quotations as the market permits. Unlike many general insurance quotations, these are not 'rule of thumb' and they incur expense for everybody concerned. It is sensible for any management to consult a specialist broker who is employed fulltime in negotiations with his market and knows its limitations and the factors most likely to influence underwriters. He (or she) has frequently had personal experience in credit management and can offer authoritative guidance on risk management and sales financing.

There is no incentive for any broking firm to enter this field unless it is prepared to invest in qualified staff and adequate *servicing* facilities. The intervention of unskilled intermediaries leads to misunderstanding and friction. There is every incentive for the insurers to encourage the brokers to find the business and nurse it carefully. The credit insurance broker has been described as 'the trustee of the insured's credibility on which the goodwill of the insurer rests'.

There are about 60 members of the British Insurance and Investment Brokers Association (out of a total of 3,700) who handle credit insurance in any way and, of these, the leading twelve form the United Kingdom Credit Insurance Brokers' Committee which negotiates terms and conditions of accreditation with Trade Indemnity and ECGD as the two main insurers. The current members of this Committee are listed in Appendix E.

8

Commercial credit insurance in the United Kingdom

vwvwvwvwvwvwvwvwvw

Commercial credit insurance is written either as specific cover on a single buyer (or a single contract) or as spread cover on a selection of names. It must always be expected that a specific risk will be underwritten more precisely than a spread of risks, with more stringent conditions and fewer concessions. Specific cover has to do with *an imminent known risk*; spread cover has to do with *risks contemplated in the future*. The specific proposer ought to be able to give more accurate details of the buyer, terms of payment, maximum outstandings and other features of the risk. At the time of application the risk must be proposed only and not yet firm. The specific insurer offers the cover to enable the contract to be made and not because the proposer has already committed himself and had second thoughts about the credit risk.

After a preliminary indication, and given full and accurate information, the insurer can give a firm offer of premium cost and conditions of cover but there is no commitment to cover until his offer has been accepted and premium properly paid. Once the premium has been paid, the insurer is liable only on the precise terms and conditions agreed and only for the risk precisely as put to him. He is entitled to disclaim liability if the risk is materially altered without his agreement and renewal is entirely at his discretion and on his terms.

PREMIUM RATES FOR SPECIFIC RISKS

The main factors which govern specific rates are the quality of the risk, the risk period and the maximum amount to be outstanding at any one time. The underwriter will look carefully at the terms of payment to see if there are peaks of risk. If, for instance, the buyer depends on payments coming in from third parties, how long can he afford to finance delays on their part? Could he afford to withhold supplies from them? What are the points in a contract programme when the buyer's cash flow is weakest? A large amount outstanding on a good name for a defined period is better than a smaller amount hanging over a doubtful name for an uncertain time. The price of reinsurance may also be a factor.

METHODS OF CHARGING SPECIFIC PREMIUM

A specific risk can be written on the basis of either 'fixed time' or 'adjustable time'. Fixed time is appropriate when the pattern of outstandings can be foreseen accurately at the outset. Premium is then related to the maximum amount and the period of risk. In other words, the insured buys a block of cover for a fixed premium. If the level of outstandings will fluctuate widely from month to month, 'adjustable time' provides for premium to be charged on the actual outstandings. Fixed time might be appropriate to a manufacturer selling to wholesalers on a regular basis or to a wholesaler selling on to retailers. Subcontractors in the building trade, builders' merchants and component suppliers to mass-production industry who simply respond to the demand might be better suited to adjustable time cover.

CREDIT AND GUARANTEE INSURANCE COMPANY LIMITED

Credit and Guarantee only transacts specific account business, mainly with its Principal Customer Default (Specific Account) Policy for contracts within the United Kingdom and for exports to certain European countries. The policy can be extended to cover work-in-progress at the time of insolvency and for which costs are admitted to rank against the insolvent estate.

A single contract must be of at least £100,000 in value but a series of contracts over a twelve-month period can be covered for a minimum total value of £250,000. Unlike most insurers, Credit and Guarantee provides a 100% indemnity for the amount admitted to rank.

'SPREAD' COVER

Full whole turnover policies covering all outstandings with all buyers are now rare except for some small policies where there is no room for any variation. Almost all other policies either exclude some risks by negotiation or they are limited to certain agreed accounts.* Business in a specified class of goods is often excluded and this may also be achieved by the reverse process of applying the policy only to certain divisions or products of a company. Over-the-counter sales and retail sales of parts

* Historically Trade Indemnity has written its Specific Account Policy to cover an agreed list of accounts but the purpose is still to secure an acceptable spread of risks and avoid unfavourable selection by the policyholder.

and materials are commonly excluded because credit control in such business is usually only cursory. Most commercial credit insurance today is 'spread' rather than 'whole turnover'.

RISK SHARING AND LOSS SHARING

A management which has invested human and material resources in good credit practice may feel able to bear a sizeable portion of its credit burden uninsured. The possibility of some loss is accepted but the incidence and scale of it should be much reduced by effective credit control, so that credit insurance can be concentrated on the major risk areas. The options open to management involve sharing the risks, sharing the losses or both. *Risk* sharing is a variation of the whole turnover contract to provide for some buyers (some 'risks') to be covered by the policy and for the remainder to be carried by the company uninsured. *Loss* sharing means that of the losses that do occur some are to be recoverable from the insurance and the remainder to be borne entirely by the company.

Sharing the risks – variations of spread cover

Consider a company with 100 active buyers and £25 million of debtors. If Pareto's theory holds good, the top twenty account for £20 million and the remaining 80 for £5 million, as the 'pyramid of risk' in Fig. 6.1 showed. One way to share the risks would be to exclude all those eighty. Some of the 'top twenty' might be excluded for other reasons – business clearly separated within the company into a division; very short credit terms making for tight credit control or the proposer may be a sole supplier able to limit his exposure more effectively. This weeding out process might leave, say, fifteen buyers accounting for £15 million and an acceptable spread of risks.

'Datum line' cover

Simple exclusion of the 'bottom 80' could be effected by agreeing a figure of outstandings and for every account to be included when it reaches the 'datum line'. Instead of selecting names on their merits or for the proportion of the total risk which they represent, datum line cover sets a level above which all accounts are insured but below which none are insured. The standard arrangement is that on inception of the policy every account which has exceeded the datum line during the previous twelve months must be offered for cover for the first year. Each buyer is still underwritten in the usual way and a limit of liability agreed.

Subsequently, any other account which passes the line must be offered for underwriting within 30 days. If approved, it remains covered for the remainder of the current policy and for the next renewal as illustrated in Fig. 8.1.

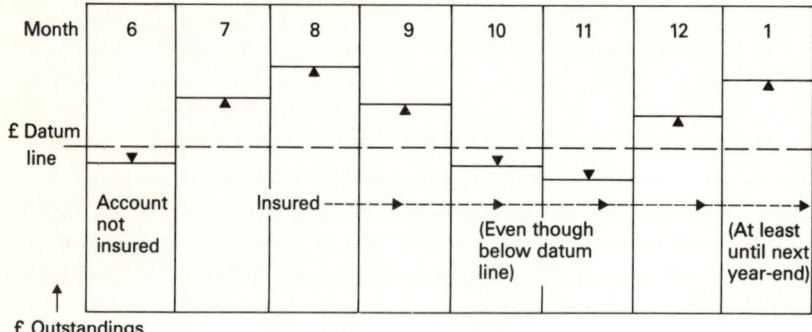

Fig. 8.1 Datum line cover

The pros and cons of datum line cover

The chief merit of datum line cover is that it uses credit insurance properly to reinforce a competent credit management regime. Day to day administration is minimal and the cost of the insurance can be related to, if not actually debited to, the insured accounts rather than spread across all buyers as an overhead. A disadvantage is that, once the buyer has passed the datum line, premium is payable even when he falls below it and there are those who feel that this defeats the object of the exercise.

There is no point in writing this form of cover unless the line is set at a level at which the company is still carrying substantial accounts uninsured. It is not a substitute for a 'first loss' (which we discuss later), and it is not suitable for seasonal trades in which outstandings fluctuate widely nor for trades such as component manufacturers in which orders are 'called off' by the buyer as and when his assembly line is ready to receive them. The peaks and troughs make datum line cover impractical. Datum line has been described as an early attempt at risk-sharing but it appears to have fallen out of fashion recently, probably because insurers prefer to market the 'catastrophe' concept for cover on selected principal names.

Sharing the losses

Not all managements are prepared to carry risks on some of their buyers with no insurance at all. A company which only has large accounts, such as a leading advertising agency, can hardly afford to select. Others place great store by the advice and guidance of a good insurer and like to enjoy some measure of support on most of their buyers. This calls for the sharing of losses rather than of risks.

The uninsured percentage explained in chapter 6 is the absolute minimum share of a loss which the policyholder must bear for his own account but the scope for negotiation lies in variations of 'first loss' before the percentage is applied.

The 'first loss deductible'

The opportunity to mitigate risk through loss-prevention measures and bear a higher proportion of losses which do occur has attracted much attention in recent years and is now a standard feature of many industrial and commercial insurances. The following four variations of 'first loss' are commonly used in credit insurance:

1. Individual first loss (sometimes called 'each and every').
2. Aggregate first loss.
3. Threshold cover.
4. Minimum retention.

Individual first loss

On every loss which qualifies under the policy, the policyholder bears the 'first loss' of £X and the remaining loss is shared between insurer and policyholder, as in Table 8.1.

Table 8.1 Individual first loss

Example: insured percentage 85%; first loss £1,000		
Total loss £950:	policyholder bears total loss	
Total loss £5,000:	policyholder bears first loss of	£1,000
	+ 15% of £4,000	600
		1,600
	insurer pays 85% of £4,000	3,400
		£5,000

Aggregate first loss

Some companies only wish to cushion their profits against an agreed figure of total losses in any given year. Instead of claiming the insured percentage of each individual loss, the policyholder aggregates the claims until he has borne the agreed first loss. The insurer is only liable for losses in excess of the aggregate figure and then pays the insured percentage of each admitted claim. Although there is no cover for losses below the aggregate figure, the losses must still be examined to make sure that they would have been admitted but for the first loss provision. In practice, losses must be notified when they occur but the final settlement of liability can only be agreed at the end of the policy period. Policies have been written which provide for both an individual first loss and an aggregate.

Threshold cover

A company with a wide spread of accounts often has a regular record of small losses at the lower end of the scale. The insurer will regard these as predictable and want to exclude them from the policy altogether. Threshold cover ignores all individual losses of less than the agreed figure.

Table 8.2 Threshold cover

Example: insured percentage 85%; loss threshold £500		
Total loss £450	policyholder bears total loss	
Total loss £600	policyholder bears uninsured percentage	£ 90
	insurer pays insured percentage	510
		£600

It can be seen from Table 8.2 that threshold cover comes to the same thing as an individual first loss when the loss is below the threshold. It responds in a very different way when the loss is above the figure. We shall see a different application of the threshold idea in 'catastrophe-type' cover where a company seeks only to protect its major exposures but is willing to bear quite substantial losses for its own account.

Minimum retention

This is probably now the most favoured form of first loss deductible. Of every admitted claim the policyholder retains for his own account either the uninsured percentage of the insured loss or the minimum retention sum, whichever is the greater. Once the minimum retention is overtaken by the uninsured percentage, the full policy indemnity is restored. The minimum retention thus only affects the smaller claims, how 'small' depending on where the minimum retention is set (see Table 8.3).

Table 8.3 The minimum retention

Example: insured percentage 80%; minimum retention £500

Loss up to £500	policyholder bears total loss
Loss £501–£2,500	policyholder bears £500
	insurer pays total loss minus £500
Loss £2,501+	policyholder bears 20% of loss
	insurer pays 80% of loss

A typical wording of a minimum retention clause might be:

The Insured shall retain for his own account and uninsured so much of the Insured Loss in respect of any Insured Buyer as exceeds the Insured Percentage subject to a minimum of £x.

There are circumstances in which a threshold or a minimum retention will produce a larger claim for the policyholder than an individual first loss. Consider, for instance, an insured loss of £50,000 in the context of an individual first loss or a threshold or a minimum retention each of £1,000 and an indemnity of 80%:

	insured loss	£50,000
less	individual first loss	1,000
		49,000
	insurer pays 80%	39,200

Whereas neither the threshold nor the minimum retention would come into play at this level:

insured loss	£50,000
insurer pays	£40,000

These examples show that there are 'horses for courses' in risk-sharing and the company's management structure and credit resources are important factors in the final choice.

CATASTROPHE COVER

Major companies with very large sums at risk on their trade debtors sometimes find that neither the conventional spread policy nor specific risk policies can conveniently be meshed in with their own credit management. They see no reason to insure the majority of their buyers and do not wish to devote management time to arranging specific covers. The solution may be the catastrophe cover illustrated in diagram form in Fig. 8.2, in which the company carries for its own account the following:

1. All non-qualifying losses.
2. All qualifying losses until the aggregate first loss has been reached.
3. Any loss after the maximum liability has been exhausted.

The maximum liability is the figure at which the company feels that any further loss is too unlikely to justify cover. Premium is a lump sum assessed on the anticipated outstandings and the quality of the risks involved. Although the policy pays 100% of every qualifying loss within the band of cover, this cannot be described as a full indemnity because the insured has already borne the non-qualifying losses and the aggregate first loss.

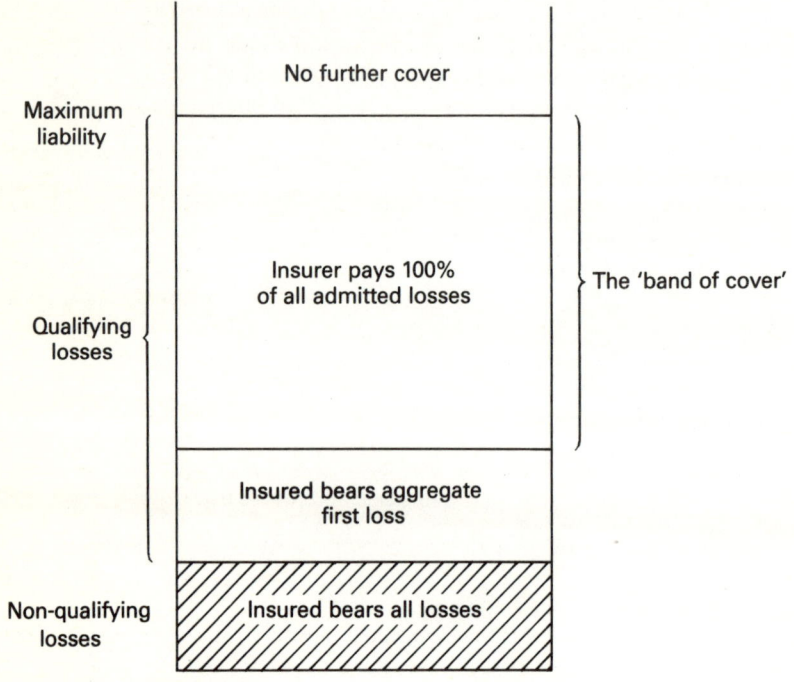

Fig. 8.2 Catastrophe cover: the insured buys a 'band of cover' between the aggregate first loss and the maximum liability

At the time of writing, catastrophe cover is generally only considered suitable for a company with an annual turnover of at least £10 million, although Trade Indemnity speaks of a minimum of £30 million. PanFinancial pioneered this form of cover (as British National) and now offers it as Insolvency Catastrophe Cover. It does not vet individual buyers but reserves the right to place a limit on its liability for a particular buyer in exceptional circumstances. It prefers to concentrate on underwriting the policyholder.

Trade Indemnity's Catastrophe Excess of Loss Policy does provide for credit limits to be approved above a high discretionary trading limit.

PREMIUM RATING OF SPREAD POLICIES

Premium is normally expressed as a percentage to be applied either to the turnover of transactions or to the balances outstanding on accounts at the declaration date. *Turnover declaring* is a simple and equitable way of charging premium when continuous deliveries are made on conventional monthly account-type terms of payment. *Balance declaring*, on the other hand, is often thought to be a more accurate measurement of risk and this is certainly true if extended credit is given. When the fall of payments is uncertain, as in the construction industry, an insurer would feel entitled to earn premium on the balances outstanding rather than on the (usually) optimistic forecast of payments which a declaration of turnover implies.

Most policies require the insured to pay a deposit premium quarterly in advance, the amount being based on the previous quarter's figures. The insurer thus holds an imprest account which the policyholder replenishes quarterly. Sometimes the deposit is a 'minimum and deposit premium', none of which is refundable on expiry or renewal. A term agreement may, for example, contain a clause such as

in the event that the premium earned in each completed twelve-month period of the policy does not amount to £x the Insured shall pay to the Insurer such amount in excess of the actual premium earned during the relative period as shall be necessary to adjust the premium to a minimum of £x for that period.

Deciding the rate

The factors most likely to influence premium rates for spread business are as follows:

1. The trade in which the company operates and status in the trade which we discussed under proposal form information. There is no tariff of rates – experience and market conditions suggest the right rate for a particular proposition.
2. The likely volume of insured turnover. At the present time Trade Indemnity's bread-and-butter business appears to be spread policies ranging from £5 million to £25 million insured turnover which gives

a good idea of the market. Smaller policies can be more expensive in terms both of risk and administration and, for the smallest, Trade Indemnity offers a simplified form of policy. The company offering more than £25 million for insurance will probably be looking for special terms such as datum line or catastrophe cover or a substantial first loss deductible.

3. The spread and quality of buyers is crucial. Knowing how promptly they pay is just as important as reading their financial statements and credit reports.

4. Terms of payment, which in some trades, commodities and raw materials for instance, are much shorter than monthly account. Longer terms, sometimes called 'extended credit' may be conceded to individual buyers of manufactured goods, often supported and financed by bills of exchange.

5. The size of accounts points to the possible scale of losses. If only one of a schedule of major buyers becomes insolvent, a large claim is a near certainty. This consideration, and in some cases the cost of additional reinsurance, affect the risk element of the premium.

6. Loss experience. Most underwriters would settle for a realistic rate at the outset rather than pare the initial rate only to have to call for an unwelcome increase after a year or two.

7. The calculation of average days' sales outstandings (DSOs) gives a rough indication of how well normal terms of payment are kept. If collection performance is poor, sanctioning procedures are suspect as well.

Credit insurers, like all others, have to watch for the right moment to 'harden' or 'soften' their rates. In the long term, 'softer', that is lower, rates do not seem to improve the flow of good-quality business. The attitude of leading credit insurers to premium rates is conservative but realistic and not too much concerned with short-term trends.

No-claims bonuses

An effective reduction in premium cost may be offered in the form of a no-claims bonus on the next renewal in a case where the insurer cannot contemplate any shaving of his present rate. It is for the policyholder to decide whether to take the claims or the bonus, a decision he may wish to defer until renewal. A novel feature of the Insurances of Credit policy is the 'reverse no-claims bonus'. A minimum annual premium is quoted subject to a retrospective increase of 50–100% if the policyholder takes up claims exceeding an agreed limit.

Special terms of business

Because trade credit is conventionally on monthly account terms, business transacted on unusual terms or conditions attracts special attention. The following are typical examples.

Consignment terms The practice of holding stock 'on consignment' at a dealer's or distributor's premises is traditional in a few trades such as timber, paper and textiles. With many distributors short of working capital but needing an assured level of stock, it has become common in other trades as well. Because there's many a slip 'twixt cup and lip, insurers must call for special safeguards. There must be a formal stockholding agreement under which invoices are drawn on the stockholder as soon as he withdraws any goods for sale. To discourage excessive stockholding, there is a limit on the 'age' of admissible stock and the policyholder is expected to monitor stock levels and movements.

Retention payments In the building industry an agreed retention, usually not more than 10%, is withheld until satisfactory completion of the contract. The insurer's difficulty is the uncertainty of the period of risk and the danger that the buyer's position may deteriorate and contribute to further delay. A sound contract should place a clear limit on the time for which the retention payment may be withheld and that is usually the initial period of cover. With the delays which are so frequent in the building and construction trades, cover for any extension is a matter for negotiation at the time.

Conditional subcontracts In building and civil engineering contracts the main contractor is often only liable to pay when he himself receives payment from the employer. Although the subcontract embodies terms of payment, the obligation to pay is conditional and so these have come to be known as 'as and when' or 'pay when paid' terms. The main contractor cannot usually afford to finance subcontractors for the large sums involved because he cannot be sure when the consulting engineer acting for the employer will accept the work done and approve the invoices for payment. The subcontractor is thus at risk directly on the main contractor and indirectly on the employer. Since much construction work is done for local authorities and public bodies, the second risk is usually one of delayed payment whereas the risk on the main contractor is clearly insolvency. The standard form of contract recommended by the Royal Institute of British Architects gives the subcontractor a limited right to present approved invoices direct to the employer but this is only intended to discourage delay and does not address the insolvency risk.

'As and when' subcontracts are not always acceptable for cover because there is often concern about both main contractors and their subcontractors. There must be an horizon of risk and Trade Indemnity, for example, only writes cover for a maximum of 180 days from the date of the subcontractor's invoice (which he must render within thirty days of completing the work). Protracted default is excluded to avoid the risk of the main contractor financing himself with subcontractors' funds.

CREDIT LIMIT PRACTICE

A credit limit service must aim for a quick and positive response to the policyholder's request. The majority of requests are agreed quickly and without qualification, the minority call for special treatment and some of that minority require very detailed consideration. Many requests need only be checked against a standing limit and agreed by simple administrative action. Only those which are sifted out are underwritten individually. The routine reviewing of standing limits and the continuous processing of new credit information are the concern of the underwriting manager. He must decide whether – and how – he should allow decisions to be taken on minimal information or even authorise 'negative vetting'. The availability, quality and cost of credit information and the level of discretionary limits have a bearing on the service which can – or need – be maintained.

The 'yes', 'no', 'yes, but . . .' decision

Any underwriting decision is 'yes' or 'no' or 'yes, but . . .'. A sound but unpalatable credit limit decision can only be changed by fresh information, by facts of which the underwriter was unaware when forming his original view. Of course, there can be genuine differences of opinion over the interpretation of information or analysis of a situation but in our experience underwriters are usually realistic. They would rather accept business and earn premium than turn it away and they more often look for a reason for agreeing than an excuse for disagreeing. The policyholder who makes a good submission is more likely to enjoy the benefit of any doubt than the one who presents a half a case with excessive zeal.

It is a common criticism that insurers are not constructive when giving unfavourable decisions. Again, it is our experience that most underwriters will explain a decision to any policyholder who is willing to listen. Nevertheless, this irritation would be removed if more of them would follow the practice of Insurances of Credit and give a coded reason for rejections which are, after all, only a minority of the total. Given a reason, the conscientious credit manager will look for firm grounds on which the decision might be modified. This is the credit insurance partnership in action.

Aggregation

The individual policyholder cannot usually be aware of the problem of aggregation of credit limits. If, for instance, an insurer has agreed ten limits totalling £500,000 on a buyer, he would count himself fortunate if none of the ten had any outstandings when the buyer went insolvent. On the other hand, there is no reason why the full £500,000 should not be outstanding. There are times when he must decide to draw the line and limit his commitments on a particular buyer. It is difficult to persuade companies to give up all or even part of existing limits and, with large figures, an insurer may have little idea of his true exposure.

Reduction and cancellation of limits

For this and other reasons it may be necessary to reduce or cancel some 'live' credit limits with inevitable difficulties for a policyholder who is committed to future deliveries and cannot easily withhold them. Trade Indemnity recognises this by allowing the original limit to apply to firm contracts already in hand at the time of the reduction or cancellation. In certain circumstances Insurances of Credit goes a stage further by indemnifying the policyholder against damages for breach of contract if it insists that he withhold deliveries from a solvent buyer.

Guarantees of payment

In chapter 6 we discussed special credit limit conditions and the insurer's general attitude to third-party guarantees. In domestic business the most common guarantor is the buyer's parent company and there are enough subsidiary company insolvencies on record to remind us that parents are not yet automatically liable for the trade debts of their subsidiaries. Some insurers specify a form of guarantee wording or approve draft wordings submitted to them. All too often nowadays a 'letter of comfort' is accepted as a substitute for a legally enforceable undertaking. Experience may show that it is not worth the paper it is written on.[†]

Reservation of property rights

Most insurers would only expect the seller to take a charge on goods wherever it would be normal practice. In some European business, for example, to omit an *Eigentumsvorbehalt* or Romalpa-type clause would be to run avoidable risk. It is always important to know whether the insurer intends that action to implement a charge is to be taken before he admits liability or whether he will pay the claim and treat the reservation of property rights as a means of salvage. We commented in chapter 6 on the policyholder's obligation to protect lines of recovery but most insurers say that they do not intend that the policyholder should incur legal costs prematurely.

Discretionary limits

There is provision in most spread policies for the policyholder to exercise his own discretion in granting credit up to a figure variously known as the discretionary limit, discretionary trading limit or non-vet limit. If a claim arises, it is for him to justify the amount and terms of credit he has conceded.

The limit was originally set at a low level intended only to filter out smaller inquiries which involved disproportionate expenditure for insurers. The policyholder's knowledge of his trade was often sufficient for him to keep minor risks under adequate control. In recent years the move towards more risk-sharing and selection of buyers for cover has made higher levels of discretion inevitable and they are now a major underwriting consideration.

Discretionary limit practice

Trade Indemnity's proposal form asks for the names of credit information agencies used to check the creditworthiness of new buyers, and the approved sources are entered in the policy schedule which also describes the limit of discretion as:

† In the particular circumstances of a recent case (Kleinwort Benson Ltd. v. Malaysian Mining Corp Berhad, *FT Law Report*, 12 January 1988) a 'comfort letter' was held to have created a legal liability but we believe this judgement may not be relevant to most of the assurances given in the course of ordinary trade credit.

(b) an amount which shall be justified
  (i) by the sum of any information in writing about the buyer obtained within a period of twelve months prior to the granting of the credit (including information from at least one of the sources specified below); or
  (ii) by the INSURED's experience of the buyer's account during that period; or
  (iii) where both information and experience exist by reference to such information and experience.

We can see that if the credit control practices outlined in chapter 5 are followed, the danger of any disagreement is negligible. Whether a discretionary limit is 'high' or 'low', it presupposes good credit control of a style and scale appropriate to the business.

Extensions of due dates

Similarly, most policies allow for discretion to give a buyer extra time to pay provided that the need for the extension arises at or shortly before the due date. Any earlier request must be seen as a request for a change of the contractual terms and an implication of more far-reaching problems. In particular, an extension must never be a contractual right on which the buyer can rely.

Trade Indemnity usually agrees a maximum extension period of 90 days from the *original* due date but where the terms are very short – seven or fourteen days for example – the period would naturally be less. Given that 'monthly account' has come to mean an average of some 70 days' debt outstanding, it is unlikely that an extension shorter than 90 days will make much difference to the ordinary customer.

Who pays for credit information?

The cost of a large specific risk inquiry may be too high for the insurer to write it off if the business does not materialise, so he may give an indication 'subject to further information' to be obtained and charged for if he is subsequently asked to make a formal offer of cover.

On spread policies for which only a few credit limits will be required during the year, the cost can usually be met as an overhead out of premium income. Some trades, steel stockholders and builders' merchants for example, handle large numbers of inquiries, many of which prove fruitless, so there may have to be a limits charge in addition to the premium. An advantage of a separate charge from the insurer's point of view is that, unlike a premium, it is not eroded by brokerage or reinsurance costs.

CLAIMS NEGOTIATIONS

A simplifying feature of commercial credit insurance is that there cannot often be any doubt about the cause of loss. The insuring clause of the standard Trade Indemnity policy, for example, reads:

in the event of any INSURED BUYER failing by reason of his INSOLVENCY or PROTRACTED DEFAULT to pay to the INSURED any INSURED DEBT . . .

The wording of Credit and Guarantee's Customer Default Policy reads as follows:

2. The loss shall have been directly and naturally suffered by the Insured as a result of the Customer having become Insolvent and thereby failing to pay the amount due to the Insured in accordance with the terms of the Contract.

Evidence of insolvency

Bankruptcy and liquidation were introduced in chapter 5 and we need only now consider the differing definitions used by insurers to implement the intention explained in chapter 6.

Trade Indemnity's definition must be suitable for a wide range of buyers from sole traders to large corporations:

2. There is INSOLVENCY when there has been taken by a Court or by an INSURED BUYER any of the steps set out below or some step which (under the law of the Court having jurisdiction) is equivalent to any of the steps set out below under English law:

    (a) a bankruptcy order has been made against the INSURED BUYER;
    (b) a composition or a scheme of arrangement by the INSURED BUYER has been approved by the Court;
    (c) a valid assignment composition or other arrangement has been made by the INSURED BUYER for the benefit of his creditors generally;
    (d) an order has been made by the Court against the INSURED BUYER for a winding up or administration under the Insolvency Act 1986;
    (e) an effective resolution has been passed for the voluntary winding–up of the INSURED BUYER;
    (f) a compromise or arrangement has been made binding on the INSURED BUYER and all the INSURED BUYER's creditors; or
    (g) An Administrative Receiver under the Insolvency Act 1986 or a Receiver on behalf of debenture holders or other creditors of the INSURED BUYER has been appointed.

Credit and Guarantee's definition is shorter only because it need only apply to the large single risk:

    There is INSOLVENCY when:
    (a) an order has been made against the Customer for a Winding-up by the Court; or

(b) an effective resolution has been passed for a Creditors' winding-up of the Customer; or

(c) a Receiver for Debenture-Holders of the Customer has been appointed.

The amount of liability

The amount of any claim settlement is determined by the following:

1. The amount admitted to rank against the insolvent estate.
2. The amount of the credit limit (either approved by the insurer or under a discretionary facility).
3. The amount of any first loss to be deducted and borne by the policyholder.
4. The indemnity in the policy.

Trade Indemnity's definition of the insured loss is:

so much of the INSURED DEBT as shall be admitted to rank against the insolvent estate of the INSURED BUYER (or in the case of PROTRACTED FAULT shall not be in dispute) taking into account the whole of any SALVAGE relating thereto.

'Salvage' means:

moneys (including dividends paid or payable out of the insolvent estate) securities indemnities guarantees rights of action counter claims or set-off or other advantages held by the INSURED or otherwise available for the purpose of reducing the amount of any indebtedness of an INSURED BUYER which has not been paid at the date of INSOLVENCY or the date for notification under Condition 3 whichever is the earlier.

Condition 3 will be discussed later.

Credit and Guarantee defines the basis of liability as:

the indebtedness owing by the Customer to the Insured in respect of the invoice value of goods or services sold . . . to the Customer.

provided the indebtedness:

(b). . . shall before deduction of Salvage be within the Permitted Limit for Post-Delivery Risk . . .

(c). . . shall be admitted to rank against the insolvent estate of the Customer in favour of the Insured.

Protracted default

This is not a common cause of claims in domestic trade because the formal insolvency procedure outlined in chapter 5 normally leads either to a settlement or to insolvency. The buyer either pays or goes under. The insurer's difficulty is that on open account terms the original due date passes and, although the seller steps up his action, each step has the effect of condoning default and putting off the evil day. It is only when the seller decides 'thus far and no further' that he can point to a final due date and claim protracted default at the end of the waiting period.

Date for payment of claims

Insolvency claims are normally paid within 30 days of submission of proof of debt and of compliance with any special conditions of cover.[‡] Claims for protracted default are examined on expiry of the waiting period during which the policyholder is expected to continue his efforts to collect and make sure that any lines of recovery are in order. Complaints, disputes and counter-claims are often not raised until the seller has put the buyer on final notice and the waiting period gives time for them to be disposed of.

The primary responsibility for avoiding and minimising loss rests with the policyholder because only he can take action under his contracts, but he is only expected to act as he would do if he were not sharing the risk with an insurer. Most claims are in some way imperfect but it is fair to say that, on the whole, insurers show sound commercial sense and considerable patience.

Potential losses

Understandably, they expect prompt notice of anything which might lead to a claim. Credit and Guarantee requires immediate notice of:

(a) the Insured having reason to suspect or having knowledge that the Customer is unlikely to make any payment or payments due under the Contract;
(b) the Insured being aware that the Customer is in financial difficulties;
(c) the Customer failing to pay to the Insured within the 'Payment Delay Period' as specified in the Schedule any amount which is due under the terms of the Contract.

Because of the special nature of specific risk insurance, Credit and Guarantee reserves the right to specify loss-prevention measures and to call on the insured to take, at his own expense, action to determine the buyer's legal liability to pay. He must also facilitate direct intervention by the insurer in the proceedings or negotiations with the customer.

---

‡ Insurances of Credit makes a payment on account as soon as it receives admission of the debt in principle from the liquidator. The payment is adjusted when IOC finally settles the amount admitted to rank.

Trade Indemnity's condition 3 likewise requires the policyholder to consult with the company as soon as the buyer fails to pay on the due date (or postponed due date) or he becomes aware that the buyer is in financial difficulties. Both insurers make clear their intention to intervene directly if necessary and this is especially important if they are covering a number of creditors.

Insurances of Credit operates a mandatory collection service which intervenes in all cases and the insured is obliged to report all overdues. The company claims that its collection and recovery rate is high and that this materially contributes to lower premium rates.

The Trade Indemnity policyholder may be able to avert or reduce a claim by employing TI's collection service as his agent in connection with an insured debt. The service is optional and self-financing.

9

Export credit insurance in the United Kingdom

vwvwvwvwvwvwvwvw

THE SCOPE OF EXPORT CREDIT INSURANCE

The distinguishing feature of 'true' export credit insurance is the interweaving of cover for the buyer risks discussed in chapter 3 and the political risks explored in chapter 4. While it is convenient to describe them separately in policy documents, the distinction is somewhat artificial because no buyer can be isolated from the economy in which he trades and no economy is immune from the depredations of politicians and bureaucrats. The commercial significance of the transfer risk, for instance, was explained in chapter 4.

The modes of underwriting

Domestic credit insurance is concerned almost wholly with revolving 'trade' credit on nominal terms rarely exceeding 60 days and with an horizon of risk usually not longer than 90 or 120 days. The export market must cater for nominal 'trade' terms of up to 180 days and for 'investment' credit of up to five years (and occasionally seven) for the buyer who finances investment in plant and machinery by buying on deferred terms. We discuss this extended-terms cover for 'investment' credit in a later section.

Short-term credit clearly lends itself to the 'spread' mode of underwriting described in chapter 8 and the two leading insurers, ECGD and Trade Indemnity, concentrate on this form of cover. Medium term credit for investment-type goods is better suited to specific underwriting, although ECGD has adapted the 'spread' mode with its Comprehensive Extended Terms Guarantee.

The special problems

Of the many differences between domestic and export credit, some are of special concern to the insurer:

1. Remoteness of the buyer.
2. Reliability of overseas credit information.
3. Longer 'trade' credit.
4. Transit time.
5. Political factors.
6. Documentation in export credit control.
7. Public sector business.

The relationship between risk management and the financing of export credit may also concern the insurer and is discussed in chapter 10.

Special country conditions Although the buyer's failure to obtain any necessary authority or consent is automatically excluded from all policies, there can still be regulations or practices which restrict his freedom to import goods or pay for them, or which are known to be conductive to delays in payment. Clearly the cover must be limited and to avoid uncertainty insurers often impose conditions which do no more than restate the regulation or define the practice. If, for instance, a certain type of licence conveys only limited foreign exchange authority, no one will expect full transfer cover.

To control expenditure by public buyers, governments often impose a system of permits or even issue official guarantees of payment, and the permit or guarantee must be a condition precedent to any liability.

Underwriting the exporter

Every insurance involves an element of risk on the policyholder and his ability to avoid or minimise loss. The export credit insurer relies heavily on the competence of the exporter in sales and credit management and ECGD certainly has many years' experience of 'underwriting the exporter'. It is disappointing that we still hear, from companies of all sizes, 'If ECGD will cover it, we'll take it' – a classical non-decision. How much more impressive to hear, 'We're satisfied with the risk – let's tell ECGD why they should share it with us.'

The company which seeks to delegate credit control to an insurer puts any underwriter on his guard. It is not the underwriter's role to make other people's commercial judgements for them but to share the risks as generously as he can with them after they have made their own judgements. How generously depends on how reliable those judgements are. Most insurers have some privileged information, especially on buyers and markets. How best to use that information often depends on the calibre of the exporter himself.

Underwriting the overseas buyer

There are special problems inherent in the underwriting of overseas buyers. Despite modern communications, they are usually more remote than the domestic buyer. Credit information is often sparse and unreliable and it is not possible to establish the close understanding with many buyers which thrives in home trade (ECGD has to insist on non-disclosure and only meets a buyer in exceptional circumstances). Knowledge of the local business scene is clearly essential and the buyer can only be assessed in the context of the surrounding economy. In parallel, an underwriter needs an understanding of local commercial practice to help him interpret credit information. There are more grey areas and more buyers who, on available information, are marginal risks.

Third-party guarantees (which we explained in chapter 6) are more common in the export scene but also present special difficulties. Very few insurers will specify the precise wording of a guarantee which they know will have to be enforced in a foreign court, and the onus of obtaining an effective guarantee must rest with the exporter. The guarantee must be irrevocable, enforceable in the appropriate courts and unconditional: that is, payable on first demand and without reference to the underlying contract so that the guarantor cannot delay payment by protracted litigation. The validity of a guarantee can usually only be proved by a favourable judgement and we find in all of ECGD's policies, for example, a standard provision that where a guarantee has been obtained:

loss shall not be ascertained, unless the Insurer otherwise agrees in writing, until . . . the INSURED has obtained a judgement against the independent guarantor or surety in a court in the country specified . . . or satisfied the Insurer that the claim against the independent guarantor or surety is a valid one.

In addition to satisfying the insurer that the condition of his cover has been complied with, the judgement opens up a specific line of recovery once he has settled the claim.

A separate instrument in the form of a prior written guarantee is obviously to be preferred for revolving business but the endorsement of accepted bills of exchange is usually an acceptable alternative. A possible weakness is that the guarantee and, therefore, the insurance cover, are not effective until the bills have been endorsed, which is normally some time after the goods have been despatched. There are many complications surrounding guarantees of payment and when an underwriter has felt obliged to call for one as a condition of cover, great care must be taken to comply with his stipulations.

The overseas distributor

For many distributors, credit from overseas suppliers is a prime source of working capital. The first danger is that the distributor will be left with unsold stock and insufficient cash to pay for it; the second is that, having sold it, he will not collect his debts promptly. Underwriting the distributor calls for a realistic appraisal of his business prospects and credit collection performance and supplier credit should be limited to his unavoidable needs. Many exporters could help distributors to raise maximum local finance (and local credit insurance) to reduce their own credit burden, especially in the extended credit field.

Insuring the transfer risk

In a sense, cover for the transfer risk is not credit insurance but bridging finance because, although he writes an insurance policy and charges a conventional premium, the insurer is, in reality, acting as long-term banker to the policyholder but without collecting interest from him.

Refinancing of foreign debt

As a government department, ECGD can only finance any cash deficit by borrowing (at interest) from the Consolidated Fund. In the last five years or so it has reduced this borrowing by refinancing some rescheduled debt through UK banks and giving the banks a fallback guarantee against political loss. Its insurance liability is unchanged but its cash position is immediately improved.

One of the handicaps facing the private market is the difficulty of rescheduling and refinancing sovereign debt.

The 'spread' in export underwriting

Given that transfer delay is the export insurer's worst risk, his attitude to 'spread' is usually dictated more by country considerations than by the quality of the buyer risk alone. A ratio of 2/1 in volume in favour of the stronger markets is commonly regarded as a standard risk – a good starting point for other considerations. A better ratio may give scope for better terms, while anything worse implies an increased risk of transfer or political claims. It goes without saying that there *are* other considerations. A proposal for the best markets only may have so many doubtful buyers or such bad loss experience that it is still a marginal proposition.

THE EXPORT CREDITS GUARANTEE DEPARTMENT

ECGD (the 'Department') has been the dominant force in export credit insurance in the United Kingdom for over 60 years.* It has been settled policy all that time that the national credit institution should be a self-accounting department of government.† While the private insurance market has demonstrated its ability to deal with large credit risks, it does not yet appear ready to carry the huge burden of transfer losses and rescheduling. Indeed, it has on occasion looked unsuccessfully to ECGD for reinsurance of political risks.

The Export Guarantees and Overseas Investment Act 1978 authorises the Secretary of State to give guarantees to, or for the benefit of, persons carrying on trade in the United Kingdom 'for the purpose of encouraging trade with other countries'. The consent of the Treasury must be obtained either by specific mandate or under the wide delegated authority which the Department already holds.

Section 1 of the Act authorises guarantees given 'in consultation with the Export Guarantees Advisory Council'. The Council represents exporting, banking and insurance interests and advises senior staff on matters of departmental policy and country underwriting limits. Certain members give final approval for very large individual risks. There is reason to believe that the role of the Council may change in line with modern corporate practice to that of the 'supervisory board', leaving all operating discretion with the 'executive board' of civil servants and the Treasury as their 'parent company'.

Under Section 2 of the Act guarantees may be given 'in the national interest' which in practice is decided in consultation with the appropriate government departments.

The present challenge to ECGD

ECGD is wrestling with a classic marketing dilemma in that 20% of its 'clients' account for 80% of its business yet its 'product' has been deliberately developed to work the other way round as if the majority of the policyholders provided the bulk of the income. At the same time, its traditional market has contracted. Its share of United Kingdom non-oil exports fell from 38.2% in 1976–7 to 23.3% in 1986 and it seems that years of concentration on 'whole turnover' have failed to attract those

---

* For the full story, we recommend the official *History of ECGD 1919–1979* available from the Department's regional offices.

† See the latest official *Report of the Committee to Consider the Functions and Status of the Export Credits Guarantee Department (ECGD)*, March 1984 (HMSO).

large exporters who can confidently carry much of their risk uninsured but would join in an excess-of-loss cover which protected them against the worst effects of a sudden accumulation of losses. The search today is for 'equitability' in the sharing of risks and losses. How far down the scale this equitability can extend remains to be seen because there must be competent and conscientious exporters for whom a near-whole turnover cover is still the only practical solution. For others a compromise could provide the protection they need without leaving ECGD with the rump of the risk. If they feel they have been rebuffed in the past, there is every reason for them to try again in today's climate, and the specialist brokers have a part to play in achieving this equitable agreement.

THE ECGD COMPREHENSIVE SHORT TERM GUARANTEE

This policy is the basic vehicle of ECGD cover and illustrates most of the generalities of the Department's credit insurance facilities. We can give only a brief appraisal of some of the salient points and for a fuller understanding we refer the reader to the formal documents, specimens of which may be obtained from the Department's regional offices. The 'core' policy is a *credit only* policy based on the twin concepts of *despatch* and *amount owing*.

'Despatch'

Cover for the credit risks begins on 'despatch' which, for practical purposes, is the point at which the exporter parts with possession of the goods for the purpose of transmitting them to the overseas buyer. Varying forms of transport and terms of delivery are thus catered for and 'despatch' merely recognises the point at which the goods are beyond any reasonable means of retrieval. 'Parts with possession' must not, however, be confused with passing of title under the terms of any particular contract.

'Amount owing'

This phrase defines the amount of ECGD's liability for credit losses and it follows that it is for the exporter to prove the amount he claims by reference to the contract and shipping documents, invoices and correspondence. It follows, too, that any dispute as to the amount owing must have been resolved.

These two concepts provide adequately for the great majority of export contracts for the sale of goods but occasionally it is agreed that no amount is owing until long after despatch – on delivery overseas or on completion of installation, for instance. The problem is more likely to arise, however, in the specific underwriting field for project–type contracts where the cover can be modified to suit the circumstances.

The contracts covered

The standard policy covers all contracts which relate to the export from the United Kingdom of:

(a) goods wholly or partly manufactured or produced in the United Kingdom; *or*
(b) imported goods (goods which have been cleared inwards through UK customs);

and which do not allow for more than 180 days' credit.

The expression 'wholly or partly produced or manufactured in the United Kingdom' has a simple intention. Very few goods exported from the UK are *wholly* of UK origin because imported materials contribute to almost all industrial production. ECGD is only concerned with the commercial character of the goods when they come to be exported and not with the origin of component parts and materials which lose their identity.

Cover for imported goods is an optional extra, and typical examples are foreign goods which an exporter holds in stock in this country or items which he brings in for calibration or adjustment.

Optional sections

Certain types of contract fall within the broad definition given above because they 'relate to the export from the United Kingdom', but by long tradition all contracts in certain categories can be excluded:

1. Contracts with United Kingdom buyers for export.
2. Contracts with overseas buyers which are confirmed for payment by a UK confirming house.
3. Contracts with overseas associate and subsidiary companies of the exporter (excluded by negotiation).
4. Sales from overseas stocks held by the exporter.

Contracts on cash before shipment terms or cash from confirmed irrevocable letter of credit are excluded from the credit risk sections of the policy.

Premium

There are normally two elements of premium:

1. An annual premium (or initial premium for a new policy) as a contribution to the cost of administering the policy and specifically for the provision of the credit limit service.
2. A risk premium calculated on the value of goods despatched each month.

For some years there has been a flat rate of premium for each exporter for all countries and all terms of payment up to 180 days. Rates have hitherto been selected from a schedule consisting of a 'standard' rate with loadings or discounts applied to it. The new underwriting regime allows the Department to quote a competitive price for whatever package of risks and cover has been agreed and to respond to market conditions. It may be that the flat-rate system will be discarded in favour of a return to 'graded' rates.

The causes of loss

We do not attempt to quote the lengthy policy definitions in full but we have retained key words and phrases to give a fair representation of what we understand to be ECGD's intention.

Insolvency: the definition includes the common events such as the legal declarations of insolvency or bankruptcy, a *court* order for administration, failure to recover a judgement debt because of insufficient assets, and a composition arrangement binding on all creditors. ECGD will consider *de facto* proof of insolvency if the exporter can demonstrate that the buyer's assets are insufficient to justify legal proceedings. It recognises that overseas legal systems may not correspond exactly to the above definitions based on English practice but, provided substantially the same conditions exist, it can accept other situations as amounting to insolvency.

Default: the wording defines this risk very clearly as, 'The failure of the buyer to pay to the INSURED within six months after the Due Date of Payment the amount owing in connection with goods delivered to and accepted by the buyer'.
    The goods must have been delivered and accepted in accordance with the contract and any dispute must have been resolved. The due date of payment includes any agreed extension and the cause of loss does not occur until the six months has elapsed. The wise exporter will, of course, be in consultation with ECGD well before that.

Repudiation after shipment: a buyer who fails to take up goods or documents properly presented to him is in breach of contract rather than in financial default, so ECGD must first be satisfied that there is no merit in enforcing the contract in the courts or suing for damages. The exporter must then sell the goods and establish a net loss. He bears a first loss equal to 20% of the contract price of the goods and ECGD pays 90% of the balance one month after the resale.

General moratorium: as defined in chapter 4.

Political intervention: the intention is to cover acts of foreign governments which effectively prevent performance of the contract. Mere delay is not of itself sufficient because the *force-majeure* provisions discussed in chapter 4 should permit of some delay without penalising the exporter or terminating the contract prematurely. The government action must be the proximate cause of loss and not just a contributory factor.

The post-shipment risk of loss from an import embargo is usually short-lived and such measures frequently exempt goods already in transit. The pre-delivery risk on specially made goods is obviously the more serious.

'Blacklists' are an embarrassing problem because if the British government does not regard the blacklist as lawful (and it may not be alone in this) ECGD cannot be expected to treat it as a cause of loss. The Arab boycott of Israel, and United States' legislation affecting UK subsidiaries are recent examples of this dilemma.

An important exclusion is the refusal of an overseas government to renew an import licence on expiry. If an adequate licence is not available when the contract becomes firm, it is debatable whether the contract is capable of performance. A decision not to renew is an administrative routine and not in any way abnormal. If the period is exceptionally long, a letter of intent from the competent authority might give grounds for special consideration. Similarly, the introduction of an import tariff or the raising of the level of tariff would not be a *prima facie* cause of loss unless it were of such magnitude as to make it impossible – not just expensive – for the buyer to take up the goods. The question is always whether the action is intended to frustrate existing obligations or simply to discourage fresh ones.

The last two risks raise the question, 'When is a government not a government?', because ECGD can only follow Whitehall's lead on recognition of a *de facto* administration.

Transfer: ECGD's wording does not require any specific action by the buyer's government:

Political events, or economic difficulties, arising outside the United Kingdom or legislative or administrative measures taken outside the United Kingdom, being events, difficulties or measures which prevent or delay the transfer of payments or deposits made. . .

Both buyer and exporter must have taken all steps, such as those listed in chapter 4, to effect transfer. The mechanics of transfer situations differ widely and the first exporters to experience delay have the difficult task of searching the regulations to ensure that they have complied as far as possible.

If, as explained in chapter 4, exchange is available to the buyer but only at an enhanced price, any delay in payment is default on his part and not a transfer loss. It is natural to ask how far this argument can be pursued if the rate threatens the buyer with bankruptcy. We can only comment that in massive devaluations, as in Brazil, buyers have paid many times the original local currency price and still survived.

Valid discharge: as defined in chapter 4.

War, civil war and natural disasters: ECGD covers war, civil war and riot occurring outside the United Kingdom which prevent performance of the contract. When a buyer is already hard pressed, it can be difficult to prove that the hostilities or disturbances are the genuine proximate cause of his failure to take up or pay for goods. The cover for the natural disasters of cyclone, flood, earthquake, volcanic eruption and tidal wave only applies where the event is the proximate cause of a credit loss and is not normally covered by commercial insurers.

UK export licence: as defined in chapter 4 but always excluding the exporter's failure or inability to obtain any licence which was required at the date of contract.

Public buyer: the nature of this risk has been outlined in chapter 4 but ECGD's definition of a 'public buyer' is relevant:

(i) a national, regional, provincial or local government authority or
(ii) such undertaking carried on or created by any such authority as the Insurer may in his absolute discretion declare to be a Public Buyer.

Our previous comment on recognition of a *de facto* administration is relevant to (i), and with regard to (ii), it must be noted that ECGD reserves 'absolute discretion' to agree public buyer status. Even then, it must still agree in writing to give the special cover for 'the failure or refusal on the part of the buyer to fulfil any of the terms of the contract'.

ECGD's intention is to respond to a failure on the part of an acknowledged public buyer which is of such a nature as to bring the contract to an end. This might be a matter of fact, the withholding of an essential facility or resource, for example, or a matter of degree such as an inordinate delay. It includes, of course, cancellation of the contract when the exporter is not in default. Public sector contracts should always provide for independent arbitration of disputes so that the buyer's failure to honour an award can form the basis of a claim.

Because the risk of repudiation is so widely recognised, a contract with a public sector buyer may be backed by a guarantee of payment and indemnity for breach of contract. ECGD makes the further proviso that any guarantee must be given by a national government authority. In other words, central government must be directly liable for non-performance.

The discretionary limit

We have discussed the principle of the 'discretionary' or 'non-vetting' limit in chapter 8. ECGD's standard policy provides for a small free limit similar to the 'quickstart' suggested in chapter 5. Thereafter, and up to the agreed limit, the credit given must be shown to be:

(i) recommended in writing, not more than six months before . . . (the date of contract or shipment as appropriate) . . . by a bank or credit information agency operating in the buyer's country or in the United Kingdom; or

(ii) justified by information in writing about the buyer and his financial condition obtained from such a source not earlier than the said six months.

For existing buyers there is a simple uplift provision based on satisfactory experience over the preceding two years. A credit limit written by the Department can be uplifted by 25% in the same way.

Although the discretionary limit in export policies was originally only intended to reduce the cost of the credit limit service, it has become an important element in underwriting the exporter. ECGD (and Trade Indemnity) with extensive information and servicing facilities can cope with the large volume of inquiries resulting from lower discretionary limits, whereas other insurers insist on higher limits as part of the risk-sharing strategy. For the smaller policy – which does not necessarily mean a small company – the question is whether to encourage the exporter to take his chance at whatever level of discretion he chooses, or to fix a lower limit but ensure a quick response to credit limit applications. ECGD appears to be moving towards negative vetting of smaller limits so that its underwriting resources can be concentrated on the larger exposures.

Extensions of due dates

The principles outlined in chapter 6 are complicated in the case of export receivables by time, distance and payment procedures and the need for a greater degree of formality, especially if bills of exchange have been accepted. The policy normally allows for a due date to be extended for a total of 90 days without reference except in any form of 'cash against documents' terms. The right to extend may be withdrawn in respect of an individual buyer or a country.

Withdrawal of cover

ECGD prefers to speak only of suspending cover in the expectation of restoring it when the situation improves. The suspension may apply to a named buyer, to a country or to non-United Kingdom goods. Suspension of cover on a buyer clearly implies adverse experience or information and future despatches are not covered. The position is more complicated if the exporter covers the pre-credit risk because, unless the buyer is already insolvent, no cause of loss has occurred. The policy provides for the exporter to ask for ECGD's agreement to shipment of the goods. If the Department declines, a claim is examined under the pre-credit cover as if the buyer had become insolvent six months after the date of the refusal.

If cover for a country is suspended because of a foreign exchange crisis, we would expect existing contracts to proceed normally, but in the event of war, civil war or serious political problems, we would expect pre-credit claims to lie.

Losses excluded

To avoid misunderstanding, certain non-negotiable causes of loss are specifically excluded:

1. The failure of the exporter or anyone acting on his behalf to fulfil the terms of the insured contract or to comply with any relevant law.
2. Any failure to obtain any import licence or other authorisation necessary for the due performance of the contract.
3. Any breach of any relevant foreign exchange authority.

Release of documents overseas

One exclusion is important enough to be spelt out separately, namely the release of documents to the buyer, except with ECGD's prior agreement against a local currency deposit in any form of 'cash against documents' transaction. In a volatile currency market, the buyer may ask for the documents (and therefore the goods) to be released to him while he finds, or awaits, a more favourable exchange rate. Not only is this a change of terms from cash to credit, but it also denies ECGD the opportunity of specifying terms such as a shortfall undertaking from the buyer.

Goods shipped to a third country

There is no objection to goods being shipped to a country other than the buyer's country provided direct shipments are not excluded for any reason. The UK export licence risk is covered but any other event which prevents the goods being exported to, or imported into, the third country is excluded. Furthermore, the buyer's obligation to pay must not depend on the goods being imported. In other words, the buyer must bear the third-country risks.

Barter and counter-purchase

Barter contracts for the exchange of goods are not covered because they cannot specify 'the terms of payment, and . . . the currency in which payment is to be made'. Contracts involving counter-purchase can be covered provided the sale of goods is separated contractually from the counter-purchase obligation.

The policy excludes any contract:

in relation to which the relevant authorisation to import goods and to pay for them is made subject to conditions as to the export of other goods from any country or subject to conditions as to the payment for such other goods when so exported.

Sales in overseas currencies

Although the policy is issued in sterling terms as to premium and settlement of claims, contracts in other convertible currencies can be covered. Conversion is calculated at the closing London TT buying rate for the currency at the date on which ECGD's liability commences.

Foreign currency recoveries

Whatever the currency of the original contract, any recovery in a foreign currency must be converted into sterling immediately it is received and handed to ECGD for allocation and division between the Department and the exporter. In accordance with the doctrine of subrogation explained in chapter 6, ECGD always retains its full portion, even if this results in it recovering more than it paid under the claim.

'Closing-out' losses on forward foreign exchange contracts

The exporter who sells foreign currency receivables in the forward market will have to buy currency at the 'spot' rate if he does not receive it from the buyer at the right time. The amount of any 'closing-out' cost can be added to the loss under the policy up to 15% of that loss. This extra *amount* of cover is free under the short-term policy. Under the extended terms policy, the exporter decides the amount of extra cover he wishes to take and for which he pays additional premium.

Cover for the pre-shipment risk

The PreCredit Risk Section is an optional extra for which an additional flat-rate premium is charged for the standard maximum pre-delivery period of twelve months. The cover begins at the effective date of contract and ceases when the Credit Risk Cover takes over on 'despatch'. Exceptionally, where the terms of payment provide for an irrevocable letter of credit confirmed in the United Kingdom, pre-credit cover continues until presentation of the documents.

The amount of loss is defined as:

(a) The actual costs, overhead charges and all other costs and expenses incurred by the INSURED in relation to the design, manufacture and supply of . . . (unshipped) . . . goods including the amount of any insurance, freight or other charges which have become payable by the INSURED on the buyer's behalf in relation to those goods; and

(b) all other sums paid or which have become payable by the INSURED in respect of obligations undertaken for the purposes of the contract to the extent to which such sums relate to those goods.

This is a generous definition which could be read to include, for example, increased costs on a fixed price contract, specific research and development costs, tendering costs or the cost of giving bonds or 'unwinding' a forward exchange purchase. There are two important limitations:

1. The exporter may not recover in a pre-credit loss more than he would have claimed if he had completed the contract. If his costs have already exceeded his selling price, he must bear the overrun himself.

2. In order to relate the costs and commitments to the intended rate of deliveries to the buyer, ECGD places a limit on the *contract price* of undelivered goods. The normal figure is four times the credit limit on the buyer. If the exporter exceeds this figure, ECGD's liability is reduced in proportion to the excess.

The merits of pre-credit cover

There are two distinct elements to ECGD's pre-shipment cover:

1. The indemnity for loss arising between date of contract and date of despatch.

2.   The commitment to cover the credit risk after despatch.

If ECGD withdraws cover on the buyer, the appeal procedure is still available. If cover on the country is withdrawn because of a 'capacity' problem, the commitment on existing contracts is unchanged. We would only expect ECGD to withdraw credit cover and invite a Pre-Credit Section claim if there was a certainty of irrecoverable loss.

Cover for foreign goods

Many credit insurers have suffered heavy losses on 'external trade', that is, the supply of goods from third countries. The reason for foreign supply is often low price which in turn attracts marginal buyers. As a government department charged with the encouragement of inter-national trade, ECGD must be primarily concerned with the export of United Kingdom goods and its support for foreign goods has accord-ingly been restrained. Private insurers, on the other hand, can view the risk strictly on its commercial merits.

In replacing its Comprehensive External Trade Guarantee in 1987, ECGD withdrew all cover for the confirming of contracts for foreign goods but introduced the Goods Originating Overseas Endorsement which affords substantially the same cover to foreign and United Kingdom goods, thus making it easier for companies which 'multi-source' goods to cover them under one policy. The main features of the cover are as follows:

1.   The foreign goods must still be 'admissible'.
2.   Provided there is an element of goods exported from the United Kingdom, any proportion of goods originating in the buyer's country can be included in a composite contract.
3.   There is no cover for any loss arising from failure or breach of contract on the part of a foreign supplier or any cause within his control.
4.   The exporter must have obtained any necessary authority to pay for the foreign goods in the currency required and comply with any UK law governing disposal of the foreign goods.
5.   Normal pre-credit cover is given.
6.   Credit cover commences when a foreign supplier despatches goods or a local supplier delivers them to the buyer.

Cover for exports of services

The problems of credit insurance for services are the problems of the contracts themselves, such as, proof of performance, absence of standardised documentation, terms of payment and the avoidance of disputes. In the export field, a government short of foreign exchange usually gives lower priority to intangibles than to goods and the buyer of services is often at the end of the transfer queue.

Nevertheless, ECGD has a long record of cover for such 'visible' services as constructional works and engineering contracts arising from large overseas projects. Smaller scale covers have been written for services ranging from interior design and management consultancy to aircraft overhauls and film processing. The Comprehensive Services Guarantee, modelled on its sale of goods counterpart, gives cover from the date of invoice for services performed. In the pre-credit period, irrecoverable expenses incurred in preparing the services can be insured. Any service for an overseas principal performed by persons normally resident in the United Kingdom can be considered for cover as United Kingdom exports. Actual performance may take place in this country (as for designing or computer programming) or overseas (as for on-site supervision or aerial survey work).

Trade Indemnity and other private insurers cover services and, in one respect, are less inhibited than ECGD which, as an official insurer, must be assured of some net benefit to the economy. To the private insurer, the origin of the services and ultimate economic gain are not immediate underwriting considerations.

Invisible exports

The financial and trading community of the City of London which has hitherto been regarded as self-insuring or uninsurable must eventually look for external protection against losses outside its control and the insurance mechanism has not yet been fully tested. The exposures, quality of risk and risk periods are often well within the capacity of the market and 'underwriting the exporter' would take on a fascinating new meaning.

Cover for bond risks

In chapter 4 we outlined the risks the exporter runs when his bank gives its unconditional payment guarantee – an 'on demand' bond. Most government insurers, including ECGD, give cover for the following:

1. A 'call' when the exporter is not in breach of contract.
2. A 'call' when the exporter is in breach as the direct result of an insured political cause of loss.
3. The failure of the buyer to honour an arbitration award following the calling of a bond.

While the calling of a bond does not, of itself, terminate a contract, it may signify an intention to do so and an insurer must obviously be consulted on any continuation of work. If an advance payment bond is called it may be desirable to continue work so as to avoid the calling of a performance bond and other losses arising from termination. ECGD takes the position that if the contract is either terminated or completed within six months of the 'call', it reserves the right of recourse to the exporter so that he only recoups his justifiable costs and expenses out of the payment the Department has made. If the contract is not terminated on a 'call', basic cover can only be continued by special arrangement.

There are those who believe that normal pre-credit cover is sufficient protection against loss from the calling of an advance payment bond. Provided a claim can be sustained for the failure of the public buyer to fulfil the terms of the contract, the basic pre-credit cover will suffice, but the contract must be drawn in such a way that an 'unfair' call is a breach of contract, and 'unfair' is notoriously difficult to define.

A further danger is that the buyer will demand that a bond be extended under threat of immediate calling – the 'extend or call' risk. While most insurers would want to cover reasonable extensions related to completion of the contract, they can neither afford to underwrite an open-ended risk nor to precipitate an avoidable call.

The bond risk endorsement to ECGD's Comprehensive Short-Term Guarantee applies automatically to any qualifying contract and the exporter need only make a simple declaration to effect the cover. The premium rate for the Pre-Credit Risk Section is marginally increased but the higher rate is paid on all contracts whether they involve bonds or not. As we shall explain later, the exporter who only occasionally needs cover may be better served in the private market.

Under the Comprehensive Extended Terms Guarantee, a separate application is made for each qualifying contract and a composite premium rate is quoted for the contract to include both basic and bond-risk cover. The exporter may select the contracts and bonds for which he wishes to take bond risk cover.

'EXTENDED TERMS' COVER

Historically, investment in capital and semi-capital goods was financed by the buyer, often through loans from London banks. Major projects, particularly in the public sector, were often financed in part by bonds issued on the London market. The supplier's contract of sale was on 'cash' terms. With the contraction of the London capital market after the Second World War, buyers looked for deferred payment terms from suppliers. A single contract providing both supply and finance is clearly attractive to the buyer and there are powerful arguments in favour of supplier credit compared with all other sources of funding for capital investment.

Most forms of bank finance require some form of security and if he elects to raise fresh share capital, he must satisfy investors (and have the good fortune to go to the market at the right moment). Government aid and other official sources may involve bureaucratic procedures and unwelcome government intervention. Furthermore, it is common knowledge that he can expect to be offered a fixed and favourable rate of interest by a seller who probably needs the business sufficiently to make concessions. All of which point to the inherent weakness of the seller's negotiating position and the problems of underwriting extended credit.

The political risk in extended credit

The customer in an advanced economy can usually best raise finance at home and is not likely to need supplier credit. The demand for deferred payment terms comes from less developed countries with all the political risks we have already discussed. They are much more difficult to assess years in advance than at short range. By the time the balance of payments forecasts are overturned and the economic indicators have gone awry, the risk is already engaged and there is little the insurer can do to control it.

The buyer risk in extended credit

The risk on the buyer in short-term trade credit is centred on his current position and immediate future prospects. When we give extended credit for plant and machinery, our concern is whether the buyer will consistently generate enough cash to meet all his current liabilities, including each instalment of principal and interest of the debt to us. We have seen that supplier credit is his substitute for fresh capital or long-term borrowing and it must be tainted with the equity risk. If the business fails, the long-term lenders will exercise their security and this may well include a charge on the plant bought with our credit. The equity shareholders stand to lose their capital, we stand to lose our debt.

Terms of payment for extended credit

Sound terms of payment are an important factor in underwriting the extended credit risk with a reasonable down payment before the buyer receives the goods and regular equal instalments of principal and reducing interest thereafter. The credit period should start when the supplier has substantially performed the contract or each identifiable part of it. In a supply of single units it is reasonable for credit to run from delivery of each unit. In the case of a composite plant it should start on delivery of the last significant item. In a project-type contract involving both supply and services, it is normal for credit to run from completion of installation or commissioning.

The length of credit

The 'revenue return' period on an every-day plant purchase is an infinitely arguable figure and no practical criterion. As we explain in chapter 11, voluntary international agreements help to discourage excessive credit, but it is generally accepted that five years should be the maximum for supplier credit, and that this period can be conceded for an individual contract value of £125,000. There are cases in which the proper length of credit should be related to the original need for credit: contractors' plant, for instance, is usually acquired for a particular contract for which the contractor will receive payment in full more or less by completion of his work. His cash flow ought, therefore, to allow him to pay for the plant during the course of his contract.

Negotiable instruments for extended credit

Instalments of extended credit should normally be evidenced by bills of exchange or promissory notes which confirm formally and without qualification the buyer's obligation to pay on the due dates. They are a vital line of recovery for the insurer – even in transfer and political losses – and the exporter will almost certainly need them to raise finance.

Guarantees and securities

Because it is so important for the supplier and his insurer to distance themselves from the equity risk, third-party guarantees (as discussed in chapter 6) are even more relevant to extended credit than to short-term 'trade' credit. The endorsement of accepted bills by the buyer's bank is an efficient form of guarantee.

A new company seeking to finance the purchase of plant largely by supplier credit is a particularly difficult risk because it may encounter unexpected problems and be unable to meet its many initial obligations from its limited cash resources. The risk can sometimes be improved by a guarantee of payment and indemnity for non-performance or by restrictive covenants. The credit insurer cannot be expected to judge whether the buyer is capable of performing the contract, only his ability to survive the financial risks involved in attempting it. The under-writer has to decide – usually with less information than the investor or long-term lender sees – whether the credit-cum-equity risk is reasonable.

Collateral security for extended credit

It is often suggested that collateral security (a chattel mortgage or other charge on the goods) improves the risk. It is difficult to see how it makes it less likely that the buyer will become insolvent or fail to pay. In a time of crisis, losing a particular piece of machinery may be the last thing on his mind. He might even prefer giving it up to being made to pay for it.

What a charge *might* do is to improve the recovery prospects. If the goods can be sold readily for a good price, there is something to be said for reducing the loss in this way, and there have been examples of successful repossession and resale, but it is very dangerous to rely on future residual values of everyday plant and machinery.

The problems of legal registration and process, feasibility of removal, maintenance and tax implications all combine to daunt the exporter and even if he can persuade an insurer to give cover with a collateral security condition, he may still find that he has bought a pig in a poke.

TRADE INDEMNITY COMPANY

Trade Indemnity's insured export turnover for 1987–8 was predicted at £2 billion (about 18% of ECGD's £11 billion) and rising to £3 billion for 1988–9. Its typical export client has a turnover of at least £2 million, with about 60% spread in developed markets. Membership of the ICIA (explained in chapter 11) gives Trade Indemnity access to credit information and recovery facilities overseas and its debt collection service can extend to many countries. With its long experience of first loss and excess of loss covers, it can respond flexibly with a package of policies to suit the individual exporter.

The Trade Indemnity Export Credit Policy

The basic policy is a variant of the home trade policy covering insolvency and default only. Terms of payment up to two years can be covered but, given a satisfactory spread policy, terms up to five years can be written as specific risks. Political risk cover is added to the basic policy by way of a series of endorsements. Because its political cover is reinsured at Lloyd's, Trade Indemnity does not intend to compete with the 'pure' political risk market for specific risks.

The political risk endorsements can be summarised as follows:

1. Endorsement A: inconvertibility (transfer)
2. Endorsement B: contract frustration through war, civil war, rebellion, import or export embargo or government intervention.
3. Endorsement C: the public buyer risk.

Waiting periods for political losses vary but claims are normally paid within 60 days of the end of the waiting period. Default claims are paid within 90 days of the final due date and insolvency claims within 30 days of admission of debt. The normal indemnity is 85% but is negotiable. Discretionary limits, maximum payment terms and premium rates vary by country. Premiums and declarations may be quarterly, semi-annual or even annual by negotiation.

A simpler single-premium, all-vetting policy is available for the exporter with a turnover of less than £2 million.

Trade Indemnity aims at the individual service for exporters that it has developed for many years with home trade clients and is willing to consider all the 'optional credit risks' outlined under the ECGD Comprehensive Short Term Guarantee. In addition, its current experience with confirming house business is good and it will cover confirming in third-country goods.

AMERICAN INTERNATIONAL UNDERWRITERS (UK) LTD (AIU)

Over the past five years AIU has written a considerable spread of business on terms up to 360 days including manufactured goods, chemicals, pulp, paper and pharmaceuticals under its Comprehensive Export Credit Policy. This is an excess of loss policy with high deductibles and discretionary limits. AIU tries to avoid vetting more than a dozen or so buyers for any one policy but for other buyers it sets country limits within its overall maximum liability. The policy can also be written to cover a single buyer on terms up to five years.

The cause of loss for the credit and political risk except transfer is 'the failure of the Buyer to pay to the Insured all or part of the Gross Invoice Value' without specifying the underlying events. For the transfer risk it is 'the failure of the appropriate exchange authority of the Buyer's country to approve and effect transfer of Policy Currency'. The practical difference is in the waiting periods applied to 'non-payment' and 'transfer' in certain markets. The waiting periods for transfer are intended to be realistic in relation to known delays. The standard indemnity for all causes of loss is 90%.

The cover applies to goods sourced and delivered worldwide except for Kampuchea, Cuba, Laos, Libya, North Korea and North Vietnam. The credit and political risk only covers loss arising after a contractual debt has been established. Premium is paid on average outstanding receivables (on 'exposure') and the policy can be written for 'losses occurring' or 'risks attaching' during the policy year.

Pre-delivery cover relates to the inability to deliver, or take delivery, as a result of the following:

1. Insolvency of the buyer.
2. War (excluding the Five Great Powers) or disturbance in the buyer's country.
3. Import or export embargo.
4. Expropriation or nationalisation of the buyer's assets.

The waiting period for pre-delivery claims is 180 days and the goods must have been scheduled for delivery within the policy period. There appears to be only limited demand for pre-credit protection in the areas in which AIU has operated so far.

AIU has a reputation for flexibility but requires very high standards of credit control and compliance with policy conditions. It looks for a minimum premium of about £10,000 for 'spread' cover and £20,000 for specifics.

POLITICAL RISK INSURANCE

The private insurance market makes a valuable contribution in the form of 'pure' political risk insurance which admirably suits certain companies and certain types of business. Public sector contracts are a case in point but a supplier or contractor dealing with a large overseas corporation is often more concerned about risks outside the buyer's control than with his solvency or ability to perform. In practice, much of the business covered in the private market is with government and quasi-government principals and some of it is excluded from state schemes by reason of the origin of the goods or services or the buyer's country.

The basis of political risk underwriting

Political risk insurers have no privileged sources of information and place little reliance on analysis of the academic variety. The analyst can always suggest what *might* happen. The underwriter must decide on the *likelihood* of its happening and the likely extent of damage if it does happen. His first view is a subjective one of the competence and credibility of the exporter and the general appearance of the contract. He then pays special attention to the economic priority attached to the business by the buyer's government. Would the government itself suffer if the contract were frustrated? Or if it were completed and the government seen to be in default? Some projects in Angola and Lebanon will still go through despite the dangers.

Premium rates quoted by underwriters – and especially Lloyd's – should not be taken as 'barometers' and used to decide whether to insure the risk or carry it uninsured. The insurer has already spread his risk through reinsurance and the rate merely reflects his view *today*. Tomorrow may bring a complete change of sentiment and confidence. What is more, when the underwriter sees this practice emerging he knows that his client is intent on selecting against him and will adjust future quotes accordingly.

The risks covered

The 'core' risks covered in the market are as follows:

1. Import or export embargo. Unilateral cancellation of contract by a public buyer when he has no contractual right to do so and the insured is not in material default.
2. The buyer's unilateral termination of the contract as a result of war, civil war, insurrection or revolution, excluding war between the Five Great Powers and between the countries of the insured and the buyer.
3. Transfer delay resulting from the implementation of a law, order, decree or regulation restricting payments between the countries concerned. (This should be compared with ECGD's current wording.)
4. Non-ratification of contract by a public sector buyer. The exporter's problem is that if the conditions precedent mentioned in chapter 4 are not fulfilled, his credit insurance (which only covers firm contracts) never comes into effect. This Lloyd's cover indemnifies him for his irrecoverable costs necessarily incurred before the date of his withdrawal.
5. 'On demand' bond risks. The insured is indemnified against his net loss:
    (a) if a bond is called when the buyer has no contractual right to call it and the Insured is not in material default; or
    (b) if the buyer has failed to honour an arbitration award following the calling of a bond.

The market

Lloyd's still leads the 'pure' political risk insurance market; as we explained in chapter 7, its members are not permitted to cover the financial risks of insolvency and default. They can only be approached through accredited brokers and this is clearly the field of the specialist who can present the risk professionally and knows when, and how best, to approach the rest of the market.

AMERICAN INTERNATIONAL UNDERWRITERS

AIU looks for specific risks of up to three years, and exceptionally five, for any combination of the following:

1. Repudiation of contract by a public buyer or seller.
2. War, civil war and disturbance.
3. Non-payment by a public buyer.
4. Transfer.
5. Import or export embargo.
6. Government intervention.
7. Bond risks.
8. Diversion of voyage by reason of political events.
9. Confiscation or expropriation of mobile assets or stocks.

For sales to private buyers, repudiation of contract and non-payment are deleted and the bond risk is limited to the buyer's failure to honour an arbitration award.

Premium is charged on exposure to risk with a minimum of about £10,000. There is always a deductible and indemnities can be as high as 95% – even 100% for expropriation risks.

AIU's waiting period for transfer claims is usually 90 days longer than the expected 'normal' delay for the country.

PANFINANCIAL INSURANCE COMPANY LIMITED

PanFinancial offers a wide range of specific covers for political causes of loss. Its Contract Completion Insurance includes all the 'core' risks covered by Lloyd's with certain additions and the exporter can select from the following:

1. Non-payment by a public buyer.
2. Failure of a public buyer or a public seller to fulfil any of the terms of a contract.

3. Frustration of contract directly attributable to a law of either the buyer's or the insured's country.
4. Import or export embargo.
5. Transfer.
6. War, civil war or disturbance in the buyer's country.
7. Additional costs of diversion of goods resulting from war.
8. Action by the buyer's government preventing performance.

Other risks which can be covered specifically are as follows:

1. Failure of an overseas issuing bank to honour the the terms of a letter of credit.
2. Wrongful calling of an 'on demand' bond (including, if required, a call resulting from import embargo or a law of the buyer's country).

For the exporter who must retain title to goods after they have been landed overseas, PanFinancial offers a unique War on Land Insurance which fills the gap in conventional marine insurances by covering goods in land transit against the following:

1. War, civil war, rebellion.
2. Capture, seizure or arrest.
3. Damage from derelict weapons.
4. Strikes, riots and civil commotion.
5. Terrorist activity.

PanFinancial will consider risks of up to three years but has developed considerable skill in shorter-term repetitive business. Working almost exclusively through specialist brokers, its policy is to foster long-term relationships with competent managements.

BLACK SEA AND BALTIC INSURANCE COMPANY

Black Sea and Baltic is controlled by, and partially reinsured with, the Soviet State insurance agency, Ingostrakh. It has a well-established marine and general insurance account and offers a form of political risk insurance for business with most of the Soviet bloc countries. Cover can be taken for the non-payment risk and the manufacturing risk but there must in all cases be a guarantee from the competent public sector bank. Black Sea and Baltic is experienced in dealing with Soviet bloc trading organisations and can usually secure payment of undisputed debts before it becomes necessary to settle a claim under the policy.

THE NEW YORK MARKET

At the time of writing, a small number of United States insurers, such as CIGNA (a merger of Connecticut and General Insurance Company and Indemnity Insurance Company of North America), and Chubb, can be approached through the London market. They generally offer similar covers to London insurers but may on occasion be able to offer more favourable terms in particular countries.

USING THE EXPORT CREDIT INSURANCE MARKET

Many exporters find the increasing variety of insurers bewildering. Some simply prefer the devil they have known for twenty or thirty years. Others believe that only governments can insure political risks adequately. How do the government and private insurers compare?

The merits of the private market

1. Private insurers are free from the political and constitutional constraints which surround the official insurer whose remit is the promotion of his country's export trade.
2. By tradition the market is flexible and competitive. Although government insurers are becoming more commercially oriented, they are never likely to be free agents.
3. There is wide scope for the negotiation of deductibles and loss-sharing.
4. Underwriters are accustomed to risk-sharing and expect a greater selectivity of contracts and risks.
5. Premium can be calculated on exposure to risk or on an agreed limit of cover rather than on turnover or contract value.
6. Specific political risks can be written after the date of contract.
7. The non-ratification indemnity is only available in the private market.
8. Risks which have been excluded (voluntarily or otherwise) from a State scheme can still be offered to the private market.
9. Policies can be written in foreign currencies which may be more advantageous than a sterling cover with an historic conversion rate.

The shortcomings

1. The maximum commitment is often three years and limited by reinsurance conditions. Subject to satisfactory experience, the

three-year period can usually be 'rolled forward' but this is not the same as a firm five-year commitment which official insurers are used to giving.

2. Cover for the war risk may be limited.

3. The cover is not so widely acceptable, nor on the whole so effective, as official insurance in facilitating export finance.

4. There is doubt as to the status of private insurers in major debt rescheduling and refinancing negotiations.

CONCLUSION

In this chapter we have been dealing with a scene which is changing so rapidly that no single picture of it can be up to the minute or all-embracing. We have tried to stimulate thought and inquiry, to reassure the doubting, prompt the hesitant and encourage the bold. The prospects for an export-led recovery in the United Kingdom are bright and we conclude that there never was a better time for the exporter to test the versatility and flexibility of this lively and growing market. He may be pleasantly surprised.

10

Credit insurance as an aid to finance

vwvwvwvwvwvwvwvw

Most domestic credit is financed from the supplier's overdraft secured on his assets so it must compete with his other working capital requirements. How much cash he needs depends on his debtors/creditors position and his style of liquidity management. Insured debt is assumed to be superior debt if only because it has survived the scrutiny of the credit underwriter. In some situations credit insurance is the key to finance from overdraft or from special facilities such as acceptance credits.

Assignment

The benefits of most credit insurance policies can be assigned and, as we explained in chapter 7, specific risk cover is often used to help a bank to finance a supplier or subcontractor. Spread policies are also assigned in some trades as a matter of course. The assignment does not in any way alter the cover and does not represent a true collateral security because it is not readily realisable. It does provide for the contingency that the assignor/borrower is unable to pay because he cannot collect his own debt, but he can offer the benefits of a valid claim on the policy. The security for the lender is the contingent liability of a reputable insurer.

It is an imperfect security because the claim may be declined either for policy reasons, such as the date of the occurrence or the proximate cause of loss, or because the policyholder has not fulfilled his obligations to the insurer. He might, for instance, have failed to report an overdue or to comply with a credit limit condition.

The 'conditionality' of assignment

The assignee cannot do a great deal to control this risk. A bank will sometimes pay the premium direct and debit its customer to be sure that the cover is bound, but this only satisfies one requirement and leaves others in doubt. When a specific cover is assigned the assignee can at least verify the extent of the cover from the policy document. With a spread policy, he cannot be sure of the amount of the current credit limit on the buyer nor of any special conditions attaching to it. Despite these defects, many banks are prepared to accept assignment as a contribution to their security.

Special finance is essential for exports because the credit often exceeds normal overdraft terms. Wherever possible this 'long' borrowing must be removed from the exporter's balance sheet. This is especially important for the successful exporter who accumulates a large debtor item and correspondingly large borrowings. Add to this the political non-payment risk and the significance of export credit insurance to the bank is clear. There are, broadly speaking, two options – to use the exporter's policy or to use a policy held by the bank.

Using the exporter's policy

The exporter can assign the benefits of his own policy (or of any 'managed' policy to which he is joined) to a financing institution. Although ECGD is still the front runner at present, some banks are already willing to consider Trade Indemnity or American International Underwriters cover. Bearing in mind the relative complexity of export credit insurance, the assignee must be exposed to a greater risk of non-compliance than in domestic trade.

The conditionality of the assignment causes concern to some institutions because, in the event of such a failure, they would rely solely on their ordinary recourse to the customer. With a good spread of business, the risk of a single loss bringing the customer down seems far-fetched. The danger lies in any concentration of risk as, for example, in sales to overseas subsidiary companies which cannot be insured against insolvency or default. This was the risk which brought to an end the ECGD Comprehensive Bank Guarantee Schemes (the CBGs) under which the banks enjoyed the Department's *unconditional* guarantees.

They must now have more regard to the ability of the customer to make sound contracts, perform them properly and maintain effective credit insurance.

'Limited recourse' schemes   In the competitive 'post-CBG' environment, most of the banks will advance the insured percentage of the debt and only reserve their right of recourse to the exporter for disputed debts or for claims rejected for 'mismanagement' of the policy. The two financing techniques most commonly used are as follows:

1.   The purchase of the debt after delivery, the benefits of the cover being assigned to the bank.
2.   The 'undisclosed principal' formula whereby the bank agrees in advance to buy the goods from the exporter and to appoint him as its agent to deliver them to the buyer (as explained in chapter 7 under London Bridge Finance Company). Because, ostensibly, the exporter's contractual status as seller has been superseded, assignment is not appropriate, so the bank's interest in the insured contract is recognised by means of an endorsement to the policy.

Some banks use both techniques, as in Barclays' Tradeline scheme. Exfinco, on the other hand, prefers the 'undisclosed principal' role.

The errors and omissions gap   Limited recourse does not satisfy all the banks and, at the time of writing, discussions are in progress between individual banks and insurers to devise a separate indemnity at the bank's expense against the exporter's errors and omissions in the maintenance of his cover. The common intention appears to be that the bank will first exercise its right of recourse against the exporter. If he is unable or unwilling to meet the demand (and it is not yet clear how strongly it is to be pressed) the bank will claim under its separate indemnity. The insurer would only be liable to pay the bank if he agreed that, but for the error or omission, he would have met the exporter's claim. It is not yet apparent whether there is to be room for negotiation or whether the banks will concede absolute discretion to the insurers.

It remains to be seen whether any of these indemnities will cover significant failures or only inconsequential mistakes over which, in practice, most insurers would exercise discretion in favour of the exporter. In ECGD's case some concern is felt that government audit may discourage any relaxation of the letter of the policy whereas, at one time, the Department could be relied on to pay due attention to the spirit. It can only be hoped that competition between banks and insurers will produce the best range of options for the exporter who takes care to insure properly, and that the brokers will make their special skills available to him. The banks and ECGD have a lot to gain from the brokers' services.

Using the bank's policy

For the exporter who does not insure himself, most of the banks offer inclusive financing packages using their own ECGD policies. The hope is that these large policies will be economical for the banks and viable to ECGD but it is, of course, for the banks to make sure that their exporting customers comply with the conditions of the cover. To the customer, an incidental advantage is that he can usually choose which business to put to the bank, whereas he might not be able to select so freely against ECGD under his own policy.

These schemes also provide a useful service to the small exporter who feels he cannot justify employing the skills needed to run a policy properly. Annual export turnover of £1 million seems to be commonly regarded as the maximum scale of business suitable for covering under a bank's policy.

It is too early to know whether bank-managed policies have, in fact, shown the economies and efficiency expected. Small or inexperienced exporters are at least as likely to make mistakes as larger ones and bank staffs bear a considerable responsibility for supervising them.

MEDIUM-TERM EXPORT CREDIT

Finance for medium-term credit (typically of two to seven years) for investment in capital and semi-capital goods may be raised either as supplier credit or as buyer credit. We shall concentrate on credit raised by the supplier because credit insurance has little immediate relevance to credit which is extended directly to an overseas buyer by a United Kingdom lending bank.

The burden on the exporter of borrowing for such long periods makes 'without recourse' finance imperative. A further complication is that fixed and favourable rates of interest are essential to secure business in some markets and, as far as finance supported by government insurers is concerned, the rates are set out in the OECD consensus described in chapter 11.

In recent years the volume of this business has diminished sharply and much of the remainder has been diverted into the *à forfait* market. Forfaiting will undoubtedly retain a large share when world trade revives and links have already been forged between forfaiters and the political risk insurers.

The ECGD Specific Bank Guarantee

Since the mid 1950s banks have been able to waive their recourse to exporters by using the ECGD Specific Bank Guarantee (the SBG), the contractual framework for which is shown in Fig. 10.1. The contract of sale provides for deferred payment terms, evidenced by bills of exchange or promissory notes and this contract must be insured under an ECGD Specific Guarantee or Comprehensive Extended Terms Guarantee. When the basic cover is fully in place, ECGD can issue to the bank its unconditional Specific Bank Guarantee for the full amount of the bank facility. In this guarantee ECGD undertakes to pay to the bank the face value of any bill or note which remains unpaid 90 days after the due date. This is an unconditional liability, so payment is immediate.

The Department's practice is to put the exporter on notice at this point that it has discharged its liability to the bank and to invite him to lodge a claim under the credit insurance cover on expiry of the appropriate waiting period. When this claim has been examined and liability

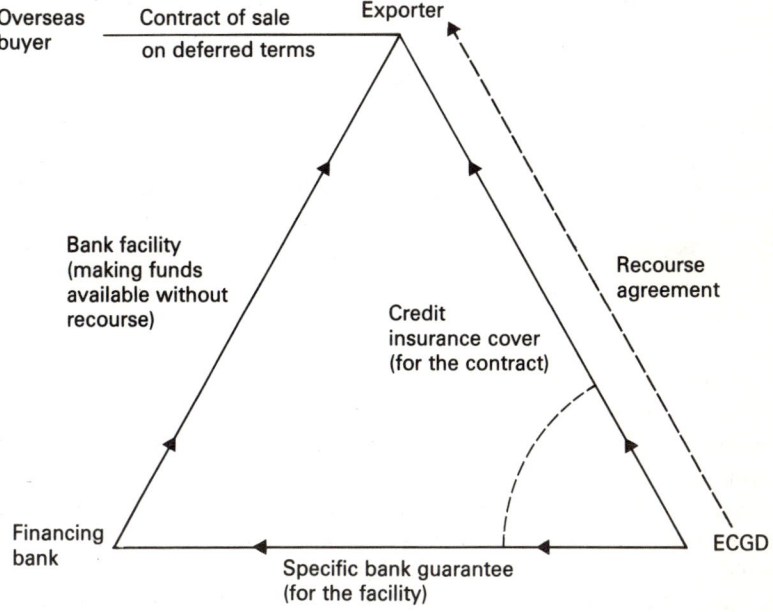

Fig. 10.1 Contractual framework of medium-term supplier credit using the ECGD Specific Bank Guarantee. The recourse agreement closes the gap between the conditional credit insurance indemnity and the unconditional guarantee to the bank.

admitted, ECGD can calculate the difference between the amount it has already paid the bank and the amount it would have paid the exporter if there had been no bank guarantee. Under the recourse agreement, the exporter is obligated to refund this difference to ECGD with interest at a commercial rate.

In the ordinary course of events, the recourse demand is only for the uninsured percentage under the credit insurance cover and the recourse interest. If there is any shortfall in the cover or, worse still, the basic claim is invalid, then the demand will be for a much larger amount. The Department must therefore be satisfied with the exporter's financial worth before it will agree to issue an SBG. It will be seen, too, that to make the whole 'framework' secure, the basic cover must be in perfect order.

ECGD support for finance houses

The small group of export finance houses based mainly in London act within the legal framework of the confirming house but specialise in medium-term credit. They originally held the standard Comprehensive Extended Terms Guarantee and were in substantially the same relationship with ECGD as any insured supplier.

Their concern was that, having in their financing agreements distanced themselves from all disputes between buyer and seller, their ECGD cover was nevertheless at risk for the non-performance of the supplier. Although the insured contract was the financing agreement with the overseas buyer, ECGD has always excluded liability for loss arising from any dispute on the underlying contract of sale.

'FINCOBES'

One answer to this problem has been to let the financing agreement take the form of a loan to an overseas bank, which would normally be a superior risk since the likelihood of a bank defaulting is remote. The borrowing bank could be expected to repay and require the buyer to institute proceedings against the supplier. These specialist finance houses are accordingly covered by the Finance Contracts (Overseas Banks) Endorsement under which ECGD insures the failure of the overseas bank to repay any instalment of principal or interest. The percentage of indemnity is higher, which recognises both the low margins on which the finance houses usually work and the special quality of the risk on the borrowing bank.

The Associated Banks Endorsement (ABE)

The specialist finance houses are, in practice, owned by major United Kingdom banks and are frequently in a position to make the loan agreement with an associated bank in the buyer's country, thus reducing the rate of premium by half. We have mentioned that the demand for medium-term credit for capital and semi-capital goods is in worldwide recession but many of the ECGD General Purpose Lines of Credit described in chapter 7 have been negotiated and operated by finance houses using this facility.

PRE-SHIPMENT RISKS UNDER BUYER CREDITS

When an ECGD Buyer Credit covers a single contract, the practice is for the loan agreement to authorise the lending bank to pay to the seller/ contractor any sums due under a termination settlement reached in accordance with the terms of the contract. Since ECGD guarantees the bank unconditionally, it invariably vets this provision before the documents are signed. The seller then has effectively the same protection as the pre-credit cover described in chapter 9. A similar provision usually applies to a Project Line of Credit for the benefit of all the participating contractors but any exporter invited to take part in a Project Line of Credit should make certain that he does qualify for reimbursement for costs incurred in the event that the contract is terminated. This is often referred to as 'complex' buyer credit.

By contrast, most General Purpose Lines of Credit are 'simple', only relating to payment for goods shipped with no provision for termination payments and no vetting of contracts (although ECGD sometimes offers useful guidance). It is for the individual exporter to negotiate his contract terms and seek pre-shipment cover from ECGD if he holds the PreCredit Risk Endorsement, or in the private market if he does not.

CAPITAL LEASING ('FULL PAYOUT LEASES')

Long-term leasing is sometimes employed as an alternative to the outright purchase of capital and semi-capital goods. The total amount to be collected in rent is calculated to equate to the credit purchase price of the goods and the lessee may have the option of buying them for a nominal consideration at the end of the lease period. The credit insurance implications are that the lessor seeks to insure what he expects will be a long-term debt payable in equal instalments, but he will retain ownership of the goods throughout. The value of any right to repossess can be debatable, as we explain in chapter 6. In most countries, insolvency of the lessee would not hamper repossession but political events anywhere certainly could. Most insurers limit the time allowed for repossession.

Insurances of Credit covers UK leases for up to seven years, charging a lump sum premium on inception based on the monthly rent and with a minimum of £50,000. If three monthly, or two quarterly, payments are unpaid, IOC takes possession of the goods and adjusts the claim twelve months later. It bears any loss on the residual value but any profit is passed to the policyholder. Investigation of the lessee is intensive. Typical leases covered have been for printing machinery, transport equipment and stand-by power plant.

Leasing is undoubtedly a high-risk activity in many trades and insurers are selective about the equipment they can cover. On the other hand, lessors are not yet minded to employ credit insurance as a support for a spread of risks and many of the risks which are offered are unacceptable. There may well be a case for catastrophe 'excess of loss' treatment.

THE PATTERN FOR THE FUTURE

This brief survey covers a period of radical change, especially in the provision of short-term export finance. In the capital goods field, several years of intensive investment by Third World countries has ended in a welter of rescheduled debt and grave concern for economic growth prospects at a time of world trade recession. The few public sector projects which can be implemented are mostly funded from government aid programmes and it has become all but impossible to finance any private investment.

In the banking world, sovereign debt has upset the balance sheets of international banks, reducing their profits, credit ratings and lending capacity. Although United Kingdom banks have generally suffered less, they have all reacted to the dramatic reduction in Third World borrowing by concentrating on short-term trade finance and diversifying into techniques such as forfaiting and factoring. Some of them are close to Bank of England limits despite having surplus funds and they are looking for ways to increase their lending and their profits while keeping within their asset ratios. A very good prospect is the use of credit insurance, not only to improve the quality of the individual risk, but also to upgrade unsecured lending in the balance sheet. This helps to explain their concern over the conditionality of assignment.

We have painted the retail picture which directly concerns the average company. In chapter 7 we mentioned the use of insurance to support the 'wholesaling' of securitised debt. Both pictures seem to give strong clues to the pattern which may emerge over the next few years, with insurers both underwriting the credit risk and helping to release funds for trade finance. All of which points to an expanding credit insurance market at home and abroad.

11

The international dimension

vwvwvwvwvwvwvwvw

'WHAT HAVE MY COMPETITORS GOT?'

Never a day goes by when the businessman does not ask himself, 'What have my competitors got that I haven't?' With more and more companies operating internationally, he should now be asking a second question: 'What have my overseas *friends and colleagues* got that we could all benefit from?' He will already be on the lookout for legal or financial advantages, marketing opportunities and human and material resources. Now is the time for the same thinking on credit insurance, because the answers to both his questions will assume greater importance as the market develops.

With overseas manufacturing increasing in most branches of industry, the credit risk pattern will change. Economic expansion will bring more competition and more business failures in the developing countries. When, for example, the enormous potential of the Pacific Basin is tapped, the business community will need sound credit insurance support.

BRINGING THE INSURERS TOGETHER

Narrow national preferences have restricted credit insurance practice worldwide for many years with government-sponsored export insurers concentrating on export promotion and the commercial insurers inhibited from operating overseas on any significant scale by licensing requirements and voluntary agreements. The majority of the insurers still only trade in their own countries. Two organisations, the 'Berne Union' and the International Credit Insurance Association, bring them together for consultation and some efforts at cooperation and regulation. Because governments are so closely involved, cooperation and regulation in the export field have been more obvious than in commercial credit insurance. In fact, the commercial underwriters have highly effective day-to-day arrangements.

THE INTERNATIONAL UNION OF CREDIT AND
INVESTMENT INSURERS

The 'Berne Union' was founded in 1934 by the export credit insurers of France, Italy, Spain and the United Kingdom. The Statutes of the Union provide that its purposes shall be to work for the following:

1. The international acceptance of sound principles of credit insurance and the establishment and maintenance of discipline in terms of credit for international trade.
2. International cooperation in fostering a favourable investment climate and in developing and maintaining sound principles of foreign investment insurance.

To achieve these aims, members agree that they will do the following:

1. Exchange information and furnish the Union with the information necessary for the accomplishment of its tasks.
2. Consult together on a continuing basis, carry out studies and participate in agreed projects.
3. Cooperate closely and where appropriate take coordinated action.
4. Cooperate with other international institutions concerned with these matters.

When business was resumed in 1946, state-controlled organisations and private insurance companies covering political risks on behalf of the state began to join the Union, all participating as insurers and not as representatives of their governments. An Investment Guarantee Committee was formed in 1970, leading to the new name and statutes adopted in 1974. In addition to regular formal meetings, there are continuous exchanges between members on general underwriting practice, commercial risks, political risks and specific cases.

Overall business transacted by the Union's members reached a peak of Sw. Fr. 473 billion in 1981 or some 14% of world exports. Although trade has declined since then, members are paying claims at an annual rate of Sw. Fr. 14 billion or double the figure of five years ago.

The rapid growth of export credit subsidies after the oil crisis of 1976 led to an interim 'gentlemen's agreement' reached by six OECD members and replaced in 1978 by a formal agreement with twenty signatories. This became the 'OECD Consensus' described later.

HELP FOR THE DEVELOPING COUNTRIES

Under the auspices of the United Nations, leading members of the Berne Union have given help, often including the secondment of senior staff, to countries setting up their own national schemes. There is much interest, too, in the role of export credit insurance in regional trade development.

In the Middle East, for example, the Inter-Arab Investment Guarantee Corporation, based in Kuwait and set up in 1974 to protect Arab investments in other Arab countries, introduced complementary credit insurance facilities in 1985. It offers a typical range of policies:

1. Whole turnover commercial and political risk policy for short-term revolving credit up to 180 days.
2. Specific commercial and political risk policy for both short and longer terms.
3. Specific political risk policy intended mainly for public sector business.

Cover for the transfer risk is limited to measures taken by the authorities in the buyer's country but includes the imposition of a discriminatory exchange rate without defining 'discriminatory'. The remaining risks are modelled on existing practice but specifically include nationalisation of the importer's assets as well as confiscation or detention of the goods. The Annex Consignment Guarantee Contract extends the political risk cover to goods held in stock, or exhibited, in another country.

A separate policy (an indemnity insurance and not an unconditional guarantee as written by ECGD) is issued to banks financing exports by means of buyer credits. These are important moves to equip the richer oil producers in the region with effective credit insurance as they diversify their non-oil exports first to other Arab States and then to the world at large.

THE INTERNATIONAL CREDIT INSURANCE ASSOCIATION

The ICIA was formed following a conference on credit insurance held in London in 1926. It now has 44 members in 28 countries who collectively earn premiums of over Sw. Fr. 3,200 million. Membership is, in principle, reserved for insurance companies who specialise in, or have a department specialising in, credit insurance or the issue of surety bonds.

The Association has four main spheres of activity:

1. Regular exchange of views on trades and economic conditions.
2. Exchange of information on individual credit risks.
3. Cooperation in collection of overdues and recoveries.
4. Cooperation in reinsurance, particularly for export business.

The exchange of credit information has been much expanded recently, many of the members using advanced telecommunications to handle each other's inquiries.

Other moves which have already begun are likely to gather pace. For many years ICIA members refrained from offering cover to companies outside their own countries unless they had the blessing of the local insurer. This 'hands-off' agreement now seems outmoded to leading insurers and Trade Indemnity, for one, has made it known that it intends to seek business wherever licensing does not preclude it (as in France). Its portfolio already includes Belgium, Holland and Switzerland and would undoubtedly extend further in a truly free market.

INTERNATIONAL AGREEMENTS

In addition to the voluntary agreements between insurers in the Berne Union, governments are further bound by the General Agreement on Trade and Tariffs (GATT) and the EEC states are subject to various Community rules. The GATT forbids export subsidies and this includes the operation of a government credit insurance facility in such a way as to conceal a subsidy. Schemes must be run on broad commercial lines and not used to fund 'loss leaders'. The Berne Union requires insurers to 'provide a satisfactory and competitive service to their exporters at a reasonable cost'.

The 'OECD Consensus'

The Organisation for Economic Cooperation and Development has a hand in two important export credit insurance matters. First, it sponsors the International Arrangement on Official Export Credit – the 'Consensus' – to which 22 countries now subscribe. The arrangement applies to credit of two years or more and specifies maximum lengths of credit, minimum down payments and minimum rates of interest which governments may support with subsidies. The object is to smooth out variations in local borrowing rates for exporters and thus remove competition on credit terms with government support. The minimum portion of direct aid which qualifies a transaction for exemption is also laid down. Countries are graded as 'poor', 'intermediate' or 'rich', the 'poor' ones receiving the best terms. Separate 'sector agreements' cover civil aircraft, power stations, shipbuilding and other types of business in which special considerations have been identified. Defence and agricultural products are excluded.

Debt rescheduling

OECD plays a key role in the rescheduling of debts insured by government insurers. The debtor government meets the Paris Club of creditor nations to reach a multilateral agreement in principle on the length of the rescheduling and the rates of interest. Individual governments, usually acting through their credit insurers, then negotiate bilateral agreements with the debtor government to implement the overall plan. This rescheduling of insured debt and the liquidation of other sovereign debt are often related to International Monetary Fund assistance.

THE EUROPEAN ECONOMIC COMMUNITY

Some of the provisions of the Treaty of Rome, particularly those regarding freedom of competition, are of interest to the credit insurance market. The Community aims to secure total freedom of trade in all classes of insurance but even if all licensing and other statutory barriers were removed, differences in local taxation and currencies could act as commercial disincentives. The main initiatives taken by the Commission so far have concerned export credit insurance but have not shown any significant benefits. In the dramatic all-night bargaining which so often determines Community policy, a subject with such a low profile is often squeezed out or traded off in favour of more popular causes. Nor has any powerful lobby emerged capable of influencing Ministers or bureaucrats. Efforts to draft a 'harmonised' policy to be adopted by all the export insurers foundered except for agreement on the common definitions for the political causes of loss. The Commission's Credit Insurance Group has, however, devoted much attention to capital goods and project-type business which, in the present world situation, has proved to be less relevant.

THE PROSPECTS FOR THE COMMERCIAL CREDIT INSURERS

Despite a decision of the European Parliament that the government agencies should refrain from insuring intra-Community trade, the Commission's directive of 1986 omitted this provision. The directive also exempted government agencies from the solvency margins which every commercial insurer must maintain on peril of suspension.

It is significant that with the contraction of Third World business, some 60% of the government insurers' portfolios is now in OECD and predominantly in the EEC and that they all have cash deficits. At the same time, most of them are insisting that because their cover is 'indivisible', they cannot segregate the buyer risk element on which the private insurers compete with them. (Trade Indemnity, at least, has no difficulty in offering buyer risk cover with political risks as optional attachments.)

At the time of writing, the only countries in which insurers can write business freely are Belgium, Denmark, Luxembourg and the Netherlands. Licensing in France operates against any foreign insurer and in Germany, although there are no formal barriers, local insurers have found ways of thwarting any incursion. The quality of cover and the requirements of the proposer are not prime factors. In Ireland, only the most persistent lobbying will secure the ministerial dispensation necessary to allow a foreign insurer to write a policy for an Irish proposer.

Unfortunately, much of the cover on offer in Europe is seriously deficient. It is mostly whole turnover with little scope for negotiation of the spread of risks. In France, Italy and elsewhere, liability for insolvency is ascertained on the 'ultimate net loss' basis, that is, when the buyer's position finally crystallises. Because in continental practice the buyer usually comes to some composition with his creditors, a claim cannot be paid until the insured receives the compromise payment and can demonstrate a net loss. Protracted default or moratorium are not covered. The underlying intention is to replace a proven capital loss rather than, as in this country, to restore working capital.

This highly artificial market must be rationalised if European companies are to enjoy true freedom of choice and the broking community will not be slow to find the right market for the available business. It is thought that some of the government agencies may, after all, withdraw from intra-Community business and concentrate on overseas buyers and political risks on whatever bases they can agree with their respective governments.

COMPARING THE INSURERS

It is not, in fact, difficult for the businessman to find out what his competitors and overseas friends have got. The difficult question is, 'How good is it?' It is one thing to catalogue the insurers and their various forms of cover; it is another to say how effectively they work. The first question can be answered from published sources or put to any insurer direct. The second can only be answered by a practitioner with first-hand experience.

Credit insurers can be divided into the following:

1. Privately owned incorporated bodies which underwrite
   (a) commercial risk reinsured in the private market;
   (b) commercial risk shared with government;
   (c) political risk reinsured in the private market;
   (d) political risk reinsured by government and private market;
   (e) political risk as agent of government.

2. Government-owned incorporated bodies (as in Canada, Australia and Hong Kong).
3. Government departments (as in United Kingdom, Japan and Denmark).

The constitution and statutory authority of an insurer have a bearing on working practices and relationships with policyholders, insured buyers and brokers. Underwriting authority may be partly internal and partly external. Certain risks may have to be referred to an outside advisory body or to a minister of government.

The questions for the practitioner

A company considering substantial business with any insurer should ask specific questions of the broker or other adviser:

1. Do they examine claims generously, fairly or stringently?
2. How often do they reject claims under a discretionary limit?
3. Are they flexible about the spread of business offered?
4. How often do they reject business altogether?
5. How good are they at covering unusual situations or new lines of business?
6. How quickly do they react?
7. Are they, in practice, their own masters?
8. Are they realistic about day to day problems such as extensions of due dates?
9. Do they encourage personal contact between policyholders and underwriters?
10. How do they set premium rates for new policies, renewals and individual risks?
11. How reliable are their *indications* of cover?
12. Do they change country conditions frequently or impose many credit limit conditions?

Taking out a credit insurance policy should not be looked on as the purchase of a product but as the setting up of a partnership. The questions we suggest are necessary inquiries as to the record and capabilities of the other party.

THE GLOBAL VIEW

One of the commonest obstacles to radical and innovative credit management is the belief that credit is a local league game. Few teams aspire to the next division. As we have seen, some of the insurers are widening their horizons and among the multi-national corporations there is some measure of international credit management but, on the whole, too few boards inquire into the global opportunities for spreading and sharing their credit and political risks.

The total devolution of responsibility for credit to local subsidiaries does not, in our view, automatically lead to the best use of resources. It is true that local management will not overcome its day-to-day problems with its hands tied by corporate decisions (or lack of them!). Equally, the corporate interest is not always best served by local executives confining themselves to local facilities. Where there are common buyers, for instance, the management and insurance of the risks ought to be coordinated at a higher corporate level. Whether negotiations are actually conducted at this level or simply directed from it is for individuals to decide, but there is no doubt that having a risk 'in one frame' helps an underwriter to be more generous. The same applies to management of overdues and loss prevention measures.

There are opportunities, too, for the underwriting of excess of loss 'catastrophe' covers on a global or regional basis. The capacity of the private market is now sufficient for any forseeable credit risk and size is not, of itself, a problem.

CONCLUSION

The last five years have set the scene for great strides in the use of the insurance mechanism to reduce and contain credit and political losses. Increased competition, especially in the London market, has encouraged a new entrepreneurial approach to the risks without discarding the hard-won lessons of the past. The trading community needs to know a lot more about managing the international risks and insuring them in local and international markets. The specialist brokers have a clear and unique role to play in advising businesses and their bankers, and influencing insurers. There will be many losers if they miss the opportunity.

12

Assessing the need for credit insurance

vwvwvwvwvwvwvwvw

In their many consultancies and training events around the UK for a variety of companies and industries, the authors have faced a wealth of talent of executives responsible for credit management. To determine attitudes to credit insurance, we have asked simply: Do you have credit insurance? And then, if *yes* – why? If *no* – why not?

The answers have been rather depressing in revealing a widespread unawareness of the range of facilities, and a lack of planned approaches to assessing what is needed.

Our experience has been that less than one in four companies has ever purchased credit insurance. When asked why they *did*, they replied in the following ways:

1. 'We always have.'
2. 'That's decided elsewhere and imposed upon us.'
3. 'I don't know why we do.'

And, quite frequently:

4. 'We had a bad loss once, so we then got cover.'

The more dedicated users stated, e.g.:

5. 'It reinforces our credit management system.'
6. 'We find it cost-effective.'

When the 75% were asked why they did *not* buy credit insurance, their replies rarely had to do with a serious evaluation. They tended to be something like the following:

1. 'Too expensive.'
2. 'We've heard you can't get the limits you need.'
3. 'They'll only cover the easy debts, not the ones you need.'

4. 'I've no idea why we don't have it.'
5. 'I've never thought about it.' (Very commonplace.)

Despite the limited nature of the sample, we have no doubt of the need for better publicity and the targeted marketing of facilities by credit insurers, and for a more detailed grasp by corporate managers of the profit protection available for their balance-sheet risks.

THE INTERESTS OF PROVIDERS AND USERS

Since this book is to benefit both sellers and buyers of credit insurance, any assessment of a business's need should consider the interests of both sides of the industry. There may be no need for the trader to insure at all or, possibly, no profit for the insurer in taking on the risks offered. However, most sellers would benefit from some degree of protection, but the problem bedevilling insurers is that of getting together with a seller in the right atmosphere to make an assessment.

A trader's view should be, 'I have an uncertain chance of bad debts in my receivables. XYZ Credit Insurance Company Ltd are willing to protect me at a cost of £x, or y% of sales p.a. Other, indirect benefits are thrown in for no extra charge. My conscious, objective decision is that it is (or is not) worth paying that price to preserve my profits.'

ASSESSING THE NEED: A MAJOR TASK

To be able to form a view, a number of things have to happen:

1. The trader has to be aware of the existence of credit insurance.
2. The trader has to accept that his receivables have some risks.
3. Insurers or brokers have to make themselves known to the trader.
4. Insurers or brokers have to work with the trader to identify risks.
5. The parties have to agree a price for cover, perhaps with different terms at different prices.
6. The trader may prefer to compare different insurers or schemes.
7. The trader has to make a decision on cost-effectiveness.

A lot of activity – marketing, analysis, negotiation, and decisions. Yet many company directors are not aware of all the benefits and most have never made detailed comparisons between the covers available. In this situation of neglect, most of those who are protected sign off routine renewals with little or no negotiation of terms. Their dependence on brokers is significant, as is the insurers', for whom, with some exceptions, brokers provide the marketing and sales force.

THE EMPATHY OF INSURERS

It is not in an insurance company's interest to take on all available business for the sake of premium income. Over-selling credit insurance to ill-organised clients leads inevitably to losses soon afterwards. It is just as unwise to persuade companies with well-spread risks of small values to buy unnecessary cover because, in the longer term, this alienates influential decision-makers against the very concept of credit insurance. Professionalism and integrity from credit insurance brokers is vital in building market respect and product credibility. Whether insurers have their own sales resource or depend on the services of brokers (whom they should instruct properly), they must empathise with the needs of industrialists, who are not only busy people but have to worry about having, usually, very slim margins to spend from.

An objective discussion of the 'who owes what?' analysis of the sales ledger is the fundamental starting point in understanding a seller's need.

ADDRESSING THE BROAD ISSUES

Existing and potential buyers of protection should consider two major questions and some consequential ones:

1. Should we cover home sales or exports or both?
2. Should we cover all our turnover or just certain sales?

How should a trader address these questions? Few have the time to assess them adequately, so there is the perfect operating situation for the 'honest broker', who needs to earn commission from an insurer but will only do so if he satisfies the trader. The trader must control the negotiations but can expect the broker to do most of the analysis and leg-work.

The other factors to be considered include the following:

1. *Credit insurance* as it now is – flexible, negotiable and part of risk management; not as it has been widely regarded in the past – as a ponderous whole turnover obligation substituting for in-house risk control.
2. The *different needs* of major corporations and smaller businesses.
3. *Balance sheet protection*: the different degrees to which this matters to particular traders, compared to, say, marketing support or information.
4. The *incidence of insolvency* in the industries of the trader's customers.
5. The *spread of risks*, good, average or poor, within a sales ledger.

6. The *size of single risks*, especially on major contracts, in relation to net profits (i.e., would any single loss really hurt us?).
7. The *indirect benefits of cover*, e.g., free information and credit opinions on customers, assistance to sales efforts and support for finance.
8. The *efficiency of in-house credit management* and its benefit of credit insurance as a 'long stop', especially with adventurous marketing.
9. *Marketing plans*: how they may be advanced by the removal of uncertainty, or how they increase exposures or generate new ones.
10. The *profit equation*, i.e., the premium as a percentage of sales compared to the percentage net profit on sales as now increased by the reduction of bad debt losses, the improved cash flow, and the savings from free credit information and, possibly, cheaper financing.

THE WRONG APPROACH

Credit insurance is often bought, and sold, for the wrong reasons. In one company it is a prop for inadequate credit management. In another, an individual manager fears for his job if a large loss is suffered. What price 'sleepability'?

It is not difficult to see how the wrong motivations of defensiveness and laziness have come about. A board of directors places all responsibility for financial risks onto the financial director who usually has little appreciation of risk management and sees credit control as a minor clerical function of his accounts department. He is usually remote from sales and production decisions. He relates credit insurance only to his own experience of bad debt write-offs and he pays scant attention to investigating creditworthiness, checking orders against overdues, or picking up warnings in every-day collection activity. Perhaps plentiful bank finance has disguised the need for shortening the collection period of receivables.

In some large groups, there is a curious ambivalence, where the head office financial director may refuse permission for a subsidiary to spend on credit insurance premiums, saying, e.g., 'It's your job to get the cash in and avoid bad debts – we're not going to pay out twice.' Yet the same director may ensure there is stoploss cover for the whole group. Why is this? Is it because he has such a high regard for the competence of his credit managers in the subsidiaries? Or does it betray his mistrust that with separate policies they would hide their incompetence behind a credit insurer? Or is his group stoploss cover just a simple way for him to protect his own corner of the hierarchy?

These common-place situations show why it has been difficult to sell credit insurance at the right policy-making level. The salesman needs exceptional skill and 'presence' to be able to make his case in the proper quarter.

Compared to home trade cover, the export credit products of ECGD carry more acceptance at board level, probably because of the respectability of governmental protection. It may also be due to the extra hazard these days of non-transfer of hard currency from so many markets, for which there is the widespread, but mistaken, belief that only governments can afford to guarantee protection to exporters. If those assumptions are correct, then perhaps the clues are there to show what is needed for greater success in selling or buying credit insurance. In the simplest of terms – national awareness of major profit risks; and respectability of insurers in the market place. It would seem to be a classic opportunity for expert marketing.

SUPPORT FOR CREDIT MANAGEMENT?

It is not an adverse reflection on line management to reinforce it with purchased services. Most companies obtain some credit information from outside sources, after all, if only a bank or trade reference. There are also bank facilities and factoring services which are sold to improve home and export credit operations. So does credit insurance.

A modern credit manager does not see the insurance underwriter as a usurper of his own authority, but rather as a helper. The company person responsible for credit is the one accountable for receivables performance – and credit insurance can field any credit problems that elude him.

The buck stops eventually in the board room for all operations. The shareholders, after all, employ the directors to apply management skills to their invested capital, and are interested in the best possible returns. The directors know that it is the duty of all of them, not just the financial director, to make sure that the business's assets are safeguarded. They need to review exposures regularly and consider every available protection of profits. Very few boards can genuinely relax in the safe knowledge that credit risk is a minor issue for their companies. Rather than theorise about the likelihood of loss, boards should take fail-safe positions which cushion any possible losses, likely or not, and use their skills to negotiate the most economical insurance facilities.

HOW A MAJOR PROVIDER EXPLAINS THE NEED

Trade Indemnity plc are the largest providers of domestic credit insurance in the UK, and their advertisements and brochures are particularly effective in drawing attention to the kind of points we have been making throughout this book. With their kind permission and some artistic licence, we are reproducing the key points from one of their documents, *A businessman's guide to credit insurance*. In our view, TI work hard to overcome the lack of client awareness we have discussed. They do this with very readable material on trade credit situations which busy executives can relate to, rather than relying on insurance-oriented messages.

Under a picture of collapsing dominoes, they state that, 'Credit failure has the classic domino effect. You may not see the first domino fall, but the last one could knock you flat. What can be your misfortune need not be your fault.' In other words, even a credit-conscious company which gets information on its own customers may not know the strength of its customers' customers, or how much they depend on them. Every good credit manager would make sure he knew all about his top few largest customers, which *inter alia*, avoids that kind of nasty surprise. But he cannot find the time to know all about all his customers and most companies do not know much about the financial condition of even their major customers.

'Credit – the lifeblood of business today.' TI explain that credit is the vital means of business existence, a statement usually applied to cash rather than credit. But since credit is the means to cash, TI are guaranteeing the cash itself.

TI talk about business risks and rewards, and give five major ways in which credit insurance helps to improve return on capital:

1. 'More capital is under your own control.' This is because insured receivables tend to be paid faster, so less of the seller's money is 'out' with customers; and also because the bad debt reserve can be reduced, thus releasing tied-up capital.
2. 'You run a tighter financial machine.' Extra attention is paid to credit control when credit insurance is in place, with benefits from faster cash intake.
3. 'More financial resources may be open to you.' Insured receivables improve the credit standing of a company and policies are assignable.
4. 'More of your sales effort is directed into fruitful enterprises.' The need to turn sales into cash on time, and therefore to sell to customers who can pay, reminds us that an insurer backs his credit opinion with his money.
5. 'More of your business forecasts have a chance of being right.' The elimination of unknown hazards in business planning, with credit insurance in place, is a major benefit to corporate managers.

TI show a pie-chart of a typical company's current assets, with 40% in uninsured debtors, calling them 'the great uncovered'. Official statistics show trade debtors are 25% of all assets and 40% of current ones, pointing to the high proportion of company wealth that credit insurance can protect.

TI show an alarm clock with a twenty minute sector, illustrating that companies fail at the rate of one every twenty minutes (even higher these days). They remind us that when this happens, the banks usually have a charge on all available assets, leaving nothing for unsecured trade creditors unless they are credit insured.

The TI document also discusses benefits in the accounting area:

1. Sounder credit control – the disciplines and defined authorities achieved to meet insurance conditions.
2. Better profitability – by suggesting more worthwhile customers for sales efforts.
3. Less uncertainty about 'book value' – the value of insured debts is as good as money in the bank (note: this is rather exaggerated!).
4. More meaning in the audit – it is easier to verify the debtor asset.
5. Self-generating bad debt reserve – meaning that insurance cover is a self-liquidating reserve, paid for at a budgetable cost.
6. Tax benefit – that credit insurance premium is allowable for tax.

TI's brochure explains cash flow with the usual diagram of income and expense going round in a circle, but with the interesting difference of showing that most business items are insured (buildings, plant, workforce, stock, etc.), whereas the vital final item – actual cash from customers – may not be.

TI then go into detail on the types of policy available. We have described these earlier in the book, in common with those of other providers, but it is worth noting that TI stress their empathy with clients' needs – a skill which must be developed by all providers. Surely the days are gone when insurers can say, 'Here we are – come and see us – that's our product, take it or leave it!'

TI rightly remind readers that an insurer's vast database of financial information on companies is accumulated from the input of various sources, Companies House, policyholders, banks and commercial agencies.

If a large customer gets into difficulties the credit insurer usually hears about it, and can collect more reliable and up-to-date information than any individual supplier. Because he has a wider, thinner spread of risks than the individual supplier, the credit insurer can afford to stay on risk longer. Very often he can stay on long enough for the insured supplier to support the buyer out of difficulty. This can bring considerable benefit to the supplier later.

Finally, TI produces a useful list of questions for risk managers:

1. Is your company's investment in its customers bigger than you knew?
2. Do you sell more than 5% of your total to a single customer?
3. 'We've never had a serious loss in the past, so I don't see why we should have one in the future.' Do you think this is a rash view?'
4. If somebody offered you a credit rating service and backed every opinion with his own money would you find this useful?
5. Do you think the debtor asset should be managed as efficiently as any other asset?
6. If you insure your production up to the point of delivery, is it not logical to insure also the time when goods are out of your hands but not paid for?
7. If your agent of undoubted financial solidity agreed to guarantee up to 80% of losses in business placed by him – would you think it fair to raise his commission from 5% to, say, 6%?

If you say yes to five or more of these questions, it will be surprising if you did not benefit from credit insurance!

THE DIFFERENT NEEDS OF HOME AND EXPORT RECEIVABLES

Domestic sales revenue is at risk almost entirely from customer insolvency, whereas export proceeds are also under attack from market insolvency, exemplified by the transfer risk, and from many other official events outside the control of both exporter and customer. Most exporters also sell in the home trade and are aware of the differences between the two that affect planned income. This is why credit managers separate home trade records from export, and review them to manage the risks separately. For example, it would be misleading to compare export losses with total company sales and conclude that the ratio was tiny, if losses were a huge, unacceptable percentage of export sales alone. Domestic sales tend to be volume-driven for most companies, resulting in a mix of all kinds of customers, with different degrees of solvency and debts often unrelated to their size or financial strength.

Export sales tend to be for fewer, more specific, contracts and are thus more capable of risk control. It is also possible to check each market separately, instead of considering the total as 'the export market' (there is, of course, no such place!).

As exports tend to remain unpaid for longer than home trade sales, the implied bad debt risk of exports is doubled because the country risk of insufficient FX must be added to the risk of buyer insolvency. Export receivables are more vulnerable and sensitive to bad debt loss and interest expense than the home trade asset.

BAD DEBTS AND THE BALANCE SHEET

Credit management exists to remove risks at an acceptable cost. One hundred per cent finance without recourse would remove debts from the balance sheet but the financing charge is invariably too high, in relation to the perceived risk.

The cost could be reduced by selling debts *with* recourse, or with, say, 10–25% recourse, but the actual credit risk then remains until the customer's payment is in. What then should be the balance-sheet treatment? Removal of the debt? Partial removal? Certainly a contingent liability until payment is in. The administration can be cumbersome and the overall cost still fairly high.

The ideal credit management 'package' for a thrusting business is to have, cost-effectively, strong in-house credit management procedures for checking orders and collecting accounts, supported by credit insurance and a low-cost financing scheme.

Effective in-house credit drills encourage insurers to cover risks at low rates and to be extra supportive with marginal risk accounts. They similarly help in obtaining lower interest rates on borrowings or, indeed, extra borrowings.

Unfortunately, not many UK companies yet have strong credit management in place. It is an evolutionary process at different levels in UK companies. Credit insurance reinforces these varying stages – so it is understandable that premium rates and conditions have to vary to reflect the risk to insurers.

THE DECISION PROCESS

The decision path involves several factors and we comment from the trader's point of view, in the belief that the resulting conclusions will be helpful to all parties in the credit insurance process.

A suggested approach

Note: as well as direct insurance guarantees of replacing bad debt losses, traders must also take account of the indirect benefits, which may not be quantifiable in money terms, e.g., credit information pointing the way to better quality business and more effective sales prospecting; disciplines which make collections easier and, in turn, reduce the probability and size of bad debts.

1. To assess how best to protect the receivables asset: look at what future losses are possible and their effect on future profitability; not backwards to actual past losses (these may be irrelevant). The *attitude* to credit insurance should be to protect against the unexpected future, just as for fire, theft, life, etc., regardless of what has happened in the past. Remember the *iceberg principle*, that bad debts usually come from the mass of slow-paying accounts.

2. Ask: 'What do we have now in our current receivables asset?' and, 'What will our sales plans give us in the future?'

3. Look separately at home and export accounts. For each category, produce a 'who owes what' analysis (see Table 12.1). The WOW will show how the asset value is spread over the accounts. Subdivide it between your own view of 'A', 'B' and 'C' risk categories. Happy? Consider also how the WOW will change with future marketing plans.

4. Look at your bad debts for the last three years. Analyse them into the following:
   (a) how many?;
   (b) what mix of values?;
   (c) which risk categories did they come from?;
   (d) which customer sectors (if you sell into more than one)?;
   (e) what was the percentage of bad debts to sales in each year?;
   (f) what was the percentage of bad debts to net profits in each year?;
   (g) has the overdue percentage of total receivables gone up?

5. Ask yourself if those figures are likely to change in the future (be very self-critical on this point – generate the widest managerial discussion before a decision).

6. Decide on future loss probability: low and no problems; acceptable levels; or too high for comfort.

7. Decide what is the bad debt value or percentage of sales in the *next* three years that would be 'painful' – however you define that. Could it happen? Are you sure? How much would you pay to ensure that no pain occurs?

8. *Now* look into the credit insurance cover available to you (bear in mind your cost limits for the profit protection).

Table 12.1 Sample 'who owes what' (WOW) analysis of debtors
by size

Number of accounts	%	Size of debts	Total value	%
8	0.3	£100,000+	£1,348,869	13.5
47	1.6	£25,001–100,000	£2,331,064	23.3
546	18.1	£5,001–25,000	£4,324,593	43.2
417	13.8	£1,001–5,001	£1,586,084	15.8
620	20.6	£101–1,001	£342,166	3.4
1,375	45.6	£0–100	£72,750	0.8
3,013	100.0		£10,005,526	100.0

Note: A computer can easily produce this kind of display. Even
non-computerised companies should make a WOW analysis at
least once a year. The display often surprises managements in
showing how few customers owe most of the revenue and how
many small accounts there are. It can be used to decide where
efforts should be applied to risk control and collection work.

9. In broad terms, consider the options of the following:
    (a) total cover – of your good accounts as well as your risky ones,
        for a *low rate* of premium percentage per £100 of sales value;
    (b) selective cover – only *your selection* of expected bad debt risks at
        a *high rate* of premium, but possibly a *low total cost* in £s and as a
        percentage of total sales;
    (c) 'Catastrophe' cover – you suffer losses yourself up to an agreed
        annual total, then the insurer picks up 100% of any further
        losses, i.e., really unexpected ones. Because nobody expects
        these losses, there is a *low rate* of premium as a percentage of
        sales.
10. In deciding, and subsequently negotiating, the form of cover
    required, traders should calculate what coinsurance percentage
    (self-retention) they can afford to take. The premium charged by
    the insurance company picking up only 75% instead of 85% of any
    loss can be significantly lower.
11. Finally, be sure that the insurer is willing to cover your actual
    customers and debts, i.e., that you can get the credit limits you
    need (or, if it is necessary, that they approve your particular system
    of credit control). Be prepared to negotiate hard on these points,
    but also be willing to listen to the warning signals if the insurer
    thinks your risks are unacceptable to them.

WHO DOESN'T NEED CREDIT INSURANCE?

The devil's advocate approach is always useful in testing the need: *if* you have access to extensive and privileged information on all your major buyers;
and you have qualified credit staff operating first-class systems;
and you have a credit manager of the highest calibre;
and a trained deputy able to take over at a moment's notice;
or you have such a wide spread of risks that no conceivable collapse of a single customer, industry or country could harm your profits;
or your resources are so huge that you (and your shareholders) could shrug off a string of major credit losses . . .
then the case for credit insurance is only marginal.

There are companies who, although they can claim most of these advantages, still appreciate the vital difference between an adviser who gives an opinion without commitment and a partner who takes a firm decision to share a known risk. That is credit insurance.

CONCLUSION

Credit insurance, whether for exports or home trade or both, must be purchased for the right reasons and not neglected for the wrong ones. It must be in the right form to suit the culture of the company and be set up and managed in a way that avoids irritating clashes on unsatisfactory credit decisions. The company must feel that the cover helps them to do more and better business. It must provide financial stability by containing those exposures which represent the greatest risk to profits and reserves. Unless these objectives can be achieved more effectively and economically by other means, then the objective decision can only be that credit insurance is the best vehicle for achieving them.

Glossary of terms

vwvwvwvwvwvwvwvw

Acceleration clause   Contractual provision which enables a creditor to obtain judgement for all outstanding instalments of a debt if any one is unpaid.

All-vetting policy   'Spread' policy with no discretionary limit.

'As and when' terms   A payment condition under which the buyer is only liable to pay as and when he receives payment from his own principal (also conditional subcontract).

Bad debt   The value of a sale which has to be written off as lost due to its uncollectability.

Ballooning   Terms of payment for medium-term credit under which the later instalments are increased so that earlier ones can be reduced.

Berne Union   The International Union of Credit and Investment Insurers.

Bill of exchange   A simple document, meeting the strict definition of the Bills of Exchange Act 1882 and drawn up by a seller to show the amount and payment date of a debt, requiring the buyer either to pay it or to accept it, by signing it, as a future obligation.

Capitalised interest   In medium-term debt, the amalgamation of principal and the total interest, and the division of the total sum into equal instalments instead of reducing the interest on reducing capital balances.

Cash discount   A contractual payment condition which allows a stated percentage of an invoice to be deducted if paid by a certain date.

Cash flow   An expression used in different ways in business. The most common use, preferred in this book, is the difference between cash received and cash paid out, in a given period.

Closing out   Settling a forward exchange sale by purchasing currency at the 'spot' rate (because the expected receivables have not been collected).

Coinsurance   Sharing of a risk by two or more insurers. One leads, the others follow on his terms and conditions. Also confusingly used to describe the uninsured percentage or portion of a risk.

Collaboration agreement   Agreement on underwriting terms and recovery action between export credit insurers, e.g., when one is insuring the main contract and the other a conditional subcontract.

Collection agency   A commercial company which undertakes collection of a seller's overdue debts from customers for an agreed fee.

Commitment cover   In 'spread' underwriting, an undertaking by an insurer to maintain conditions of cover unchanged. Most commercial credit insurers are committed to covering firm contracts already in hand when they reduce or withdraw a credit limit. ECGD has recently agreed to give to selected exporters undertakings to cover business on existing terms and conditions in specified markets regardless of changes in the normal country conditions.

Conditional subcontract   See 'as and when' terms.

Credit enhancement   A device by which a company's credit rating is improved, e.g., a financial insurance policy to raise a Standard and Poor's 'AA' rating to 'AAA'.

Credit limit   A value decided by a seller up to which credit can be allowed on sales to a customer, i.e., an assessment of the maximum amount a customer can probably afford to pay by the due date. In credit insurance practice, the limit (as defined in the policy) to the insurer's liability for loss on a named buyer.

Crédit mixte   In medium and long-term credit, a mixture of government-aid funds and government-insured commercial funds.

Datum line cover   A form of risk-sharing in which only accounts exceeding a certain level of outstandings are insured.

Deadweight debt   Debt on which the debtor cannot afford to pay the accumulated interest.

Discretionary limit   A figure of outstandings below which the insurer does not underwrite credit limits but expects the insured to justify his discretion in the event of a claim (also discretionary trading limit or non-vetting limit).

Double financing   The raising of excess funds, e.g., by a distributor on credit sales which have already been financed by the credit given by the manufacturer to the distributor.

DSO   Abbreviation for days sales outstanding, being the ratio of unpaid debts to total sales. The DSO expresses the average time to turn sales into cash.

End-buyer paper   Bills of exchange, promissory notes or other instruments held by a distributor to secure credit given to his buyers.

Ex gratia   'As an act of grace': an insurer may make an *ex gratia* payment against a claim for which he has no strict liability, e.g., when an insured cause of loss has occurred but the insured has failed to fulfil some minor term of the policy. Contributions to salvage costs are sometimes paid *ex gratia*.

Facultative reinsurance   A specific reinsurance for large or unusual risks which fall outside a quota share treaty.

Financial default exclusion   At Lloyd's, the mandatory exclusion of loss arising from insolvency or default of a private sector buyer.

Five Great Powers   China, France, United Kingdom, USA, USSR.

Full percentage facility   In ECGD extended terms cover, 100% indemnity given at underwriters' discretion in certain markets after the first year's payments have been made satisfactorily.

FX   The standard abbreviation for foreign exchange. Used in exporting to refer to a currency other than the seller's.

Going-concern basis The valuation of a company's assets on the assumption that it will continue to trade. (NB In a gone-concern valuation, a break-up situation, the assets are always worth less than their book value, while liabilities remain as large as ever).

Hands on Colloquial expression from the USA meaning 'personally performing a task', rather than viewing it theoretically or delegating to others.

ICIA The International Credit Insurance Association.

Inadmissible goods Non-UK goods specified by the Department of Trade as inadmissible for ECGD support, e.g., to prevent unfair competition with UK manufacturers, protect endangered species, etc.

Inception date Date on which an insurer's liability commences.

Liquidity The ability of a company to meet its current debts out of its turnover of current assets.

Losses occurring Cover only applying to losses occurring during the policy period even though the risks may have attached before the inception date (see risks attaching).

Marginal risk The extreme area of risk in business taken on credit.

Margin cover An additional amount of loss to cover costs incurred in 'closing out' a forward foreign exchange contract.

Market limit In export credit, the maximum amount of liabilities which an insurer wishes to assume in a particular country.

Matching credit In capital goods and project-type business, agreed procedures for matching terms which a competing insurer is known to be offering and which exceed the international consensus.

Negative covenant See restrictive covenant.

Negative vetting Relaxed underwriting of small credit limits provided nothing adverse is known.

OECD The Organisation for Economic Cooperation and Development to which 22 major developed nations contribute information, financial support and economic planning.

P & L Profit and loss account, the book entries to accumulate all the business's income and expenditure in a period.

Private market Generic term for all non-government providers of credit or political risk insurance.

Progress payments See stage payments.

Quota share reinsurance A blanket treaty under which all the reinsurers take agreed shares of all risks written by the prime insurer within specified limits of size and substance (see also facultative reinsurance).

Quick ratio (or 'acid test') The ratio of a company's liquidity after excluding stocks/inventories, i.e., its ability to meet current debts from cash and near-cash such as debtors.

Recourse agreement In ECGD-supported *supplier credit*, the exporter undertakes to pay to ECGD any sum which ECGD has paid under its guarantee to the bank which it would not have paid to the exporter under his credit insurance policy. In *buyer credit*, his maximum liability is limited to a percentage of the total facility and ECGD can only exercise recourse if the exporter is in default under the contract.

Recourse indemnity   An indemnity given by Lloyd's to ECGD at the exporter's expense to enable ECGD to raise its recourse limit in suitable cases.

Receiver   Person appointed by a debenture holder (usually a bank) to take control of a borrower's business with a view to recovering the lender's debt. A receiver has powerful legal rights.

Reservation of property rights   A provision either in the contract of sale or by a separate instrument (e.g., a chattel mortgage) under which the seller retains property in the goods until final payment is made.

Reserves   Accounting entries which set aside a portion of profits against possible future losses or costs.

Restrictive covenant   An undertaking by a buyer not to incur significant new liabilities, e.g., major borrowings, nor to forfeit assets or securities, e.g., parent company loans, without the seller's approval. It may include the maintenance of financial ratios.

Retention of title   A contractual provision under which goods sold remain the property of the seller until final payment is received. (Unless the buyer is contractually liable for any shortfall, there may be no insurable loss.)

Risks attaching   Cover only applying to risks attaching during the policy period (see losses occurring).

Risk categories   Codings applied to customers or markets to indicate the degree of risk, e.g., 'A' = no risk, 'B' = average, 'C' = high risk.

Roll over (roll forward)   Subject to satisfactory experience, and amended terms if appropriate, the insurer extends the cover for a period equal to the expired period. Thus a five-year risk might be covered for the first three years with successive rollovers after the first two years. Not to be confused with a five-year commitment. In foreign exchange, a forward commitment is often rolled over, usually at some cost to the seller.

Securitised debt   Collections of individual debts, e.g., property mortgages, 'packaged' for the purpose of sale or use as collateral security.

Self-insurance   Not insurance at all, but a decision to bear losses rather than pay an insurance premium. Also confusingly used to describe the uninsured percentage.

Seller's risk insurance   An insurance which holds the seller covered if title to the goods reverts to him, e.g., if the buyer fails to take up documents. Usually an extension to an open transit cover.

Shortfall undertaking   In export, the buyer's undertaking to make up any shortfall in a local currency deposit due to devaluation in a transfer situation.

Solvency   The excess of a company's total assets over its external liabilities, i.e., its overall ability to meet its commitments.

Sovereign debt   Debt for which a government has assumed direct liability, e.g., rescheduled transfer losses.

Split risk   An export risk involving more than one overseas country, e.g., shipment to a destination outside the buyer's country.

Stage payments Payments to be made during the execution of a contract usually but not necessarily related to the delivery of goods.

Subrogation An insurer's right, having paid a loss, to any rights of recovery open to the insured.

Tail-end risk If outstandings exceed an insured credit limit, any payment received allows part of the uncovered portion to be brought into the cover until only the insured limit, the 'tail end' is left. Under a turnover-declaring policy, premium is payable on all the turnover because the insurer is committed to covering all the outstandings.

Term agreement The insurer quotes terms and conditions for, typically, a three-year period but in the form of three separate one-year policies. This is important in any division of insured loss and 'first loss' for each policy year.

Transfer risk The danger that the buyer's country will have insufficient hard currency available to enable the invoiced amount to be remitted to the seller on the contractual date even though the buyer has paid the local currency.

Under-capitalised The situation of a company which has inadequate assets and reserves to finance its current activity – usually exemplified by stretching payments to suppliers.

Unwinding An exporter wishing to withdraw from a forward foreign-exchange commitment may be able to 'unwind' at lower cost than waiting for the delivery date and 'closing out'.

'Who owes what' analysis A summary display of a seller's accounts from his sales ledger, grouped by size of balances, showing the number of accounts in each size group, the percentage it represents of all accounts, each group's combined value and percentage of the total. Useful for determining the spread of risk and comparing debt values with acceptable losses.

Working capital The excess of a company's current assets over its current liabilities, indicating the surplus funds available for current activity.

Appendix A

A short history of credit insurance in the United Kingdom

vwvwvwvwvwvwvwvw

THE EARLY BEGINNINGS

In mid-nineteenth-century England, when the distributive sector was burgeoning, merchants and manufacturers had to protect themselves as best they could from the credit risks of a growing volume of sales to wholesale traders. The British Commercial Insurance Company had been formed in 1820 in the expectation that credit insurance could be provided 'with perfect safety and certain profit to the company and benefit to the public'. Its activities are not well recorded but it appears to have done only a small amount of business before being amalgamated and eventually wound up in the 1860s. It had, however, acknowledged that the quality of debt varied between trades. Trade in staple goods was regarded as a 'common' risk. Sales by woollen drapers, hosiers and retail drapers were a 'hazardous' risk while trade in all kinds of fancy goods was 'doubly hazardous'.

The Debt Insurance Society, formed in 1871, itself became insolvent as the result of a financial crisis in Australia in 1893. Two years later the Ocean Accident and Guarantee Corporation began to write credit insurance and made a valuable contribution by abandoning the practice of selection of risks by the insured and insisting on covering all of a company's credit sales. This was the 'English–Hamburg' system or, as we now know it, 'whole turnover' or 'spread' underwriting, the principle which has governed most domestic and export credit insurance for many years.

In the late 1890s a group of Lloyd's underwriters who had already covered some credit risks under the leadership of Cuthbert Heath, the 'father of Lloyd's', set up the Excess Insurance Company which eventually took part in the British Trade Corporation formed by the Board of Trade during the First World War. In March 1918 the Trade Indemnity Company was registered, the major shareholders being the British Trade Corporation, the Excess Insurance Company and C. E. Heath and Company.

Although he never achieved his ambition of a credit insurance market at Lloyd's, Cuthbert Heath remained a director of Trade Indemnity for many years.

The potential for a Lloyd's market was frustrated by a scandal which engulfed a not very successful underwriter named Harrison who wrote financial default policies to support the financing of hire-purchase debt on motor cars and taxi cabs. Having embroiled himself with the dubious Industrial Guarantee Corporation, he generated premium income by insuring unsold vehicles still in the hands of dealers and by covering accommodation bills, bills of exchange drawn and accepted, not to finance trade transactions, but simply to be discounted in the money market. Having also been persuaded to underwrite fictitious sales of taxi cabs, he collapsed in a welter of unpaid claims and his own fraudulent accounts. His obligations were discharged by a unique policy underwritten by every member of Lloyd's. Ever since, the insurance of financial default has been forbidden in the Lloyd's market.

Shortly after these events Cuthbert Heath formulated his famous eight principles:

1. Credit insurance should be concerned with credit risks for goods sold and delivered by merchants and manufacturers to their customers on credit terms in the normal course of business.
2. The cover should be against loss due to the insolvency of the customer and the debt should be admitted as a claim against the insolvent estate.
3. A credit insurance policy should not guarantee payment of a debt at due date and should not cover disputed items.
4. Insured debts should be self-liquidating, preferably out of the proceeds of onward sale of goods by the debtors.
5. Terms of payment for the goods should be normal for the type of transaction and credits should be short or medium term – two or three years at the outside – for capital goods.
6. A credit insurance policy should not cover more than 75% of a risk and it should be a condition that the insured retain the uninsured part for his own account.
7. Insurance of existing commitments, including current contracts, should be avoided.
8. Financial credits such as loans by banks or finance houses should not be insured.

Although Trade Indemnity had covered some overseas insolvency risks, the polarisation of commercial and export credit insurance was completed in 1932 when ECGD introduced transfer risk cover in response to mounting apprehension over the worldwide abandonment of the gold standard and the threat of exchange controls in many countries. For some 50 years thereafter ECGD and Trade Indemnity held their respective virtual monopolies, ECGD being constituted as a Department of Government in 1937 with the passing of the Export Guarantees Act.

THE POST-WAR OPPORTUNITY

The immediate post-1945 period was marked by the concentration on whole turnover cover to ensure adequate spread and to support the best terms and quality of cover. Although from about 1960 Trade Indemnity adopted a more flexible approach, it was not until the early 1980s that ECGD acknowledged the need to compromise with those companies who, because they could bear a greater share of their risks, rejected the whole turnover concept.

Trade Indemnity continued to build up its store of credit information and its close surveillance of credit patterns in individual trades. It often played the 'caretaker' role, exerting a steadying influence on a company in difficulties by keeping credit to a prudent level but giving both the debtor and his suppliers the assurance of continued support.

In 1956 efforts to set up the Credit and Guarantee Insurance Company in direct competition with Trade Indemnity were thwarted by the Capital Issues Committee and when it was finally registered with a much reduced capital, it operated only as underwriting manager for the New Era Insurance Company of the National Employers Mutual Group. For two or three years before this Norwich Union had written hire-purchase default insurance but withdrew when government restrictions were relaxed in 1958. In 1960 the Norwich embarked on a domestic credit insurance venture using the Credit Indemnity Company, a subsidiary of a specialist broker, as its underwriting agent. This business was terminated after some three years when the Norwich decided to reduce the overall exposure of its Accident Branch.

In 1975 Credit and Guarantee Insurance Company was reconstituted under the ownership of British, Danish and Dutch insurance interests and proceeded to develop its distinctive style of specific risk and surety underwriting.

Two important newcomers arrived on the scene in the early 1980s, American International Underwriters and PanFinancial Insurance Company, previously the credit insurance operation of the British National

Insurance Company. AIU at first only wrote specific political risks, adding its Comprehensive Export Credit Policy later, whereas Pan-Financial entered the market with Insolvency Catastrophe Insurance and branched out into specific political risks in 1985.

In export credit, ECGD had decided on a strategy of maximum spread and minimum selection; between 1945 and 1949 its insured turnover quadrupled from £52 million to nearly £200 million. In the 1950s and 1960s a perceived obligation to offer cover to almost all comers, the insistence on whole turnover and the absence of effective competition allowed the Department's business to expand relentlessly. Major transfer situations in Brazil, Colombia and Chile brought political risks into the foreground. The upsurge in project business (financed with OPEC dollars) and extended terms cover for semi-capital goods and the coupling of preferential export finance to basic cover then combined to drive insured turnover to a peak in 1982–3 of over £19 billion. ECGD's 'market share', the proportion of non-oil exports covered, rose to 37.6% in 1976–7 but fell to below 20% ten years later. Nearly 12,000 policies contracted to fewer than 9,000.

Like all the 'official' insurers, ECGD took heavy losses in the Iranian revolution and has since seen its cash reserves wiped out by transfer claims in over 40 countries.

Approaching the end of a decade which has bred opportunities, encouraged competition and stimulated some radical thinking, we find ourselves attempting a very different book from the one we might have offered ten years ago.

Appendix B

Summary of major official export credit insurers

vwvwvwvwvwvwvwvwvw

All the official insurers now offer combined credit and political risk cover and write both spread and specific risks but they vary in their interpretation of the acceptable spread of risks. All provide cover for the pre-shipment risk but sometimes only within spread policies. Names and addresses are included in appendix C and for fuller details we recommend *Export Credit Financing Systems in OECD Member Countries* (ISBN 92–64–12291–5) published by the OECD.

Australia	EFIC	Government corporation.
Belgium	OND	State-guaranteed public agency. Exporter must enter into underlying insurance agreement with OND before any cover, spread or specific, can be offered.
Canada	EDC	Crown corporation which also participates directly in financing of large contracts.
Denmark	EKR	Autonomous council responsible to Minister of Industry and financed from the Government-guaranteed Danish Trade Fund.
Finland	VTL	Government agency.
France	COFACE	Government-controlled company.
German Federal Republic	HERMES	Private insurance company underwriting for account of government.
Japan	MITI	Department of Ministry of Trade and Industry but most underwriting is delegated to trade associations.
Netherlands	NCM	Privately owned insurance company reinsured by government for political and exceptional commercial risks. Exporter can offer political

risks only but most prefer combined commercial and political cover.

New Zealand	EXGO	State-owned corporation under administration of State Insurance Office. Whole turnover comprehensive cover is preferred for short-term credit but specific policies covering commercial and/or political risk are offered for longer-term business.
Norway	GIEK	Government agency.
Sweden	EKN	Government agency.
Switzerland	GERG	Government agency but underwriting delegated to trade associations.
United Kingdom	ECGD	Self-accounting department of government.
United States	FCIA	Consortium of insurance companies underwriting for account of EXIMBANK.

Appendix C

Members of the International Union of Credit and Investment Insurers (Berne Union)

vwvwvwvwvwvwvwvwvwvw

Secretariat	Telephone (44 1) 409 2008
17/18 Dover Street	Telex 28263 (EGERTN G)
London W1X 3PB	FOR BERNE UNION
	Telefax 629 0559

ARGENTINA (CASC)

Compania Argentina de Seguros de	Telephone (54 1) 394 7171
Crédito a la Exportacion S.A.	394 7777
Sarmiento 440–4° Piso	394 7979
1347 Buenos Aires	Telex 24207 CASC AR

AUSTRALIA (EFIC)

Export Finance & Insurance	*Mailing Address*
Corporation	PO Box R 65
Export House	Royal Exchange
9th & 10th Floors	NSW 2000
22 Pitt Street	Telephone (61 2) 231–2655
Sydney, NSW	Telex EFIC AA 21224
	Telefax (02) 251 3851

AUSTRIA (OEKB)

Oesterreichische Kontrollbank	*Mailing Address*
Aktiengesellschaft	Postfach 70
Abteilung Exportgarantien	A-1011 Vienna
Strauchgasse	Telephone (43 222) 53127–0 or Ext.
A-1011 Vienna	Telex 132785 OKBE A
	Telefax (43 222) 53127–250
	(Panafax UV-400)

BELGUIM (OND)

Office National du Ducroire
Square de Meeûs 40
B–1040 Brussels

Telephone (32 2) 512 38 00
Telex 21147 OND B
Telefax 010 32 2 513 50 59

CANADA (EDC)

Export Development Corporation
151 O'Connor Street
Ottawa
Ontario

Mailing Address
Box 655
Ottawa, Ontario KIP 5T9
Telephone (1 613) 598–2500
Telex EXCREDCORP OTT 0534136
Telefax 237–2690 (Xerox 495)

CYPRUS REPUBLIC (ECIS)

Export Credit Insurance Service
Ministry of Commerce & Industry
Nicosia

Telephone (357 2) 40 –3441
Telex 2283 MINCOMIND CY

DENMARK (EKR)

Eksportkreditradet
Codanhus, Gl. Kongevej 60
DK-1850 Copenhagen V

Telephone (45 1) 31 38 25
Telex 22910 DEF DK
Telefax 01 31 24 25

FINLAND (VTL)

Vientitakuulaitos
Eteläranta 6
SF-00131 Helsinki 13

Mailing Address
PO Box 187
SF- 00131 Helsinki 13
Telephone (358 0) 661811
Telex 121778 VTL SF
Telefax +358 0 651 181
(Nefax 3500)

FRANCE (COFACE)

Compagnie Française d'Assurance
pour le Commerce Extérieur
12 Cours Michelet
La Défense 10
92800 PUTEAUX

Mailing Address
Cédex 51
F-92065 PARIS La Défense
Telephone (33 1) 49 02 20 00
Telex ASEXP Z 614884 F
Telefax 49 02 20 49

(SFAC)
Société Française d'Assurance
Crédit
1 rue Euler
75008 Paris

Mailing Address
19x Cedex 10
F-75460 Paris
Telephone (33 1) 4070 50 50
Telex SFAFC A 630850 F

GERMANY (HERMES)

Hermes Kreditversicherungs-
Aktiengesellschaft
Friedensallee 254
Hamburg-Bahrenfeld

Mailing Address
Postfach 50 07 40
D-2000 Hamburg 50
Telephone (49 40) 88 70
Telex HK D 212631–90
Telefax (040) 887 7744(a)

(TREUARBEIT)
Treuarbeit
Aktiengesellschaft
New York-Ring 13
Hamburg

Mailing Address
Postfach 60 27 20
D-2000 Hamburg 60
Telephone (49 40) 6378–0
Telex TAHH D 2174118
Telefax (49 40) 6378 103
(Group 3. Tenofax 31)

HONG KONG (HKEC)

Hong Kong Export Credit
Insurance Corporation
South Seas Centre, Tower 1
2nd Floor, 75 Mody Road
Tsimshatsui East
Kowloon
Hong Kong

Mailing Address
Box 98548 TST Post Office
Hong Kong
Telephone (852 3) 7233883
Telex HKXC HX 56200
Telefax 852 3 7226227
Group 3

INDIA (ECGC)

Export Credit Guarantee Corporation
of India Limited
10th Floor, Express Towers
Nariman Point
Bombay 400 021

Mailing Address
PO Box 373
Bombay 400 021
Telephone (91 22) 202 2587
          202 4852
          202 6768
Telex ECGC IN 11 3231

ISRAEL (IFTRIC)

The Israel Foreign Trade Risks
Insurance Corporation Ltd
65 Petah Tikva Road
Tel Aviv 61201
Israel

Mailing Address
PO Box 20215
65 Petah Tikva Rd.
Tel Aviv 61201
Telephone (972 3) 5611351
Telex IFTI IL 341179
Telefax (972 3) 5610313
Ricoh Model FX210 (Group 2 X3)

ITALY (SACE)

Sezione Speciale per l'Assicurazione
del Credito all'Esportazione
Piazza Poli 37
00100 Rome

Mailing Address
CP 253 Roma Centro
Telephone (39 6) 67361
Telex 613160 SACE I
Telefax 0039 6 6736225
(ITT 3533 Group 2 & 3)

(SIAC)
Società Italiana Assicurazione
Crediti S.p.A.
Via Raffaello Matarazzo 19
00139 Rome

Mailing Address
Casella Postale 2446 A.D.
I-00108 Rome
Telephone (39 6) 81691
Telex 620616 SIACREDI
Telefax 8820424
        8820413
        8820548
        8820512

JAMAICA (EXIMJ)

National Export-Import Bank
of Jamaica Limited
Bank of Jamaica Building
Nethersole Place
Kingston

Mailing Address
PO Box 3
Kingston, Jamaica W.I.
Telephone (1 809) 92 29690
Telex 2165 RESERVE JA
        2167

JAPAN (EID/MITI)

Export Insurance Divison
International Trade Administration
Bureau
Ministry of International Trade &
Industry
1–3–1 Kasumigaseki
Chiyoda-ku
Tokyo 100

Telephone (81 3) 501–1665
Telex EIDMITI J 22916
28576

EID/MITI – LONDON

Export Insurance Division
127 Cheapside
London EC2G 6BP

Telephone (44 1) 606 2500/2509
Telex 886079 EIDLDN G
Telefax 600 8107

KOREA (EIBK)

The Export-Import Bank of Korea
16–1, Yoido-Dong, Youngdungpo-Gu
SEOUL 150

Mailing Address
Yoido PO Box 641
Seoul 150
Telephone (784) 1021, 7071
Telex EXIMBK K 26595
Telefax 784 1030

EIBK–LONDON

The Export–Import Bank of Korea
Plantation House
31–35 Fenchurch Street
London EC3M 3DX

Telephone (44 1) 623 1831
Telex 8812140 EXIMBK G

MALAYSIA (MECIB)

Malaysia Export Credit Insurance
Berhad
29–3 & 29–4 Jalan Medan Tuanku
50734 Kuala Lumpur

Mailing Address
PO Box 11048
50734 Kuala Lumpur
Telephone (60 3) 2910782
Telex EXCRED MA 31190
Telefax (60 3) 2910353

MEXICO (FOMEX)

Fondo para el Fomento de las
Exportaciones de Productos
Manufacturados
Banco Nacional de Comercio Exterior
SA
Camino A Santa Teresa No. 1679
Colonia Jardines Del Pedregal
Delegacion Alvaro Obregon
CP 01900 MEXICO DF

Mailing Address
App No. 389
Telephone (52 5) 652 6600
    (52 5) 652 6738
Telex BNCEME 1764393
    BNCEME 176494/95
Telefax 52 5 6526662
    52 5 6526703

NETHERLANDS (NCM)

Nederlandsche Credietverzekering
Maatschappij NV
Keizersgracht 271–285
1016 ED Amsterdam

Mailing Address
Postbus 473
NL 1000 AL Amsterdam
Telephone (31 20) 5539111
Telex 11496 NCM NL
Telefax 20–5532811

NEW ZEALAND (EXGO)

Export Guarantee Office
State Insurance Building
143 Lambton Quay
Wellington 1

Mailing Address
State Insurance Building
Box 5037
Wellington
Telephone (64 4) 720 –265
Telex STATINS NZ 31239
    FOR EXGO
Telefax (64 4) 725 824

NORWAY (GIEK)

Garanti-Instituttet for Eksportkredit
Dronning Mauds gt 15 IV
0250 Oslo 2

Mailing Address
Postboks 1763 Vika
0122 Oslo 1
Telephone (47 2) 20 51 40
Telex 76783 GIEK N
Telefax 42 68 55

PORTUGAL (COSEC)

Companhia de Seguro de Créditos, EP
Avenida da Republica 58
1094 Lisbon Codex

Telephone (351 1) 760131/766055
Telex 12885 COSEC P
Telefax (19) 734 614 (m)

SINGAPORE (ECICS)

Export Credit Insurance Corporation
of Singapore Limited
10 Shenton Way
17–03/09 MAS Building
Singapore 0207

Telephone (65) 220–8344
Telex ECICS RS 21524
Telefax 2242887
    (Toshiba Model 6350)

SOUTH AFRICA (CGIC)

Credit Guarantee Insurance
Corporation of Africa Limited
Credit Guarantee House
31 Dover Street
Randburg 2194
Johannesburg

Mailing Address
PO Box 9244
Johannesburg 2000
Telephone (27 11) 886 3010
Telex 420508 + 426525 SA
Telefax 27 11 886 1027
    (Group 3)

SPAIN (CESCE)

Compania Espanola de Seguros de
Crédito a la Exportacion, S.A.
Velazquez, 74 Telex
28001 - Madrid

Telephone (34 1) 401 70 00
        401 30 62
Telex 45369 CESCE E
    23577
Telefax 435 61 75

(CESCC)
Compania Espanola de Seguros
de Crédito y Caucion S.A.
Raimundo Fernandez Villaverde 61
E–Madrid 3

Mailing Address
Apartado Correos 524
E–28023 Madrid
Telephone (34 1) 253 6800/8704
Telex 43163 SCYCE
Telefax (34 1) 253 7685

SRI LANKA (SLECIC)

Sri Lanka Export Credit Insurance
Corporation
278/5 Union Place
Colombo 2

Mailing Address
PO Box 2213
Colombo 2
Telephone (94–1) 547508/9
        22815
        22806
Telex 21404 SLECIC CE

SWEDEN (EKN)

Exportkreditnämnden
Norrlandsgatan 15
Stockholm

Mailing address
Box 7334
S-103 90 Stockholm
Telephone (46 8) 23 58 30
Telex 17657 EKN S
Telefax + 46 8 11 81 49
    (Nefax 3500)
    (CCITT group 1 & 2)

SWITZERLAND (GERG)

Geschäftsstelle für die
Exportrisikogarantie
Kirchenweg 8
CH-8032 Zürich

Mailing Address
Postfach
CH-8032 Zürich
Telephone (41 1) 47 66 54
Telex 816519 VSM CH

(FEDERAL)
The Federal Insurance Company
Limited
(Eidgenössische Versicherungs-
Aktiengesellschaft)
Flössergasse 3
CH-8039 Zürich

Mailing Address
Postfach
CH-8039 Zürich
Telephone (41 1) 208 44 22
Telex 815353 FED CH
Telefax (41 1) 2012804
    Type Panafax UF-400
    (CCITT- G 3/2A)

UNITED KINGDOM (ECGD)

Export Credits Guarantee Department
PO Box 272
Export House
50 Ludgate Hill
London EC4M 7AY

Telephone (44 1) 382 7000
Telex 883601 ECGDHQ G
Telefax 1 382 7649
    (Canon 401H Group 3)

ECGD–CARDIFF
Crown Building
Cathays Park
Cardiff CF1 3NH

Telephone (44 222) 824100
Telex 497305 ECGDCF
Telefax 0222 824003

(TIC)
Trade Indemnity plc
Trade Indemnity House
12/34 Great Eastern Street
London EC2A 3AX

Telephone (44 1) 739 4311
Telex 21227 TICLON G
Telefax 729 7682

UNITED STATES OF AMERICA (EXIMBANK)

Export-Import Bank of the United
States
811 Vermont Avenue NW
Washington DC 20571

Telephone (1 202) 566–2117
Telex EXIBANK 89461
(In-Safe No) 6710607 EXIBANK
Telefax 202 566 7524

(FCIA)
Foreign Credit Insurance Association
40 Rector Street
New York NY 10006

Telephone (1 212) 306–5000
Telex 428807 FCIA NY
    428818
Telefax 1 212 306 5099
    (Rapicom 330)

(OPIC)
Overseas Private Investment
Corporation
1615 M Street N.W.
Washington DC 20527

Telephone (1 202) 457 7200
Telex 440227 OPIC UI
Telefax 202 457 7158

ZIMBABWE (ZCIC)

Zimbabwe Credit Insurance
Corporation Limited
67/69 Second Street
Harare

Mailing Address
PO Box 1085
Harare
Telephone (263 0) 738944/8
    706101/5
Telex 4424 ZCIC ZW
Telefax (263 0) 732945
    (c/o M&G)

NB The telephone numbers shown include the United Kingdom call prefix.

Appendix D

Members of the International Credit Insurance Association (ICIA)

vwvwvwvwvwvwvwvw

MAILING ADDRESS	OFFICE ADDRESS

ARGENTINA

Aseguradora de Créditos y Garantias SA San Martin 379 1004 Buenos Aires Argentina	San Martin 379 Buenos Aires Telephone: (1) 394–1018 1023 1076 1154 Telex 24334 JUNCA AR Telefax: (1) 393 2566

AUSTRALIA

Trade Indemnity Australia Limited 267 Collins Street Melbourne Victoria 3000 Australia	7th Floor 267 Collins Street Melbourne Telephone: (3) 654 3322 Telex: 31341 TICMEL AA Telefax: (3) 654 7350

AUSTRIA

Österreichische Kreditversicherungs- Aktiengesellschaft Postfach 237 A-1011 Wien Austria	Stubenring 24 Wien Telephone (222) 51 5540 Telex: 112756 OEKV A Telefax: (222) 52 4415

BELGIUM

Compagnie Belge d'Assurance-Crédit
S.A. (COBAC)

15 Rue Montoyer	15 Rue Montoyer
B-1040 Bruxelles	Bruxelles
Belgium	Telephone (2) 513 8930
	513 9530
	Telex: 22337 CREDAS B
	Telefax: (2) 513 8621

CZECHOSLOVAKIA

Ceska Státni Pojistovna
(Section Credit)

PO Box 841	Nove Mesto Spalena 16
114 00 Prague	Praha
Czechoslovakia	Telephone: (2) 29 8641
	Telex: 121112 CPOJC
	Telefax: (2) 29 9146
	CSP Foreinsure 1

DENMARK

Dansk Kautionsforsikrings-
Aktieselskab

PO Box 2168	Gl. Torv 14
DK-1016 Copenhagen K	Kobenhavn
Denmark	Telephone: (1) 91 1900
	Telex: 16414 DANKAU DK
	Telefax: (1) 12 4730

Copenhagen Credit Insurance Co. Ltd

PO Box 2168	Vestergade 5
DK-1016 Copenhagen K	Kobenhavn
Denmark	Telephone: (1) 91 19 11
	Telex: 27127 GARANT DK
	Telefax: (1) 91 19 17

FINLAND

Pohjola Insurance Company Ltd

Lapinmaentie 1	Lapinmaentie 1
SF-00300 Helsinki 30	Helsinki
Finland	Telephone: (0) 5591
	Telex: 124556 PLA SF
	Telefax: (0) 565 2205

FRANCE

Société Française d'Assurance
Crédit (SFAC)
19 Cedex 10
F-75460 Paris
France

1 Rue Euler
Paris 8e
Telephone: (1) 4070 50 50
Telex: 630850 SFAFC F
Telefax: (1) 4070 50 17

Compagnie Française d'Assurances
Pour le Commerce Extérieur
(COFACE)
Cedex 51
F- 92065 Paris - La Defense
France

12 Cours Michelet
La Defense 10, Puteaux
92800 Puteaux
Telephone: (1) 4902 20 00
Telex: 614884 ASEXPOR
Telefax: (1) 4902 20 47

Caisse Franco-Néerlandaise
de Cautionnments
82 Rue Saint-Lazare
F-75009 Paris
France

82 Rue Saint-Lazare
Paris 9e
Telephone: (1) 4285 46 20
                 4874 56 40
Telex: 283069 FRANCAU
Telefax: (1) 4281 29 19

GERMANY

Allgemeine Kreditversicherung
Aktiengesellschaft
Postfach 1209
D- 6500 Mainz 1
Germany

Ernst-Ludwig-Strasse 2
Mainz
Telephone: (6131) 1431
Telex: 4187676 AKV D
Telefax: (6131) 22 47 11

Gerling-Konzern Speziale
Kreditversicherungs- AG
Postfach 10 08 08
D-5000 Koln 1
Germany

Hohenzollernring 62
Koln
Telephone: (221) 1441
Telex: 881132 GK D
Telefax: (221) 144 3970

Hermes Kreditversicherungs-
Aktiengesellschaft
Postfach 50 07 40
D-2000 Hamburg 50
Germany

Friedensallee 254
Hamburg-Bahrenfeld
Telephone: (40) 8870
Telex: 2126310 HK D
Telefax: (40) 887 7744

GREECE

'L 'Ethniki'
Société Anonyme Héllenique
d'Assurances Générales
Rue Karageorghi Servias 8
Athens 105.62
Greece

Rue Karageorghi Servias 8
Athenae
Telephone: (1) 3222 121/9
Telex: 215400 ETAS GR
Telefax: not available.

IRELAND

The Insurance Corp. of Ireland plc
Burlington House
Burlington Road
Dublin 4
Ireland

Burlington House
Burlington Road
Dublin 4
Telephone: (31) 601377
Telex: 25131 INCO EI
Telefax: (31) 609220

ITALY

Intesa Credito e Cauzioni
Casella Postale 6317
1-0010 Rome - Prati
Italy

c/o UIR
Via dei Giochi Istmici 40
00194 Rome
Telephone: (6) 36 5931
Telex: 610348 611529
614386 UIR I
Telefax: (6) 327 3398

Societa Italiana Assicurazione
Crediti SpA
Casella Postale 2446 AD
1-00198 Rome
Italy

Via Raffaello Matarazzo 19
00139 Rome
Telephone: (6) 81691
Telex: 620616 SIACREDI
Telefax: (6) 8820424
8820413
8820548
8820512

Societa Italiana Cauzioni
Casella Postale 30078
1-00100 Rome 47
Italy

Via Crescenzio 12
Rome
Telephone: (6) 653 0848
Telex: 611 050
612 390 SIC I
Telefax: (6) 687 4418

JAPAN

Taisho Marine & Fire Insurance Co.
Ltd
9 Kanda Surugadai 3-Chome
Chiyoda-ku
Tokyo 101
Japan

9 Kanda Surugadai 3-Chome
Chiyoda-ku
Tokyo
Telephone: (3) 259 34 81
Telex: 24670 KALMSEA J
Telefax: (3) 291 5466

The Tokyo Marine & Fire Insurance
Co. Ltd
Credit & Guarantee Insurance Section
2-1, Marunouchi 1-Chome
Chiyoda-ku
Tokyo 100
Japan

2-1, Marunouchi 1-Chome
Chiyoda-ku
Tokyo
Telephone: (3) 212 6211
Telex: 24858 STILWTR J
Telefax: (3) 214 3944

KOREA

Korea Fidelity & Surety Company
CPO Box 1553
Seoul
Korea

136–74 Yeonji-Dong
Jongro-Ku
Seoul
Telephone (822) 744 0021
Telex: 28485 KOSURE K
Telefax: (822) 743 0016

MEXICO

Compania Mexicana de Seguros
de Crédito SA
Apartado Postal 27–320
03810 Mexico DF

Insurgentes Sur 587
Col Napoles
Mexico DF
Telephone: (5) 687 35 16
(5) 523 53 28
Telex: 1773909 SECEME
Telefax: (5)238620

NETHERLANDS

NV Nationale Borg-Maatschappij
Postbus 19625
NL-1000 GP Amsterdam
Netherlands

Keizersgracht 165
Amsterdam
Telephone: (20) 239 011
Telex: 12610 BORG NL
Telefax: (20) 22 3189

Nederlandsche Credietverzekering
Maatschappij NV
Postbus 473
NL-1000 AL Amsterdam
Netherlands

Keizersgracht 271-287
1016 ED Amsterdam
Telephone: (20) 5539111
Telex: 11496 NCM NL
Telefax: (20) 5532810

NORWAY

Kreditt-Atlas Forsikrings-
Aksjeselskapet
PO Box 461 Sentrum
N-0105 Oslo 1
Norway

Radhusgaten 1–3
Oslo 1
Telephone: (2) 33 10 20
Telex: 74929 KREAT IN
Telefax: (2) 41 1455

Kreditt-Garanti A/S
Forsikringsselskapet
PO Box 3540
N-5033 Bergen-Fyllingsdalen
Norway

Folke Bernadottesvei 50
Fyllingsdalen
Telephone: (5) 17 10 00
Telex: 40867 VEFIN N
Telefax: (5) 171 898
171 899

Norsk Kausjon Forsikrings-
Aksjeselskap
PO Box 533-Sentrum
N-0105 Oslo 1
Norway

Kirkegt 1–3
Oslo
Telephone: (2) 33 50 50
Telex: 77669 NOKAU N
Telefax: (2) 412336

PHILIPPINES

Malayan Insurance Company Inc.
PO Box 3389
Manila
Philippines

Yuchengco Building
484 Quintin Paredes Street
Manila
Telephone: (2) 48 75 61
Telex: 63228 MICO PN
Telefax: (632) 49 79 57

POLAND

'WARTA' Insurance & Reinsurance
Company Limited
ul. Traugutta 5
00–916 Warszawa 51
Poland

ul. Traugutta 5
Warszawa
Telephone: (22) 263997
266481
Telex: 813549 REWA PL
Telefax: not available.

PORTUGAL

COSEC Companhia de Seguro
de Créditos, EP
Avenida da Republica 58
1094 Lisboa Codex
Portugal

Avenida da Republica 58
Lisboa
Telephone: (351–1) 76 01 31
76 60 55
Telex: 12885 COSEC P
Telefax: (351–1) 73 4614

SINGAPORE

Export Credit Insurance Corporation
of Singapore Limited
10 Shenton Way
17–03/09 MAS Building
Singapore 0207

460 Alexandra Road
18.00 PSA Building
Singapore 0511
Telephone: 220 8344
Telex: 21524 ECICS
Telefax: 224 2887

SOUTH AFRICA

Credit Guarantee Insurance Corp.
of Africa Limited
PO Box 9244
Johannesburg 2000
South Africa

31 Dover Street
Randburg 2194
Telephone: (11) 886 3010
Telex: 4–20508, 4–26525
Telefax: (11) 886 1027

SPAIN

Compania Espanola de Seguros
y Reaseguros de Crédito
y Caucion, SA (CESCC)
Apartado Correos 524
E-28023 Madrid
Spain

Raimundo Fernandez-Villaverde 61
28003 Madrid
Telephone: (1) 253 6800
253 8704
Telex: 43163 SCYC E
Telefax: (1) 2336735

Compania Espanola de Seguros
de Crédito a la Exportacion, SA
(CESCE)

C/Velaquez, 74   C/Velaquez, 74
E-28001 Madrid   Madrid
Spain   Telephone: (1) 401 7000
                                     401 3062
                     Telex: 23577 CESCE E
                     Telefax: (1) 435 6175

SWEDEN

Svenska Kreditförsäkringsaktiebolaget
Box 7435
S-103 91 Stockholm   Norrmalmstorg 4
Sweden   Stockholm
                     Telephone: (8) 22 10 60
                     Telex: 10124 SVENSKA S
                     Telefax: (8) 20 16 82

SWITZERLAND

Eidgenössische Versicherungs-
Aktien-Gesellschaft
Postfach   Flössergasse 3
CH-8039 Zurich   8039 Zurich
Switzerland   Telephone: (1) 208 4422
                     Telex: 815 353 FED CH
                     Telefax: (1) 201 2804

UNITED KINGDOM

General Surety & Guarantee Co.
Limited
PO Box 10   Hawthorn Hall
Wilmslow   Hall Road
Cheshire SK9 5BZ   Wilmslow
England   Telephone: (625) 52 7242
                     Telex: 668448 GSG G
                     Telefax: (625) 53 5943

Trade Indemnity plc
12–34 Great Eastern Street
London EC2A 3AX
England

Trade Indemnity House
12–34 Great Eastern Street
London
Telephone: (1) 739 4311
Telex: 21227 TICLON G
Telefax: (1) 729 7682
          (1) 739 4397

UNITED STATES OF AMERICA

American Credit Indemnity Company
300 St Paul Place
Baltimore
MD 21202
USA

300 St Paul Place
Baltimore
Telephone (301) 332 3300
Telex: 87907 ACI BAL
Telefax: (301) 332 7811

Federal Insurance Company
PO Box 1615
Warren
New Jersey 07061–1615
USA

15 Mountain View Road
Warren NJ
Telephone: (201) 580 3472
Telex: 279839 CHUBB UR
Telefax: (201) 580 3656

Fidelity & Deposit Company of
Maryland
PO Box 1227
Baltimore
MD 21203
USA

Fidelity Building
210 North Charles Street
Baltimore
Telephone: (301) 539 0800
Telex: 62226380 EASYLINK
Telefax: (301) 539 7002

Insurance Company of North America
PO Box 7728
Philadelphia
PA 19103
USA

1600 Arch Street
20 Tower
Philadelphia
Telephone: (215) 523 4171
Telex: 834 442 INA PHA
Telefax: (215) 523 7595

Appendix E

Members of the United Kingdom Credit Insurance Brokers' Committee

vwvwvwvwvwvwvwvw

Alexander Stenhouse
Norman Insurance House
Kings Road
Reading
Berkshire RG1 4LW
Telephone 0734 61100

Bain Clarkson Credit Ltd
Alpha House
Suffolk Street
Queensway
Birmingham B1 1LS
Telephone 021 632 4211

CT Bowring and Co. (Insurance) Ltd
PO Box 145
The Bowring Building
Tower Place
London EC3P 3BE
Telephone 01–283 3100

The Credit Insurance Association Ltd
13 Grosvenor Place
London SW1X 7HH
Telephone 01–235 3550

Credit Insurance Services Ltd
89 High Road
South Woodford
London E18 2RH
Telephone 01–505 3333

Gibbs Hartley Cooper
Bishops Court
17–33 Artillery Lane
London E1 7LP
Telephone 01–247 5433

Jardine Credit Insurance Ltd
PO Box 71
Thames House
1–4 Queen Street Place
London EC4R 1JA
Telephone 01–489 1994

Lowndes Lambert UK Ltd
Aspen House
Temple Street
Swindon
Wilts SN1 1SH
Telephone 0793 26252

John Reynolds & Co.
(Credit Insurance) Ltd
Byrom House
21 Quay Street
Manchester M3 3JA
Telephone 061 832 9022

Risk Administration Ltd
Woodruffe House
Cooper's Row
London EC3N 2NL
Telephone 01–488 3288

Sedgwick Credit Ltd
Sedgwick House
The Sedgwick Centre
London E1 8DX
Telephone 01–377 3456

Willis Wrightson Credit
10 Trinity Square
London EC3P 3AX
Telephone 01–488 8111

Membership of the UKCIBC is proof of the specialist broker's commitment to the provision of a continuous service in the credit insurance market. A non-member firm may, however, provide an acceptable service in particular circumstances. Non-specialist brokers may place occasional credit business, e.g., standard 'small business' proposals which require minimal negotiation and servicing.

Index

vwvwvwvwvwvwvwvwvw